T0371952

WHAT WE SOW

WHAT WE SOW

On the Personal, Ecological, *and* Cultural Significance *of* Seeds

Jennifer Jewell

TIMBER PRESS · PORTLAND, OREGON

Image credits as follows: Dreamstime/Ekaterina Kilaniants, pages 73, 75;
Dreamstime/Ernest Akayeu, page 230; Dreamstime/Geraria, pages 17, 31, 57, 96,
152, 202, 322; iStock/ilbusca, pages 151, 229, 286, 321; iStock/ZU_09, pages 128,
263; Sarah Crumb, page 12; Shutterstock/Hein Nouwens, pages 18, 185

Published in 2023 by Timber Press, Inc.,
a subsidiary of Workman Publishing Co., Inc.,
a subsidiary of Hachette Book Group, Inc.
1290 Avenue of the Americas
New York, New York 10104

timberpress.com

Printed in the United States of America on responsibly sourced paper
Text design by Sarah Crumb
Cover design by Hillary Caudle

The publisher is not responsible for websites (or their content)
that are not owned by the publisher.

The Hachette Speakers Bureau provides a wide range of authors for
speaking events. To find out more, go to hachettespeakersbureau.com
or email HachetteSpeakers@hbgusa.com.

ISBN 978-1-64326-107-2

Catalog records for this book are available from the Library of Congress
and the British Library.

For Delaney and Flannery
my most beloved, bright, generative, and generous seeds

CONTENTS

PREFACE   8

INTRODUCTION: TO SEE OURSELVES IN SEED   12

SEEDING:
THE END AND THE BEGINNING

October: The Energetic Nature of Seed   18

November: The Circular Setting of Seed   31

December: Seedshed   57

SEED BEDS

January: Seed Life Linking Us   75

February: Seed Shares and Seed Laws   96

March: Seed Commerce   128

SEED READING

April: Seed's Human Banking History   152

May: The Wild Side of Seed Banks   185

June: Seed Libraries and Literacy   202

SEED SAVING

July: Seed Conservation   230

August: Seed Memory   263

September: Seeds of Culture   286

SEED FUTURES

October: Going to Seed   322

ACKNOWLEDGMENTS   341

SELECTED REFERENCES   343

ADDITIONAL READING AND RESOURCES   366

INDEX   373

PREFACE

In mid-March 2020, California became the first state to order its nearly 40 million residents to stay home and all nonessential in-person businesses to close down in an effort to stop the spread of COVID-19. Cases of the novel coronavirus had been in the news, at first sparingly and then ever more urgently, from January to that moment in March, so the crisis response was not a surprise, but the halting of life as we knew it was as novel as the virus.

My partner, John, and I were traveling in the early days of a long-planned speaking tour as the concern and confusion regarding the crisis reached its first fevered pitch. Tour events disappeared in front of us wholesale. But my first thought upon hearing about the California lockdown orders was not "How do we get home?" or "How do we keep from getting sick?" or "How do I stem the ebbing of my work and income?" As gardeners, our first thought was "We need to order seeds."

We were not, apparently, the only gardeners to have this instinctive thought. When I got online the day after the lockdown orders, before being able to get on a flight home, "Out of Stock" and "Back-ordered" popped up on our computer screens over and over again from our favorite organic seed sellers: Redwood Seeds, Peaceful Valley Seed, Territorial Seed, Fedco Seeds, Hudson Valley Seed, Seed Savers Exchange, Southern Exposure Seed Exchange, Kitazawa Seed, Johnny's Selected Seeds, Baker Creek Heirloom Seeds. As a gardener, to feel a sense of scarcity in the seed supply was an alarm bell ringing—and ringing loudly in my mammalian brain, triggering survival anxieties, and triggering a determined instinct to engage with my own survival. Our collective survival.

Seed is important: botanists know this, ecologists know this, farmers and horticulturists know this, and most gardeners have a pretty good basic understanding.

But, if many of our (human) species are overwhelmingly "plant blind," even more of us are stunningly seed stupid—many of us are not sure exactly how they work, how they've evolved, how they are being handled at legislative, commercial, or perhaps most importantly, cultural levels, and why this matters.

In the midst of climate crisis, a precipitous rate of biodiversity loss in our world, a global pandemic, attendant financial chaos, global social-justice reckoning, and now the most globally reverberating war in the last 50-plus years, we as humans, and in the United States as an industrialized society, are being offered an intense short course in what we need most in this world, what is in fact *essential* to our lives: community, family, health, dignity, clean water, clean air, access to some open space and sufficient food are all unquestionably on this list of essentials. Foundational to clean water, clean air, and sufficient food are ... plants. Foundational to the vast majority of plants on our planet—the seed-bearing plants (yes, there are non-seed-bearing plants. More on that soon)—are their seeds: the smallest form of, the very *essence* of, these plants.

In this bizarre moment of colliding urgencies for life as we have known it, we are collectively being offered an opportunity to remember and really understand the essential importance and power of seed in our world: for food, for medicine, for utility, for the vast interconnected web we include in the concept of biodiversity and planetary health, for beauty, and for culture, whatever that might mean to us.

This recognition of the importance of seed on micro and macro levels did not just happen in March of 2020 with the COVID-19 pandemic in full form, with increasing climate extremes of the last several years, or with the Russian invasion of Ukraine disrupting geopolitical stability and global food security and health.

On the contrary, the stewards of the "seed world," that dedicated sector of our independent plant-engaged world, have been sounding the alarm and preparing the soil for a likewise global seed-literacy and seed-protection revolution of sorts for many years.

The seed world is rich with scientists, spiritualists, growers, activists, and protestors who have been keeping seed alive, accessible, shared, and safe. These seed stewards have been preparing for the battle ahead as seed (its integrity, its diversity, and our open access to it) has become increasingly threatened. These seed keepers have been declaring loudly to all who would listen why we should join in the work to know and care for seeds ourselves as one of the most proactive steps we can take to rebuilding our human food systems, our social systems, and the global ecosystems of biodiversity on which we all depend.

Since the 1980s, when the first GMO seed patent was issued, and the 1990s, when reporting began in earnest about seed supply strategically (and stealthily) being consolidated into the holdings of large agribusiness-chemical corporations, the smaller seed sowers, growers, banks, and knowers have been recording and responding. Their strategic, heartfelt, ground-level actions—documenting, saving, sharing, and protecting seed—protects us all.

As I write this in mid-2022, I have been struck by an image in the *New York Times* of the largest wildfire on record in New Mexico, and specifically of one Paula Garcia, executive director of the New Mexico Acequia Association, a nonprofit protecting traditional, historic, and cultural irrigation waterways. In the face of the fire, the first thing Paula packed in order to evacuate was a large jar of maíz de concho seeds, shared through generations in her family; I am struck by the news of Russian forces targeting fields and silos of grain and seed in Ukraine, and the bombing of some or all of Ukraine's national seed collection in Kharkiv, the tenth largest collection in the world, supplying seeds to breeders around the globe, including Russia. Our important but often frayed connections to seed have *always* been important, and this needs to be far more visible to more of us if we are to protect them for future generations.

If water, air, soil, and fire are the four primary elements, it takes seed as a fifth element for humans to make the first four equal life here on earth. Seed is life.

I hope my own journey here through veins of the history, biology, social and cultural arc of seed in the United States, seen through a lens of my own life, will inspire readers and gardeners to be ever more loving, knowledgeable, vigilant, and proactive in your own advocacy on behalf of our connection to the natural world. Starting with the seeds you buy, the seeds you sow and share, and the seeds—literal and figurative—you save. You, your garden, and other relations have a green and growing stake in the future.

—*Jennifer Jewell, Butte County, California, May 2022*

INTRODUCTION

To See Ourselves in Seed

A seed is the dormant dream of a new life.

A hope, a prayer, the smallest version of an entire life.

Creation stories the world over are often germinated from just one green life—seed or seedling—nourishing and making possible all other lives who are then able to reproduce and radiate out from there.

In a heavy old wooden chest that sits at the foot of my bed, among the many treasures tucked inside is a green felt tree shape onto which one or the other of my daughters in their second-grade year pasted the little shapes of birds, a nest, leaves, and fruits. At the bottom, she has pasted an abridged excerpt from the parable of the mustard seed from the Christian Bible, Luke 13:18–19: "What is the kingdom of God like? And to what shall I compare it? It is like a grain of mustard seed that a man took and sowed in his garden, and it grew and became a tree, and the birds of the air made nests in its branches."

I like the tree, the bird life, the seed references. Though we are not a religious family, and I am not a religious person, it is not lost on me now that seed is to plant life what a messiah is to Western religions: the alpha and omega, the beginning and the end, and the beginning again.

Posted in my home office is an old Welsh proverb: "A seed hidden in the heart of an apple is an orchard invisible."

The notion of it, *a seed*, and the very act of it, *to seed*, permeate our collective cultural fabric and imagination. Seeds are the flesh of life and one of the smallest visible units of its meaning, they are the future of that flesh and meaning, and they hold the metaphoric bounty of it all wrapped up in the enormous diversity of their relatively tiny forms.

Linguistically, seed is a wildly and fascinatingly compounded word in the English language—think seed money, seed bed, bad seed, seed stitch, seed pearls. We seed clouds, we seed thoughts, we seed imaginations, we seed fields of athletes. As a gardener, I was intrigued to learn that in athletics, seeding players dates back to the 1800s when tennis first began distributing players by ability more equally across the span of a competitive series so that the best players didn't compete directly until the end of the competition, increasing interest for both players and audience—and mimicking the idea of planting the seeds or seedlings of the biggest plants at the back of a garden bed so as to not outcompete and overshadow the smaller specimens in the front.

There are seeds of love, seeds of war, seeds of hope, seeds of success, and seeds of change. We spill our seed in intimate union (the Latin for seed being *semen*), ecstatically or recklessly; we become seedy in self-neglect; we go to seed in our senescence and old age. These linguistics are fabulous. And profoundly pregnant with possible meaning. This parallel, just like seed itself, holds an abiding interest for me. Why is this so?

No doubt similarities exist in other natural processes or aspects of the plant, animal, and geological spheres, but it occurs to me through just these simple linguistic observations that we as humans understand ourselves better in some small way as a result of our metaphoric identification with seed. We—humans and the seeds that surround and support us—live distinctly different and yet interestingly parallel lives.

This all speaks to the capaciousness of the figurative as well as literal cultural importance of these life-bearing forms. And to their symbolizing our larger understanding of life itself, carried in these smallest individually viable versions of our planet's seed-bearing plant lives, which make up more than 96 percent of all plants.

Many seed keepers describe seed as embodied prayers for the future from the past, full of adaptive and encoded history of time and place, full of the history of peoples, places, and cultures, full of environmental lessons and learning, all of which imbue surviving seed with strength, with resilience.

In this way, the state of our seed reflects who we are as people. One measure of who we have been and who we will or could be.

Seeds are the holders of the genetic ingredients and recipes ensuring biodiversity in our plant lives across ecosystems everywhere. These plant lives are arguably the basis on which a vast majority of other life forms are built and dependent.

Successful seed set is an indication of health, vigor, and vitality. A barren landscape is a common theme of many world myths indicating that the divine has forsaken us humans, wherein all is lost and doom imminent. I have heard it said that good seed set is the point at which we know we as humans have passed the great test—we have assured future food stores and will reap the reward of a bountiful harvest.

In the fifty-sixth year of my life, as a gardener and human, I immersed myself in the study of seeds as one way to understand more my own path through the greater life of which I am but a very small part.

I have been a student of seed, like many of us, for the entirety of my life; in some ways, I have been a student of seed since I popped the first white oak acorns into my young self's pocket while visiting grandparents, since I blew my first dandelion into the wind, hoping the seeds would fly off to find (and grant?) my wishes. More professionally, I have been a student of seed since moving to Northern California in 2007 and beginning to study the natural history of this new-to-me region in my roles here as mother and woman, as gardener and citizen, as native plant garden curator at the Gateway Science Museum in Chico, California, and as creator and host of the public radio program and podcast *Cultivating Place: Conversations on Natural History and the Human Impulse to Garden.*

But this most recent discipleship and immersion is different— catalyzed by great losses in the world: by the Camp Fire of 2018 in my home region, followed by the COVID-19 pandemic and the long overdue social-justice turmoil and hoped-for awakening of 2020 and 2021, which also marked back-to-back and unusually hard drought and fire seasons in interior Northern California—a region accustomed to both drought and fire, but not like these seasons of both.

My most recent personal study has been catalyzed as well by important thresholds in my own phenological life: my daughters both fully fledged in this time period, I undramatically moved out of my own childbearing (seed-bearing) years, and I passed the age my mother had attained when she died. I found myself with a growing number of questions, and deep griefs, and few answers.

Readers may wonder why the resulting ruminations and lessons on seed are nestled inside this quasi-memoir structure of a year in my life. What are seeds if not a microcosm of the stages of being that mirror our own lives? And what are our lives if not contextualized by the larger life cycles on this planet?

These phenological checkpoints in my life—the death of my mother, my own mothering, partnering, menopause—are pure parallels to the lives of the plants around us. When we recognize intimate similarities between ourselves and another, we care more.

When we are separated from this complex relationship, when it is sanitized into sterility for us, we all lose. As a gardener, I ardently believe that in re-seeding these intricate, delicate and brilliant, stubbornly persistent relationships there is hope for me, for us, and for them.

I began this purposeful immersion in October of 2020 with the harvest and end of the growing season and the associated "new year" as recognized by many cultures' calendars, which coincides patly with my own birthday in early November.

Over the years producing *Cultivating Place* and writing my first two books, my mind has been expanded by most people I've spoken with, their passions and knowledge driving my own curiosity to continue learning. Their insights into our growing world so often simultaneously offering insights into our human condition—and into how to perhaps better tend both. But with recurring consistency, it has been the seed of the garden, of the native landscape, and the seed keepers of all kinds who I have felt most drawn to, and it is to all of them that I listen most closely to find the universal lessons in the particular. To separate—as it were—the chaff from the seed.

SEEDING:

THE END AND THE BEGINNING

The Energetic Nature of Seed

NEW MOON, OCTOBER 16
FULL MOON, OCTOBER 31

OCTOBER 16

Just past the autumnal equinox of late September, I am sowing seeds for winter greens—lettuce, arugula, spinach, and rainbow chard; carrot seed went in at the end of August. By the end of this month, we will plant out the season's garlic bulbs as well.

I try to plant in accordance with the season and by the phase of the moon, setting out each kind of annual seed at a time when the length of day and the energetic lunar pull will best support each seed's own way of growth, putting faith in the power of these celestial bodies to positively impact our planet's seasonal cycles and our plant and soil friends for my own little vegetable patch as they have for the entire earth for eons.

This keeps me in touch with the seasons, the moon phases, our planet's position in time and space—my own position in time and space.

For the long view—far beyond the life cycle of my human self—the mature native oak trees here know best. They are "planting" their acorns with abandon right now. The ground is covered in the beautiful plump fruit, and the seed inside will grow powerfully both up and down. Those that survive the first year, and then the first ten years, will provide food and shelter for many, many other lives—floral and faunal—for the next 100 to 200 years, if not more.

This perspective of the one and the many, the here and now running inside future here and nows, a single season inside a century or centuries of seasons—this is all held in an acorn resting, still, in the palm of my hand.

OCTOBER 29

It is hot in the canyon, in all of interior Northern California, again today. And dry—so dry. Dust storm clouds rise behind the car as I drive the winding dirt road. It is unseasonably warm for this late in October, although what is seasonable or not seasonable seems in constant flux now. Humidity levels are in the single digits most days, while the thermometer rises into the high nineties, low hundreds still.

The soil is tired. The oaks and manzanita, toyon, scrub of the slopes and even the grasslands of the lower flats in this small canyon are tired. In this summer-dry climate, though many native plants and animals are adapted to summer's heat and know enough to go dormant to withstand the lack of resources in this season, everyone is tired. Before early autumn's lapsing light has begun reducing the chlorophyl in the nondormant plants for the season, with this prolonged heat and drought, all the greens and even the summer browns that form the normally harmonious plant palette of this place look pale and wan. Shadowy, bloodless versions of their normal painterly selves.

The north wind is up and with it an edgy electricity is in the air. An alertness holds the collective attention. We are all listening and straining to hear: the oak and pine trees, the creek, the canyon creatures—from bumble bees to squirrels, hummingbirds to vultures, deer to turkeys, these last two being frequent companions in the grassland—we all listen. The bear, coyote, rattlesnakes, and mountain lion are no doubt edgy too—waiting, listening—but they are out of sight (though never far from mind).

The great oaks of this canyon, as the world over, hold, house, and hide, welcome, feed, and nurture these many creatures—natives, residents, migrants, and migrators alike. California is home to a great biodiversity of plant life in general. The California portion of the California Floristic Province, a designation for the plant life in an area covering most of California, up into Oregon and down into Baja California, Mexico, and sharing a similar Mediterranean climate, is home to more than 20 distinct species and more than 20 known hybrids of oaks, and some of the species lines date back more than 20 million years. Oak woodlands became a dominant feature here after the last ice age, according to current scientific research and thought. For the past 5000 years or so, these oaks have been coevolving with humans. With improved tools for historical analysis of plant and landscape—from dendrology to carbon testing of lake beds and soil cores—it becomes more and more clear that the Indigenous peoples of what is now California have actively managed the landscape with sophisticated thinking and oversight for thousands of years. The Mechoopda of this region have used, and still use, low-intensity, high-frequency fire regimes to maintain the health and structure of the oak woodlands. These accomplish several things—they keep small conifers under control in oak-dominated environments so that oak succession and therefore acorn production are ensured for both wildlife and humans. This traditional use of fire simultaneously reduces dead dry wood and grass buildup in these same areas so that naturally occurring brush fires (often started by lightning) do not get too big, and so that each year's acorns have a better chance of reaching fertile soil. Subsequent oak seedlings then also have a greater chance of establishing without overwhelming or overshadowing competition. And all of this shows a remarkable understanding of place and keen observation of the most productive natural cycles by the people who have long called it home.

Here in this small canyon, through which a 150-year-old dirt road is sistered to a small year-round creek, at least four native oaks continue to coevolve: valley oak, blue oak, interior live oak, and now too the oracle oak—a natural hybrid cross between the interior live oak and the black oak, which is not present in this canyon, but lives north a few miles uphill, upwind, and upstream, based on the prevailing winds and the topographical course of this little canyon.

Late September and October are traditionally the retreating edge of "high fire season" in the northern Sacramento Valley—a tense seasonal transition zone for a place mired in a 100-year drought. A roiling cloud of dust can, with a single spark introduced from the sky or by human carelessness, morph into a violent column of smoke and fire within milliseconds. It happens every year now.

But it is also the front edge of high seed season—the great harvest of the year's (and by extension millennia's) work for many of the plants of this place.

The valley oaks (*Quercus lobata*) are masting this year. While mast refers generally to the fruit and nuts of a variety of trees and shrubs, mast*ing* is when any one species produces an unusually large crop in a given region. For oaks, this can happen every two to five years. While the cycle of masting is understood generally, a lot of mystery and theorizing remains as to how they know when to do it, or why a whole region will mast at the same time. Could it be due to the previous season's rainfall, or summer heat, or overall temperatures, or which way the wind blew during spring pollination? No one theory is reliably predictive. What is clear is that when the oaks are masting, acorns fall in remarkable numbers, with a mature oak (between 40 and 120 years old) producing upwards of 10,000 acorns. This abundance can alter migration routes of acorn eaters—from mice to deer and bear, to jays and acorn woodpeckers. The generous food source affects the life cycles and populations of acorn-eating wildlife as well as the oaks' own succession success. The more acorns they are healthy enough to produce, the greater chance some will survive to maturity.

I've been watching the thick bunches of green acorns forming and growing fatter all season. In their development stage, these acorns are bright young-apple green and clearly visible even from some distance against the restrained and contrasting late-season leathery, forest-green valley oak foliage. The acorn clusters, which will age over their six-to-seven-month development to a deep chocolatey brown, speckle the canopies of these largest and most stately of our oaks.

Valley oaks, along with the blue oaks, are a keystone species here—the entire ecosystem depends on them to exist in its current iteration. They are the charismatic megaflora, so to speak, of this plant and human community. The valley oaks, which can live up to 600 years and reach 100 feet high and almost as wide in ideal circumstances, favor the lowest elevations of the canyon for its deep, rich soils. The blue oaks (*Quercus douglasii*), stouter and somewhat shorter lived (between 100 and 400 years), prefer a little rise in elevation, and are the dominant species partway up the small canyon's slopes.

The intermingling gray pines (*Pinus sabiniana*) are often taller than many of the oaks around them—they shoot up to 80 feet quickly. As evergreens, with their very specific glaucous blue-green-grayish needles arranged in airy bundles, they stand out to the eye amid the oaks. Their cones are among the largest in the pine genus and, where the valley and blue oak acorns can swell to three rounded or pointed inches in length, the gray pine's seed-bearing cones easily reach nearly a foot in length.

Similarly, though, both the valley and blue oak acorns and the nuts filling the large and heavy gray pine cones are critically important food sources for all manner of life along the food chain here. Collectively, valley oak riparian—creek or riverside—forests, which are endemic to California, support 67 nesting bird species, more than any other California habitat.

This little riverine canyon occupies an ecotone seam, a transition zone between the north central valley and the central valley foothill and mountain environments of California. It is characterized by valley floor grasslands and meadows, by oak savanna, and by open oak woodlands rising with elevation gains to Sierran mixed hardwood forest. Like most ecotones it is endowed with the rich diversity of such overlaps.

Over time and space, this little cross section of the world—in many ways a mirror of the wider world—and the fruits and bodies of some of these exact trees or their parents or grandparents have been feeding and sheltering fungal, plant, and animal life along this creek and human path for a very long time, since well before European colonization.

Plant life grows hand in hand with rock and soil life. Geologically, the canyon shows all the layers of time that sculpted my region: the uppermost layers of the canyon walls are known as "Tuscan Formation lava cap," hardened mudflows from an ancient volcanic eruption some 50 miles northeast of here 3 million years ago. Beneath the Tuscan Formation cap is "Lovejoy

Formation" basalt from 15 million years ago, and beneath that is sandstone ranging from pale cream color to reddish mineral-rich clays from an even more ancient river system that flowed from significantly farther northeast of here traveling southwest to an ancient ocean edge, which left its own marine layer of history.

This geologic underwriting paved the way in these various stones—and the protective stability they subsequently provided—for the California Floristic Province to become a biodiversity "hotspot" on the planet, home to some 6500 distinct taxa of plants. The diversity of mountain and coastal formations aggregated over time have offered dozens of microclimate options from which living beings could choose—a little wetter, a little drier, a little more basalt, a little more sandstone or clay—increasing the possibilities for survival and gradual adaptation.

The sheer number of plant genera, species, and subspecies native to the Floristic Province, to say nothing of the endemics that occur only here, means that there is a corresponding richness of plant communities and ecosystem types. Wildlife likewise coevolved to be interdependent with and take full advantage of this cornucopia of plant life. In the simplest symbiotic terms, wildlife needs the plants for food, and the plants need the wildlife for pollination, seed dispersal, for pruning, and to achieve other kinds of evolutionary selection. And we as humans—no matter where we live or how divorced or "protected" we believe ourselves to be from this environment—are ultimately reliant on the success of them all. If we want to make the places we have chosen to insert ourselves our true homes, we must remember that we have things to learn from these diverse lives, cycles, and epic adaptation stories.

What makes us feel at home? Some combination of family and familiarity, I think, as I make my home among the multitude of lives that preceded me here.

Increasingly dire reports of sprawling rather than strategic urbanization and biodiversity loss at staggering rates make me feel ever more pressed—daily—to learn from and return love to *my* chosen home. It offers prismatic hope, lessons, and opportunities for adaptation, for starters. The more of us who become intimately and fiercely understanding of and interdependent with our own home grounds, the more we become like the masting generation of 10,000 acorns—improving chances for *all* succession.

While the dry, windy weather of late October equals anxiety right now, the many clusters of fattening valley acorns, along with the other fruits, berries, and nuts—the seeds of the season—mean feasting.

We are all waiting for this too.

OCTOBER 30

The north wind rises through the night, announcing itself as a discordant chorus of tree leaves frenetic and unsettled in the dark. It is an uncomfortable sound—like friends in distress. Dust—more dust—sieving through the screens of any open windows. Acorns, buckeyes, and gray pine cones (the megaseeds of our seed shed) pelt the ground, the deck, the roof. A fury of flying life—plant life in its most mobile form hurled across the garden, into the creek, across the road.

On the hot breath of the night, a fire kicks up some ways off. Its acrid smell wafts in as the night turns to morning. Whole burned leaves— like telegrams of bronze—arrive on thermals like offerings from a fiery overstory 8–10 miles away. So estimates John, my partner, who has lived with this land and in this canyon for more than 35 years. Bigleaf maple, tan oak, black oak, perhaps madrone? This is not a "large event" as fire and wind are categorized by meteorologists these days, and yet it still reminds us that these are crucible times and we are in a crucible place.

But then, aren't we all?

We travel to see the aftermath of this spot fire. On land adjacent to the active fire, much of the ground is textured by burned leaves, and by windfall seeds. They are both wounded and wounding with the tumult of hot, dry weather. A poststorm apocalypse of shredded leaves, lichen-adorned twigs, and countless acorns.

I choose one acorn—they nearly all call out to be picked up, for me to admire their heft, their smooth protective skin, the luster that shines up with just a light brush of my sleeve. And their caps! Also called a cupule, the cap is in fact formed from the bracts beneath the oak's flower. These caps are calling cards announcing each species' unique nature in the shape of them, the size of them, their texture, the tilt of them positioned with personality on the apex of each nut.

One this morning, about the size and thickness of a pointer finger down to the second knuckle, is beginning to ripen. Its protective enclosing shell, or pericarp, is just cracking from the tip, becoming a permeable and slightly more pliable sheet enfolding the interior life, and from inside the creamy soft flesh of the acorn, the developing cotyledon leaves are visible.

It is a petite and perfect parcel provisioned with everything it needs to grow from this small and unlikely projectile into the discrete universe that is a mature oak.

Something about this view into this acorn proffers the sensation of a privileged peek behind the veil of life's mysteries. An unnervingly small unity of opposites and possibilities.

These acorns foreshadow almost everything about this place. These are not *just* acorns—no, no, affirm the canyon's loud, bossy acorn woodpecker clans, excited by the wind's harvest. These, like all seed, spark thoughts of food, family, impossibly elegant engineering ... and the possibility of having our futures literally flung at us by forces beyond our control, to fall where they may. A baptism by wind and fire.

The nubbly cupule of the acorn I hold, despite the pericarp cracking, remains firmly attached at the top, and the connective stem that held cap to tree is tipped jauntily, making it look like some kind of botanic beret. I recall my own infant babies just out of an evening bath—their towels positioned diagonally, their healthy fat bellies peeking through, like acorn endosperm flesh.

In past years, in much larger nearby wind and fire "events" in fall (such as the disastrous November 2018 Camp Fire that killed 85 people, destroyed nearly 15,000 homes, and burned 70,000 acres), the world has sounded like one large percussive cacophony—frenzied canopies being blown, ashes-to-ashes-tree-trunks crashing into the creek, acorns and buckeyes popping and hissing, the warlike sound of propane tanks exploding in a terrifying sequence above us in the canyon, and beyond that in the nearly destroyed town of Paradise.

It is not unheard of in such moments for those of us listening to wonder, to in fact plead with the universe: What are they saying, these sound-ings? Did and do the Mechoopda or Mikćapdo, Yamani, and Koncow or Koyom'kawi—the Maiduan peoples original to this land—wonder the same thing on a stormy night along the creek? Their relationship and generational knowledge stretches back many, many centuries with these same oaks and their community of plants and animals, their creek-side footpath a long-standing wayfinder through life—and no doubt a pre-liminary version of what would become the dirt road we now travel daily. Did they have the same questions as the mining and logging settlers in the 1840s? As us now working remotely from home and wondering if the internet will hold?

In many things present and past, we have little choice: mast years, fire season, creek levels; pandemics, the exacerbations of climate change to date; genocide, erasure, and suppression of Indigenous and other land-based peoples and their cultures and knowledge. These have all happened, some—like mast years and fire season—we know with certainty will happen again. We have little control except in how we understand the past and what we do from here.

But we have a great deal more control than we might think. As a mother and a gardener, I know this to be true.

Because, here we are: holding life in our hands and wondering what it is saying to us, asking of us.

Out of crucible ashes, we can make choices.

And the seeds show to us, sing to us, and even shout at us many of these choices.

Are we even in "shouting distance"? Can we hear?

OCTOBER 31: ALL HALLOWS' EVE, SAMHAIN, FULL MOON
I am very interested in the "moral arc of the universe," in the words of the nineteenth-century abolitionist Theodore Parker, referenced regularly by both Dr. Martin Luther King Jr. and spiritual explorer and public radio voice Krista Tippett.

No matter how long that universe is arcing from unity and a receptiveness to redemption back over to misery, separation, and self (and other) destruction, no matter how long it takes to "bend back toward justice," as these seekers before me believe that it does and will, I believe that a garden occupies the center of this moral universe. And it is a garden of Edenic beauty, a "paradise" born of the gifts—the justice, the mercy, the grace—of seeds and seed-bearing plants that ornament, feed, house, clothe, and breathe for the rest of us living beings on the planet.

If you go all the way back and then go back one step further: clean water, clean soil, clean air, and healthy civilizations across time and space on this abundant planet are all in large part based on the seed-bearing plants, and seed-bearing plants are perpetuated by ...

Seed.

The origins of Halloween on October 31 are said to go back to the ancient Celtic festival of Samhain (pronounced *sow-whin*). Celtic cultures of more than 2000 years ago, in what are now Ireland, England, Wales, Scotland, and northern France, considered November 1 their New Year—marking the end of harvest and the beginning of autumn and winter, seasons often associated with the abundance of the season before, and subsequent decline, aging, and death.

Celtic cultures believed that at this time—halfway between the autumnal equinox in late September and the winter solstice in late December—the boundary between the worlds of the living and the dead were especially porous. For Celtic cultures, not unlike the cultures of what is now Mexico honoring Dia de los Muertos, Day of the Dead, Samhain on October 31 was when the ghosts of the dead returned to earth, when our understanding of the known world, our universe, included most poignantly forces both seen and unseen.

Most of our Western cultures have today eschewed this earlier attention to the difficult moments in the cycle of life—like in so many other ways, we prefer to chase after only the pleasant, the blousy blooms, the juicy fruits. It's little wonder, then, that we've essentially also come to consider inert seeds "dead" or "unseen" forces. But they are always there, communicating. We are simply not listening.

If we as a species, in this postmodern day and age of the Anthropocene and of loneliness, suffer from a generally acknowledged "plant blindness," we are by and large not only blind when it comes to seeds, but deaf and mute as well.

Some of our plant blindness, unsurprisingly, correlates directly with how the demographics of the United States have shifted over the past century and a half. In 1921, for the first time the census discovered that more people in the United States lived in cities than in rural areas: 51 percent to 49 percent. By 1970, it had skewed 74 percent urban.

Does this physical remove from nature, a clear and direct contributor to the "plant blindness" that exists today, also play into our inability to grasp climate change, to grasp global habitat loss and degradation, and to grasp the scale of biodiversity loss in our world?

If people are not routinely made to or do not have opportunity to look at, to see, to think about plants, they are reduced as a source of knowledge and of essential literacy. In our increasingly urbanized world, even with today's standard school curriculum, how and when *would* new generations learn to truly see or know plants, let alone their seed?

Places for this *do* exist *everywhere*, but we don't take much advantage of urban environments. A small pocket park, community garden plot, along an urban riverbank, on a roadside or sidewalk verge, or remnant lot left to its own devices. We will see that life finds a foothold, but we now have to be *taught* to look for it.

Most who have been given any chance to garden come to this revelation quickly: every seed that germinates is a renewal of an outright miracle. How the hell does it work? Even once successfully? Continue, year after year and seed after seed? It is a *miracle* we take for granted daily.

NOVEMBER

The Circular Setting of Seed

NEW MOON, NOVEMBER 14
FULL MOON, NOVEMBER 30

NOVEMBER 6

I am now 55 years old; 55 in 2020. There's something oddly symmetrical and balanced to the numerology. Strength in numbers? It's been an odd, hard, illuminating, contracting, and expanding few years.

My first thought on waking on my birthday morning was this: my mother waking on her fifty-fifth birthday had less than one year to live.

She was a gardener—the gardener who grew me. She did not graduate from college. Through her life as a gardener, she was as knowledgeable and caring a gardener and human as I've known. I remember her cutting "seed" potatoes down to one or two "eyes" each and letting them sit on cookie trays overnight to callous over a bit before planting out the next day; I remember small porcelain teacups soaking her peas (sweet and edible peas) overnight to soften the smooth dark seed coats and jump-start germination.

I wonder quite specifically: Had she known she had less than one year—and she knew she did not in all likelihood have very long, being in the end stages of metastasized breast cancer—what seeds would she have planted differently knowing it was her last planting season?

I will never really know. Here's what I do know. Being the most avid gardener of her three daughters, I was given my mother's garden journal at the time of her death in April 1998. She had written in it mere weeks before. Her last few entries show a disintegration in distinctive hand-writing—from square, straight, and bold to shaky, wispy even—but they also show a tenacity for life. Her list waxed, even as her life waned.

Her entries read, in turn:

Planted: Lettuce seeds

Planted: native Rain Lily bulbs

Planted: Moonflower seeds

The progression of this last list of life my mother planted into her garden along the marshy coastal islands of South Carolina mirrored the grow-ing season as well as the seasons of a human life. We also go from the full-sun vigor of salad-days lettuce, to feeling comfortable in our native midlife habitat like the rain lily bulbs (*Zephranthes* sp.), to finally acknowl-edging the evening of life as does night-blooming moonflower (*Ipomea alba*). I like to think of her spirit similarly, dreamily and fragrantly making its way in the dark into the star-filled reaches of an old, gnarled, and moss-festooned live oak tree.

So at 55, in 2020, seeds—metaphorically and literally what I can still tend and grow in this world—are very much on my mind.

My father, a PhD wildlife biologist, also molded me to observe the natural world. He recognized that the animals he studied and loved could only be as healthy and strong as the wild plants and seeds that made their habitats. Our hiking and camping outings invariably included discussing both creatures and environments. To understand the health and habits of fish, my father evaluated streams' insect life and the health of the adjacent plant communities. While cleaning fish or game birds, he always looked at what they had been eating. He would have us opening guts and sifting through them, splaying the crops of seed-eating upland game birds such as dove, quail, pheasants and evaluating their recent food—predominantly seeds and grains of the fields.

Even being raised in this very connected way, it was not until hiking in the foothills of Northern California my first year of living here that both the miracle and the tangible life (and importance) of seed really landed. And stuck. And germinated.

It was autumn. In an effort to get to know my new home, I took a local native plant society tour of the oak grasslands and woodland plant communities with Dr. Wes Dempsey, emeritus professor of biological sciences at California State University, Chico.

It was a warm, dry day, the oaks were golden, and I was beginning to grasp the general features that distinguished the blue oaks from valley oaks, the interior live oak from the canyon live oak. I was learning to identify (very roughly) some of the shrubs: toyon, yerba santa, buckbrush, poison oak (!). When we came to a tall, old gray pine, Dempsey crouched down to examine one of the large intact cones on the ground beneath the tree. Scattered around the pine's drip line were reddish woody chip piles, the detritus of squirrels having investigated and eaten from those same cones with their clawed feet and sharp, well-adapted teeth.

He shook the cone—wider than the span of his hand—and peered up into its scales. He tapped it against a nearby rock and out dropped several perfect, meaty pine nuts. With his pocketknife, he peeled back a little strip of the rust-colored coat and then bisected the nut from top to bottom. He held out his palm displaying the insides of the two halves. There, clear as day, was the outline of an entire pine tree running down the center of each side.

This tiny, grub-sized nut could grow into that entire conceptualized pine tree.

Bam!

❖

Where do you start in a study of seeds? As Carl Sagan notes, "If you wish to make an apple pie from scratch, you must first invent the universe." Which came first, the universe or the apple seed?

Which came first, the seed or the seed-bearing plant? The answer is of course a circular continuum repeating itself ad infinitum: seed germination, plant, flower, pollination by wind, animal, water, or some or all of these, followed by seed formation, seed ripening, seed dispersal, seed dormancy (with some exceptions) of whatever length, and then germination—and again.

And again.

I asked myself whether I would start my study with seed biology (their life cycle), morphology (what they look like), or their phenology (what they look like when, or the timing of important life moments, from pollination and formation to dispersal to dormancy and ripening, to germination ... or their loss of viability or vigor one way or another).

This was not an easy question to answer because there is no one right answer, but also because, often by intention, we can't see the state of seed in our world.

But before scrutinizing the creep and reach of the purposefully opaque industrialized seed industry, and the worldwide renaissance of on-the-ground independent seed stewarding that has flowered in response, let's start with the plain and simple miraculous fact of the seeds themselves in the places we live.

What do we *need* to know about seed? What *should* we know?

Let's start with what we can actually see.

Most simply, a seed is the fertilized ovule(s) of a plant that, when mature and ripe and exposed to the right conditions of air, light, soil, and water, is capable of germinating and growing into a new, related, plant.

However, not all plants produce seed. So let's go way back.

The current and general understanding of the evolution of plant life on the planet is among the greatest of creation stories.

For our purposes here, a short and simplistic version: According to NASA, Earth achieved its current form about 4.5 billion years ago, and sometime over 2 billion years ago, photosynthesizing bacteria evolved. Thanks to a few hundred million years of photosynthesis, these bacteria released enough oxygen to tip us toward the atmosphere we enjoy today—78 percent nitrogen and 21 percent oxygen, among other gases.

Early life forms (including bacteria) continued to evolve in concert with the atmosphere. Eventually, complex multicelled organisms developed (eukaryotes). These earliest organisms were free-floating ocean dwellers gathering and transmitting nutrients and reproductive materials in their watery environment. Very, very slowly, terrestrial land volume increased, the atmosphere became more hospitable with the development of the ozone layer (approximately 200 to 600 million years ago), and these early organisms began adapting to and colonizing the shorelines, fresh water, and in time, dry land itself.

According to spore fossil records, land plants existed some 510 to 439 million years ago, "a time when the global climate was mild and extensive shallow seas surrounded the low-lying continental masses. The earliest photosynthetic organisms on land would have resembled modern algae, cyanobacteria, and lichens, followed by the bryophytes—spore-bearing rather than seed-bearing, nonvascular plants—liverworts and mosses, which evolved from a group of green algae. Then, about 425 million years ago, evidence of vascular plants appeared.

"The evolutionary adaptation of vascular plants, with roots and shoots and the capacity to internally move water and nutrients between these roots and the rest of their living structure, meant that these organisms did not have to rely on external environments for their own water and food. If their roots could reach water, they could control their own survival far more precisely within their own bodies." This evolution in plant form led to a comparatively rapid and remarkable diversification of land plants.

Most biological fields agree that it was the appearance and evolution of seed—small, transportable, and adaptable forms of plant life—that allowed for the global reach, diversification, and wild success of the vascular, seed-bearing plants. The earliest relative of seed-bearing plants arrived to this global and exuberant life party sometime between 2 and 4.5 million years ago.

As a group, the seed-bearing plants of today are known as the spermatophytes. Spermatophytes include both gymnosperms (which evolved first) and angiosperms. Gymnosperms (derived from the Greek words for *naked* and *seed*) currently comprise less than 10 percent of vascular plants and notably include the cone-bearing species—think pine and fir trees. Angiosperms (derived from the Greek words for *container* or *vessel* and *seed*) comprise around 80 percent of all vascular plant life. The remaining 10 percent are the persistent spore-bearing plants still abundant around us, including the ferns and fern allies.

A primary difference between gymnosperms and angiosperms is the way they form and offer out their seed. Gymnosperms are a little like the ferns and other sporophyte plants that came before them in that they have an added gametophyte phase, or generation, in their reproductive cycle. However, unlike the ferns and other spore-reproducing plants, all the steps of the gymnosperm reproductive cycle (except pollen dispersal) take place within their reproductive structures—their cones. Gymnosperms have pollen-producing and seed-producing cones: so-called male cones produce male gametophytes (essentially an evolutionary intermediary relict phase from spore-producing plants), and these gametophytes mature to produce the pollen grains neces-sary for fertilizing the seed-producing eggs. Seed cones produce spores on their scales, and these develop into so-called female gametophytes that produce an egg inside an ovule, again on the scale itself—not in the enclosed ovary that characterizes the later evolution of the angiosperms. The wind-dispersed gymnosperm pollen allows fertilization of the mature egg, from which the final seed (like a pine nut) develops and disperses when ready. Gymno-sperms are known as "naked seeds" because the egg, and the seed, are relatively exposed to the environment, not housed within a protective ovary or fruit.

All seed-bearing plants have cotyledons—leaves formed within the seed that are the first to appear after germination. Cotyledons help provide nutrients to the germinated seedling. Gymnosperm seeds have a varying number of cotyledons, but always more than two, to support the seedling's early growth. Angiosperms are largely divided into monocots (one cotyledon) and dicots (two cotyledons).

Whereas gymnosperms have the gametophyte generation in their reproductive cycle, angiosperms have two fertilization steps before the formation of the seed: the first is fusion of the sperm from the pollen with the egg in the ovary to form the embryo. The second is the fusion of the sperm and the nuclei in the embryo sac to form the endosperm with the nutrients for the seedling after germination (although not all angiosperms, such as those in the orchid family of Orchidaceae, form endosperm).

Here is a quick reminder about botanical Latin and taxon-omy, the scientific practice of organizing, classifying, and naming plants, and all living things, based on presumed relationships, a system proposed by Swedish botanist, zoologist, and physician Carolus Linnaeus in his *Systema Naturae* in 1758. Botanical Latin is a universal language that allows plant people the world over to understand each other and the plants they are talking about. Currently, all known living organisms are grouped by these classifications, starting with the most general and ending with the most specific: domain, kingdom, phylum, class, order, family, and finally the "binomial": genus and species. A few variations on this have developed over time, and within this basic hierarchy you may find subfamilies, tribes, subtribes, subgenus, or subspecies.

That said, of greatest interest for our exploration into seed and seed-bearing plants is from family (and subfamily) down: (tribe and subtribe as needed), genus, subgenus, and species (and beyond to subspecies and varieties). The Latin family name is capitalized and ends in *-aceae*, which translates to "from the family of," so Iridaceae means iris family, Rosaceae means rose family, and so on.

Within angiosperms, the largest and most diverse form of land-based plant life, it's generally accepted that there are currently 406 families, a little over 14,000 genera, and somewhere over 273,000 known species. It has long been thought that flowering plants evolved 145 to 140 million years ago in coevolutionary partnerships that continue to this day. Animals of all kinds (birds, insects, mammals including humans) are attracted by flowers, their nutrient-rich pollen and nectar, and their nutrient-rich seeds, and, via one mechanism or another, help to disperse that seed. However, fossilized angiosperm-like pollen found in Switzerland in 2013 dates to more than 240 million years ago, suggesting our beloved flowering plants (and their partnerships) have been here far longer than we previously understood.

And from all of those millions of individual evolutionary tweaks from the beginnings of seed-bearing plant life, we are currently in the glorious company of an immense diversity, symphony, and panoply of their collective seed.

This very riotous diversity of seed forms and methods of attraction and dispersal is one of the primary reasons that the angiosperms were able to take a relatively short amount of time to go from being the new plants on the shoreline to dominating our earthly lives.

Plants are generally (and historically) grouped according to similarities in their floral parts, rather than similarities in their leaves or trunks or other vegetative parts. The reason for this is that the shape, color, habit, size, etc. of leaves and stems are far more adaptable and immediately impacted by new, or challenging, or seasonal, or just different conditions. So while foliage and other structural aspects of a plant can look very different under different conditions, their flowers—their reproductive parts—will still look and work with predictive similarity.

And as we drill down into a plant's classifications, we find that plants in the same family or subfamily often have notable (and helpful) similarities to the look and structure of their seeds and related structures.

There are some accepted anatomical elements shared by most seeds—angiosperms *and* gymnosperms. But, as we know with plants (and life?), where there is a "rule" there are a healthy handful of notable exceptions.

Generally speaking, with angiosperms, after the pollen successfully finds the flower's stigma with the help of wind, water, or animal, the pollen grain (pollen grains themselves displaying an amazing diversity of complex structures, shapes, and color, often complementary to the surface shape and texture of their partner stigma) germinates in its own way to grow a pollen tube that moves down the style to the ovary, which the pollen tube penetrates to reach the ovule(s). Together the whole female reproductive unit of stigma, style, ovary, and ovule is called the carpel. A flower's pistil is made up of one or more carpels.

Inside the ovule, the pollen grain delivers three haploid (having a single set of unpaired chromosomes carrying the genetic-information-bearing genes) cells. These cells unite with the haploid cells found inside the ovary. One cell from the pollen grain goes to the formation of an embryo, and the remaining two cells help form the nutrient-rich endosperm.

The ovary containing the fertilized ovules matures into the fruit of the plant, which encloses the seed. While the word *fruit* might connote a soft or fleshy food, like an apple or peach, botanically it means the matured ovary enclosing a matured ovule (seed). In this sense, a fruit can be soft and sweet, like the peach, or hard and dry, like most grains or nuts. The ovary wall then matures to become the pericarp, the outer layer(s) of the fruit, often as the husk, rind, or skin of an enclosing fruit (think banana peel or orange rind or acorn shell). The wall of the ovule becomes the seed coat or testa, the outer protective layer of the seed often helpful in regulating germination. On some fruits the pericarp looks indistinguishable from (or is fused with) the seed coat itself. On many dispersed or detached seeds, the seed coat is marked or scarred at the place where the seed was attached to the plant stem. This "belly button" of the seed is the hilum.

The seed matures as the fruit around it matures and ripens. Ultimately, the seed consists of the outermost seed coat; the nutritious, starchy endosperm, which the embryo and then seedling live on until roots and photosynthesizing leaves are up and running; and the embryo itself, consisting of the cotyledon(s); the radicle, which will become the first depth-seeking root; the hypocotyl, which will become the first single stem bearing the seed leaf; the epicotyl, the portion of the stem that will grow up beyond the first seed leaf/leaves and off of which the first true photosynthesizing leaves will grow; and the plumule, which consists of the epicotyl and the embryonic growing bud tip.

The science of the seeds and dispersal mechanisms of the seed-bearing plants is a vast field of botanical study known as seed ecology, or carpology. Seeds and their diverse dispersal structures (together known as diaspores), as well as their modes of pollination (wind, water, animal) and dispersal (more on that as we go) are remarkable feats of nature's engineering.

Seed biology is a mind-blowing marvel. Every aspect and element has its own vocabulary and distinct and specialized areas of study. Botanists would assert that there is likely as much still to be learned as we "know" today.

As Thor Hanson muses, "If evolution [as many contend] progresses towards singularity, then how do we explain diversity— the 20,000 different grasses, the 35,000 different dung beetles, the profusion of ducks, rhododendrons, hermit crabs, gnats, and warblers? Why are the most ancient life forms on the planet, bacteria and archaea, [even now] more diverse and prolific than all other species combined? Given time, evolution is much more likely to provide us with a multitude of solutions than it is to give us one ideal form." And yet, we are living in a time when gardeners and homeowners continue to pamper 40 million acres of synthetically fertilized, fossil-fuel-mown, and overwatered monoculture turf grass in the United States (more acreage is dedicated to turf grass than most of our largest national parks put together). Why don't we see more beauty in diversity than homogeny?

In 2019, the United Nations (U.N.) reported that "the average abundance of native species in most major land-based habitats has fallen by at least 20%, mostly since 1900, and that around 1 million animal and plant species are now threatened with extinction, many within decades, more than ever before in human history."

But, this same 2019 U.N. report also noted, "it is not too late to make a difference, if we start now at every level from local to global. Through 'transformative change,' nature can still be conserved, restored, and [engaged with] sustainably—this is also key to meeting most other global goals [like managing water more effectively, and curbing greenhouse gases, and improving urban air and water quality]. By transformative change, we mean a fundamental, system-wide reorganization across technological, economic, and social factors, including paradigms, goals, and values."

Where does seed figure into this pervasive need for transformative change? Clearly in the very center, but how do we translate it into useful acts?

Seed is illegible to many of us.

Why is that? Complacency? Conspiracy?

NOVEMBER 7

The road through the canyon where John has made his life these past
35-plus years, and where I have been making much of mine these past
5 years, mirrors the contours of the creek running alongside. Hugging
close here, veering more distant there, crossing and crossing back, much
like the lives of the plants that call this creek, road, and canyon home.

All along the road, a buffet of seeds is offered out most days of most
seasons: from lower-lying grasses and bulbs to skyward-reaching vines,
the largest of persistent shrubs, mighty trees, and back down to the most
petite and fleeting of spring's ephemeral wildflowers. Native and non,
invasive and non, they all share the same survivors' goal—to survive, and
to be noticed by pollinators and seed dispersers, as a means to that end.

Today the iris and the *Calochortus* seed heads catch the eye higher up
on the road, where a spring seeps off the canyon's eastern slope and
forms rich green swathes of plant life along it. These spring-blooming
friends are now in their fall clothing—their ever-returning seed form. Iris
and *Calochortus*, I will look forward to meeting you in green growth and
flower again, but despite a fall full of smoke and fire, COVID-19, rampant
and long-lived social injustice, and all else that might make us despair,
it is my favorite season to watch you, as you cloak your essence in suspended animation.

If seeds, among the greatest teachers on this planet, can show up and
keep teaching, it feels loud and clear to me that I have a duty to show up
and keep learning.

The iris occurring all along this canyon is a local strain of the
native endemic California *Iris douglasiana,* and while we have
at least three kinds of *Calochortus* in the canyon, the seed
heads here are of *Calochortus albus.* Its graceful, translucent,
lantern-shaped flower is formed by three white pendent petals
tinged with pink-purple that overlap each other slightly to form
a globe. The flowers nod on their stems as they seem to climb
the canyon's shaded slope beneath oak and pine, intermingling

throughout the seasons with surrounding grasses, other herbs, and shrubs—especially poison oak and toyon. These little blooms light up a spring scene, and their common name—fairy lantern—is descriptively perfect.

Now, in the autumn seed harvest and sometimes final-shaking-out dispersal season, the seed heads themselves catch my eye as much as their blooms do in spring.

Both the iris and the *Calochortus* are monocots and are among California's many native geophytes. And like all geophytes—plants with rhizomes, bulbs, or corms—they hold a good portion of their nutrients in their below-ground structures, which allows them to withstand a lot of above-ground disturbance, from flood, to fire, to our extended seasons of drought.

Both of these plants have rugged and tough seeds as well—seeds and pods that have persisted intact through a long and very hot, dry summer and early fall to now. While the seed pods themselves have dried and cracked open (dehisced) to allow the seed to disperse, some seeds still hang on—and will perhaps be released into the world to eke out a place among so many larger plants with the next wind or rain event, or by the chance nudging of a passing mammal or bird, or by a falling cone or twig.

It's absolutely miraculous that even the smallest of the seeds and seed-bearing plants—the tiniest of wildflowers and herbs—are as tenacious, fierce, and resourceful in finding ways, means, and places for their seed to succeed as their largest kin, the trees.

Darwin, Mendel, Linnaeus: titans in the West's seed ecology world, students of seed of a very high order. These are dead white men from whom we can learn a great deal.

And yet . . . and yet. I want more perspective than their glass lenses or their guiding sights and insights can provide. I want to get before, behind, beyond them to experience life without the blinders they may have unintentionally applied to this science, to re-hear, re-see the seeds and their inherent knowledge all around us. I want to learn through other notable seed teacher-students of our time who bring their own passions and lenses. I would like to learn more about seeds and seed people by establishing my own direct relationship with them.

The seeds have been here far longer than we have—if we listen, they will share. We are all students of seeds, if unknowingly.

As a mother and gardener, I want to believe we have the capacity and the desire to re-seed a better future from this low (hopefully turning) point.

Because sometimes in understanding more fully how the smallest essences thrive, we can better support the larger whole.

Because I feel sure that gardens and gardeners can save the world and that those gardens and gardeners are born of more fully understood, valued, heard, and heeded seed.

And I think many others believe this too.

NOVEMBER 10

On our morning walk we notice that the narrowleaf milkweed (*Asclepias fascicularis*) pods, known as follicles, have finally opened. They're just dry enough that the pointy ends crack and split along the seam (or suture), expanding enough to reveal the pure shimmering white of the silky hair plumes inside—each attached precisely to the end of one rounded, shiny, chocolate-colored seed. The seeds are arranged in an overlapping pattern, like fish scales. They look orderly and patient, but the wider the seam of the slightly warty follicle casing opens, the more wind and moisture from the outside enter, and the more the plumes ruffle and become untidy. At this point in the progression, each seed looks to be jostling impatiently for the next step—the loosening from its stillness and dormancy to its first ride on a breeze into the big, wide world—to wherever the wind might float it.

The big, bold buckeyes too are ripening and swelling within their sturdy outer shells.

Seeds might seem still, quiet, passive. But in them all is a forceful dynamism not to be underestimated.

Just observing closely the physical attributes of seed and their structures can tell you something about how they work in the world. The milkweed's plumed seed helps it take flight on the wind; the buckeye's solid orb falls heavily and sturdily with the aid of gravity to the ground below.

You will often notice that while a flower can bloom upright (like the buckeye), advertising itself boldly to passing pollinators, a plant's ultimate dried seed heads will not always have the same orientation. Once a flower has been pollinated, the subsequent seed head or pod can either be pendent or upright. Sometimes they can start out upright and then mature to be pendent, bowing under their own weight, or vice versa, allowing for the seeds to spread more easily via their dispersal method of choice.

NOVEMBER 11
The first measurable rain! Less than 0.10 of an inch, we guess. The redbud (*Cercis occidentalis*) at the end of the deck sparkles in its sunset orange-red-pink coloring.

This small multitrunk tree is loaded every year with dangling, dried seed-holding pea-pods that turn a lovely light burnt red. We select its seedlings to plant on and continue this coloration.

NOVEMBER 12
The 2021 Whole Seed Catalog arrives in the mail—500 packed pages of seeds and seed stories from around the world curated by Jere Gettle, founder of Baker Creek Heirloom Seeds. On page 249 is a full-page photo of one of Jere and wife Emilie's daughters under a full moon holding two large white moonflower blossoms.

The image would make my mother smile.

NOVEMBER 13

John's house is nestled into the western slope of this canyon. From the road we walk daily to his house, there is about 180 feet of elevation gain; from the creek bed to the top of the canyon on either side, east and west, you gain almost 400 feet of elevation. The topography of the canyon—with the road and the creek the primary conduits in and out—serves as a microcosm for the study of plant and seed isolation, dispersal, and distribution.

For instance, the range of the oaks. Oaks come in two large groups, the red oak and the white oak groups. The valley and the blue oaks are both members of the white oak group and are capable of interbreeding. Throughout the canyon, crosses and cross-backs between the lineages result in a large number of variations. Different relative gene pools are visible everywhere: some tall, some branching, some squat and arching. You can see these crossed siblings and cousins marching up or down a slope, across a wide field—like extended family members coming for a picnic. And bringing most of the food.

At the highest, northern end of the canyon, bigleaf maple (*Acer macrophyllum*) lines the creek bottom of the canyon but does not occur as far south as our part of the creek; western sycamore (*Platanus racemosa*) rise ghostly white and statuesque both north and south of us along the creek—at the mouth of the canyon and farther up—but they do not make it to us in the middle of the canyon, and we're not exactly sure why: Wrong elevation? Different temperature ranges? Eradicated sometime in the history of the place, or have the seeds simply not successfully dispersed to this locale? Each—the maple and the sycamore—seem to like their respective places, and so we, and the oaks, mingle with them where they are.

NOVEMBER 20

Last year's alder "cones" are dropping from upper branches of these creek-side trees right now—the new catkins nearly fully formed, perhaps pushing the last season's produce just above them off their shared branches.

Making room for the new is a recurring theme in the plant and seed world.

The little staggered clusters sprinkle small seeds when you shake them—like coarse ground pepper the color of cinnamon.

Communities of native white alder (*Alnus rhombifolia*) line the creek the length of the canyon. They are quick growing and fix nitrogen, benefiting the other riparian community members. They grow up and are pulled down with the rise and fall of the creek throughout the years, seasons, winter storm surges. Alders bear pollen-producing flowers as well as seed-producing flowers—both relatively insignificant in the flower stages. The pollen-bearing flowers appear in early January here and eventually coalesce into droopy, slender catkins between two and eight inches long, in groups of three to five. The small seed-bearing flowers also form catkins, but these range in length from less than an inch to under three inches, in clusters of two or three. It is inside these smaller, squatter catkins, which mature from fleshy green to woody and cinnamon colored, that the winged nutlets are enclosed until dispersal—at which point you can shake the little woody catkins like a pepper shaker to release the seeds. It is these seed catkins that closely resemble a small conifer cone. Individual alders produce both the pollen- and seed-bearing catkins. The brown seed catkins from the previous season, and their elongated pale green winter-bright pollen-producing catkins of this season are easily visible throughout the trees' deciduous stage. So, despite first appearances, they are not wind-pollinated gymnosperms, like the gray and ponderosa pines of the canyon, but wind-pollinated angiosperms.

Resident and very recognizable conifer (and gymnosperm!) gray pines are a reliable companion of blue oaks (angiosperm) in these foothill environments. The gray pine nut, so rich in fatty nutrients, is not dramatically different from the 100 or so other species of pine and pine nuts growing across the Northern Hemisphere—some of which live to over 1000 years old. *Pinus longaeva*, the famous Great Basin bristlecone pines (so-called for the sharp bristles on their seed cones) of the limestone, alpine reaches of California's White Mountains south and east of here are the oldest non-clonal plant species on the planet; the oldest living individual (discovered in 2012) is estimated to be more than 5060 years old.

The fact that blue oak and gray pine coexist so well across interior Northern California comes down to, at the very least, the fact that both species are well adapted to the long, hot, dry summers of the region. Both can thrive in poor, lean soils—and sometimes in serpentine soils, whose chemical composition rich in magnesium, iron, and nickel has caused plants to evolve such that they grow *only* in this unique environment. Both have adapted to withstand fire, or to resprout and regenerate in its wake. But where some oaks and conifers will compete for resources like light, water, and ground, these two live fairly harmoniously. The blue oak is deciduous, allowing ample rain and sun through its bare canopy in winter, and its small leaves let in light and water in summer. Its winter leaf fall feeds the soil and organisms around both species. The gray pine is noted as having among the airiest of conifer canopies, long and loosely arranged needle clusters. It often grows on an angle and on slopes, thereby minimizing shade cast and maximizing precipitation and light shared.

Being competitive in challenging conditions is important, but perhaps there is a lesson here in learning to live in community?

For the various Maiduan peoples the gray pine nut was a very important food source. Ali Meders-Knight is a plantswoman of Mechoopda Maidu descent. A leader of traditional ecological knowledge here in Northern California, Meders-Knight says that the "gray pines and the oaks are buddies, just as the willow and the mugwort are friends," growing better together. When she sees any one of these without their favored plant companions, she thinks they feel and look lonely.

Pine nuts feed a multitude of birds who have coevolved to seek them out, to crack them open, and to feast on the endosperm of the nut, which is said to have almost 600 calories per gram.

Remember Darwin's observations of finches from *The Voyage of the Beagle*, and their place in his development of the theory of natural selection, wherein the finches on the Galapagos had a wide variety of beak shapes and sizes? Darwin posited they'd all descended from one mainland ancestor but that over time different beak adaptations had naturally selected—or coevolved—the large-beaked finches to thrive because they could feed more easily on the larger hard-shelled seeds of the islands. The smaller-beaked finches had likewise been naturally selected over time for their ability to thrive on the smaller, softer seeds.

Seeds have lessons for anyone who looks, from eminent scientists to creek-side amblers.

Interestingly, pine nuts are often most easily dispersed by being released from their cones after the cleansing, scarifying effects of fire. The heat opens the often resin-sealed cones and weakens the seed coats on the nuts. Blue oaks, by contrast, prefer to resprout from crown or stump, rather than seed bank, after a fire.

The point here is that acorns and pine nuts, two different adaptations, grow one climate-adapted forest full of life, and help feed human and avian and bushy-tailed rodent economies along the way. If "ecology" is considered the relations of organisms to one another and to their physical surroundings, the blue oak and gray pine woodland is a simple embodiment of a thriving seed ecology.

Seeds are not just in the woods; they are everywhere humans might find themselves. Or are we everywhere seeds are? There is no one "seed" season—seeds form on different kinds of plants throughout each seasonal cycle, providing a wide range of habitable earth for the ecologies that support us.

Once you really see one plant's seed, you begin to see seed everywhere. Learning to identify a plant's seed form is to instantly begin to know that plant more fully, more truly in all its phases, seasons, voices, and garb. Understanding involves not just seeing, but truly knowing another; and in more fully knowing this other form life can take, we can also have a greater understanding and more intimate, accurate, and real relationship with the world around us.

NOVEMBER 22
John collected a stem of scarlet monkeyflower (*Erythranthe cardinalis*) seed pods for me, and they have been sitting in a glass on the kitchen counter for a few days. He shows me the dustlike coating at the bottom of the container to remind me to hop to storing them properly if I want to save any for spring germination in pots. I gently snip the dun-colored papery capsules (some just opening, others already wide open) into a small envelope. The almost spore-like seeds are obvious against the white of the paper.

Seeds have distinct traits and personalities, and seed people often have very particular relationships with particular seeds: for example, Cheryl Birker, manager of the seed conservation program at

California Botanic Garden (CalBG, located in Southern California and focused on documenting, studying, and conserving plants of the California Floristic Province) loathes cleaning minute seeds, like those of monkeyflowers, while Naomi Fraga, manager of the CalBG conservation programs, is dedicated to those same monkeyflowers (which have long been in genus *Mimulus* but in 2018 were botanically divided into *Mimulus*, *Erythranthe*, and *Diplacus*). Ephemeral and small-flowered, they lead bright and tough little lives. Fraga loves their mysterious ways, all contained in a dustlike speck of life.

Beyond the cardinal monkeyflower, at least two other varieties of the *Erythranthe* genus live in the canyon, all along the creek: the yellow (a.k.a. seep) monkeyflower (*Erythranthe guttata*), and the shield-bracted monkeyflower (*Erythranthe glaucescens*), their seeds dispersed by wind and water, swirling and eddying in the currents and breezes of the riparian corridor, finding their tiny but determined way in the world.

Every summer that John can remember, one particularly tenacious (and well-rooted) cardinal monkeyflower has persisted in blooming from the slenderest of cracks in a large basalt rock in the middle of the creek, in a shady bend near where we like to swim or wade on hot days. Several scientific sources have pointed out that cardinal monkeyflower, with other species in this genus, are of scientific interest for studying pollinator-based reproduction in relative isolation. This stream-channel specimen's nearest relative is downstream at least 500 winding feet. This has meant that while in the creek ourselves on said hot, hot afternoons, we have often been joined by the visiting hummingbirds whose beaks are fitted perfectly for its deeply red and deeply tubular flowers.

How do the hummingbirds find these flowers with such precision, we wonder? Sight, sight, sound, memory?

NOVEMBER 24
The sandhill cranes are in.

You can hear them overhead day and night and in the rice checks and dairy meadows around the nearby towns well before you spot them. Tall, gangly creatures on the ground and long, gray, painterly streaks across the smooth sky, they have stilts for legs, gray plumage, a characteristic red forehead, and yellow eyes. We go to watch them sometimes, stopping along the fence line of a nearby rice farmer's checks. Their paired dancing and distinctive calling make them an annual winter treat along our part of the Pacific Flyway. Their duets are part of the mating ritual, and these churring, trilling, bugling, yodeling call-and-response routines are performed between the same pair sometimes for years, according to the Cornell Lab of Ornithology, before they breed. Serenades before sex.

Despite being omnivores and supplementing their diets with insects, snails, and the like, the sandhill cranes are among the world's seedeaters, like the granivorous California quail and dove (whose diets are up to 80 percent seed), frugivorous robins and cedar waxwings (whose diet is up to 60 percent fruit and seed), and omnivorous wild turkeys and acorn woodpeckers, all of whom live their full lives in the canyon. These seedeaters need seed.

And the seeds need these animals and insects for reliable processing and dispersal.

A loss of animal and insect diversity and the degradation and loss of habitats through human development and human-caused climate change results in a vicious disruption to this vital exchange.

This extinction cascade can create a negative feedback loop: lose seed-eating and seed-dispersing animals and insects and lose plant resilience; lose plants and seeds and lose animal resilience and survival.

This is a lose-lose situation.

We humans live not apart from this situation, but very much *within* it, along with the rest of our wildlife planet-mates and family. According to journalist Carolyn Fry, "Although 7000 food crops are cultivated or harvested from the wild, [in the 21st century, most] humans derive half our plant-based calories from just three: rice, maize, and wheat. Sorghum, millet, potatoes, sweet potatoes, soybean and sugar (from beet and cane) account for a further 25% of our energy intake."

NOVEMBER 26
The roadside toyon (*Heteromeles arbutifolia*) berries have colored up for the season; ripening from pale green to a yellowy orange to a full rich red is a process that marks time between Halloween and the winter solstice here. Their jolly red clusters hang heavy and high on branches covered in leathery, serrated evergreen leaves. It makes for a very seasonal scene. Is the ripening triggered by waning light, by growing chill? I am not sure. But the overwintering robins are quick to report that they are ready for them, as are the migrating cedar waxwings.

Local journalist Sue Rosenthal writes, "Cedar waxwings and toyon berries: It's one of those iconic California food-web pairings, like black bears and manzanita berries or southern sea otters and sea urchins ... One of the few true frugivores (fruit feeders) among birds, the cedar waxwing can assimilate nutrients solely from fruit—low in calories and protein compared with insects— for weeks at a time. Toyon berries are technically pomes, like apples, and their seeds contain similar toxins. Green toyon berries are loaded with poisonous cyanogenic glucosides, but as they mature, their toxins shift from pulp to seed and the berries turn red, signaling their edibility. Waxwings safely pass the toxic seeds through their guts and back into the environment intact, in the process dispersing toyons to new areas."

In this, Rosenthal offers just one example of the incredible importance of seed to wildlife both winged and four-legged with the mention of bears and manzanita berries. Similarly, brown bears (and other megafaunal seedeaters) are critical to the continuation and genetic diversity of the plants whose seed they eat: in one study, brown bears were found to have consumed seeds from "at least 101 fleshy-fruited plant species belonging to 24 families and 42 genera, of which the blackberry/raspberry genus—Rubus family (Rosaceae)—and blueberry/huckleberry genus—Vaccinium family (Ericaceae)—constituted the largest quantity eaten." Seeds eaten by bears germinated at higher percentages than seed from whole uneaten fruits (meaning this fruit had no seed coat preparation or removal as the seeds that went through a bear's gut did), and at similar percentages as manually cleaned seeds. Thus, "brown bears are effective and important seed dispersers as they consume large quantities of seeds that remain viable after gut passage. The decline of these megafaunal frugivores [or other declining fruit-and-seed-eating animals] may compromise seed dispersal services and plant regeneration processes."

Dr. Doug Tallamy (and Dr. E. O. Wilson before him, to some extent) has spent the lion's share of his entomological and advocacy career researching and reporting on the importance of insects and their larva to the persistence and health of all life on the planet. In an urgent call to action to stanch the increasing loss of biodiversity we are witnessing in this age—variously referred to as the Anthropocene, the Sixth Extinction, and not incidentally or ironically, the Age of Loneliness—Tallamy makes a plea to regular homeowners, gardeners, and in particular bird lovers, to eliminate their use of toxic chemicals (synthetic fertilizers and biocides, including herbicides, fungicides, rodenticides, and especially insecticides), and to significantly increase their planting of a diversity of native plants well known to support the full life cycles of insects (from larva to adult). Because, he points out, it is the larval, caterpillar stage of insect life that is the foundation on which so much of the food chain above it rests and relies—caterpillars are many birds' preferred morsel. It is, Tallamy and Wilson warn us, the stability of that larval and insect foundation that allows for the great biodiversity on which our entire planet's quality of life depends. Eliminate or severely diminish insect life at our own (and everyone else's) peril.

It's no great leap to realize, then, that what the caterpillars themselves have to eat—and, by extension, what seeds gardeners plant for them—is also critically important and also a severely overlooked and underappreciated aspect that contributes in an outsize way to worldwide health.

Diminish the diversity of seed, diminish its quantity or quality, its integrity, or its complexity, and you degrade life for all living organisms here on earth.

On the walk today, at the top of the road just a little farther along than the iris and *Calochortus*, the backlit coyote brush (*Baccharis pilularis*) glows spectacularly. Each bush looks like it is in full white flower—and just like flowers in their season advertise a readiness to be fertilized (pollinated) via color, form, scent, and pheromones, the white, parachute-like plumes (known as pappus) at the top of every tiny seed in these fluffy flower-like clusters are just beginning to open in invitation to the wind and the wildlife.

DECEMBER

Seedshed

NEW MOON, DECEMBER 14
FULL MOON, DECEMBER 30

DECEMBER 1

John and I take a field trip to Plumas National Forest with a Forest Service tree-cutting permit in hand. We are in search of a Christmas tree; our decoration will simultaneously help to thin a fire-prone forest so long as we cut according to their guidelines.

It is a sunny, cold winter day, and we are glad for the fresh air, the outing taking us further afield than everyday life for this interlude in annual and seasonal ritual. We hike along the logging and forest service roads, entering into clearings or carefully working our way through low brush whenever we see a likely spot to look for a crowded juvenile grove we could choose from in the mixed forest. As we hike, our heads down to navigate around stems and branches, through sometimes dense brush of dead grasses, low-growing shrubs, we identify trees of this place (and thus the makeup of the forest) by way of their fruits and seed dotting the ground or scattered across hardened snowpack: black oak, with their heavily scaled cups and thick, dark nuts; Douglas fir, with their whiskered, malty-brown cones; white fir, studded with roundly columnar, horizontally layered scales; fleshy clusters of textured, orange-to-red berries of the broadleaf evergreen madrones; and the firm, rounded berries of green or chestnut brown of several manzanitas. All are evident. We even note the mealy algal-green clumps of mistletoe, bunches of waxy, sticky, ivory-colored berries, in the canopies and branch joints of some trees.

Know your forest and you will learn your cones, nuts, and berries; know your cones, nuts, and berries and you will know your forests.

In fact, a deliciously specific vocabulary exists to help us learn the names of seed shapes, sizes, and structures. From *pappus* for the feathery appendages on seeds of the Asteraceae, to *pome* for the fruit of some members of the rose family, to *loculicidal follicle* describing the seed pods of the milkweed family—Apocynaceae. Seed scientists employ special names to designate the differences—sometimes obvious, sometimes nuanced—in the form and function of *diaspores*, the word for seeds plus their physical dispersal structures.

Here is a primer on some of the common form, shape, or function terms, with examples:

accessory fruit: develops from an ovary or ovaries, but some portion of its whole develops from nonovarian tissue near the carpel (female reproductive part) (e.g., strawberry, rose hip, apple, fig, pineapple).

achene: small, dry, indehiscent fruit with a single chamber and single seed, attached at a single point (e.g., sunflower, strawberry seed).

acorn: hard, dry, indehiscent fruit of oaks, with a single large seed and cuplike base.

awn: a hair- or needlelike stiff bristle that aids in dispersal. For example, attached to the lemma (chaff-like bract enclosing the floret) of many grasses, such as wheat, barley, purple needle grass; the central column of the pappus of Asteraceae; and the central column of the mericarp of Geraniaceae.

berry: fleshy fruit with several or many seeds. Usually lacking a pit or core (e.g., tomato).

burr: fruit armed with hooked or barbed spines.

capsule: a dry, dehiscent fruit composed of more than one carpel (e.g., poppies, lilies).

caryopsis: dry, one-seeded, indehiscent fruit with seed coat fused to the seed body (e.g., grains).

drupe: fleshy, indehiscent fruit with a stony endocarp surrounding the seed (e.g., peach). Fruits like raspberries are aggregates of small drupes, or drupelets.

follicle: dry, dehiscent fruit composed of a single carpel (e.g., milkweed). Opens on one side.

fruit: mature, ripened ovary of a plant, along with the contents of the ovary. The ovary is the ovule-bearing reproductive structure in the plant flower.

hesperidium: a berry with a leathery rind (e.g., citrus).

hip: berry-like structure composed of an enlarged hypanthium (tube beneath the petals) surrounding numerous achenes (e.g., rose hip).

legume: dry, dehiscent fruit formed from a single carpel and opening along two seams (e.g., pea).

nut: hard, dry, indehiscent fruit usually with a single seed (e.g., styrax, buckeye).

pappus: hairs, bristles, or scales on some fruit, specifically achenes of plants in Asteraceae, aiding the seed in wind dispersal (e.g., dandelion, thistle, lettuce).

pepo: a berry with a hard, thick rind (e.g., melons, gourds, pumpkins).

pome: ovary or core surrounded by edible, fleshy tissue (e.g., apple, pear, quince, loquat). The actual ovary or core is usually not eaten, at least by most humans.

samara: dry, indehiscent winged fruit (e.g., maple).

schizocarp: dry, indehiscent fruit that splits into one-seeded segments when ripe (e.g., mallow, and most species in borage, carrot, and geranium families).

silicle/silique: dry, dehiscent fruits of the family Brassica, with two valves separating from the persistent placentae and septum (e.g., mustard, broccoli). Silicle less than twice as long as wide; silique more than twice as long as wide.

DECEMBER 4

Two small packets of Palestinian heritage wheat seed I ordered after interviewing Vivien Sansour, founder of the Palestine Heirloom Seed Library (PHSL), arrived in the mail today. The mission of the PHSL is to find and share heirloom seeds of cultural importance to the history and people of Palestine; centuries of war have taken a toll on all agriculture, but especially on traditional small farmers there. Vivien hopes to help get that seed into the hands and soils of people who can steward it for future generations of farmers and so the Palestinian diaspora—like her—still have access to something of where they came from. Palestine, as part of the ancient Fertile Crescent, is a center for biodiversity of wheat and its wild relatives.

My region of California was a wheat-growing center after the gold rush in 1849 (before wheat was literally supplanted by our current large commodity crops: rice, almonds, walnuts, prunes and plums, citrus). Wheat is well suited to our hot, dry summer and wet winter climate, but the commercial wheat industry quickly depleted the soil by overplanting and monocropping. Then came drought. The major markets were at that time still in the east as well, so shipping was another hurdle. It was simply easier to grow wheat at scale elsewhere.

As a gardener, I am excited to meet these storied wheat grains, try them out in the dryland canyon garden. To become a small part of their story of preservation and perseverance. In thinking about planting even this small packet of wheat, I conjure romantic visions of dried wheat-stalk bouquets in fall, of threshing, winnowing, and then grinding the rich grains, of baking with the flour from that small harvest. I open the little white packets scrolled with bold, black Arabic lettering—but no seed! In their three-dimensional living place along with informational papers from Disarming Design, Palestinian distributors of some of Vivien's PHSL offerings, is an official notice from US Customs saying the seed has been "seized."

I have no seed-importing license—apparently a requirement to receive even a single packet.

This is no doubt intended as genetic (and financial) protection for our agricultural industry, maybe even for the environmental seedsheds of the United States—I don't discount these issues. But I can't help feeling that seizing a small packet of home garden seed for a noninvasive food crop from an accredited vendor is also simply obstructing small growers and breeders. It is exerting control and censorship of the free exchange of seed.

A delicate and tricky tension exists in ongoing efforts to balance preserving a way of life with efforts to preserve an existing ecosystem. Could my planting and sharing historic Palestinian wheat have helped to save that wheat for the future? Could planting that wheat here, well out of its historic range, have irreparably damaged this canyon? The remaining commercial wheat growing of Northern California and our regional food and seed security?

DECEMBER 10

Watersheds, foodsheds, viewsheds, fibersheds. If you harm one aspect of the related systems and their carefully calibrated processes—you harm the whole.

Violence against the seedshed is violence against the seed; violence against the seed is violence against the seedshed and the community of life within it: all the organic organizing elements of the web of life in which we find ourselves—the geology, the seeps and springs and creeks and rivers moving to the oceans, the grasslands, and the forests, the birds, the reptiles, the mammals.

As the watershed and seedshed and historic human web of relations are to this little canyon, so too is this canyon to the planet. We as humans have done a great deal of damage in the name of things we believe in, from religion to transportation to farming; we can never seem to get past protecting our own survival or comfort rather than protect the needs of future generations.

From war-ravaged and culturally torn areas of the world like Palestine and Israel, to the more than hundreds and hundreds of current EPA Superfund sites (many agro-industrial) across the country (more than 90 in the state of Pennsylvania; more than 110 in New Jersey; close to 110 in California), these conflicting but interrelated dilemmas—for better or worse—seed our collective futures and our immediate understanding and decision-making.

DECEMBER 21: WINTER SOLSTICE
The moon is bright and clear, rising through a precise notch in the canyon wall directly east of John's house. It's some 20 degrees north of its position just three months ago, at the autumnal equinox. An annual and seasonal reminder of our constant planetary journey.

The coyote brush (*Baccharis pilularis*) is still in such wide-open, big-hearted, full-throated seed "bloom" that it glows by day and even more luminously by moonlight on the meadowy hillside at the top of the road. Torch-like branches are held high, positively resplendent with the white seed plumes ... even a little breath of the cold night air sends them trembling and jostling and then ...

hesitantly at first ...

lifting

upward

from their assigned places and ...

shh ...

phshh ...

whshhhh.

Down and up and off onto the air current—

into the world.

Little parachutes of life and hope, past and present.

Ripe ...

rich ...

redolent.

DECEMBER 24

Winter is a season of final seed dispersal here, a culmination of the celestial and seed year—a very literal ending-beginning line between not only seasons, but generations of life. Acorns in October, iris and *Calochortus* in November, and now alder catkins and coyote brush at the solstice.

If seeds are going to get out into the world, for at least a percentage of them to find good growing grounds and continue their species, they need to be separated from their mother or parent plants. They need to be dispersed. And in a lot of cases, seeds (and therefore their otherwise mostly stationary parent plants) need help. They need to attract that help in order to send the seed off in the best way, at the right time, and under the best conditions.

Seeds may simply drop and roll, but they are also flung, they fly, hitchhike on animals, are transported by birds and bears, carried and buried by ants and beetles, and moved from one place to another by water and wind.

To find that perfect niche, a plant may need to move across mountain ranges, up and down canyon slopes, or stay right close to its place of origin in its currently successful community. It needs mechanisms that increase the probability of finding a foothold, whether the consistently moist habitats that the stream orchid (*Epipactis gigantea*) requires, or the crisp, draining alluvial fan in which California's desert lavender (*Condea emoryi*) grows.

Often plants have several methods to send their seeds out into the world—primary *and* secondary dispersal adaptations. The seeds of the California native bush poppy (*Dendromecon rigida*), for example, are flung out and away from the parent plant with impressive torque created by the drying silique. Once the seeds are on the ground, a fleshy appendage (known as an elaiosome) on the seed attracts ants. Ants carry the seed and the elaiosome back to their nest, eat the elaiosome or share it with their larvae, and the still-intact seed is either left in the nest or removed as waste by the ants, allowing it to potentially germinate and grow nearby.

These are the most common forms or modes of seed dispersal:

Wind Dispersal: Anemochory

Over the hundreds of millions of years since seed-bearing plants began their evolutionary journey, a large number of seed structures have adapted and evolved to take successful advantage of the wind as their primary or secondary mode of transport to new growing grounds.

Parachutes, propellers, wings, sails, tumblers, and even balloon-like structures, have all evolved to improve dispersal by wind. These developments have often been modifications of other plant parts—such as the style or the calyx. The silvery filaments (the pappus) that form the "parachutes" on many plants in the aster family, Asteraceae, are actually modified calyces from the flower.

Wind dispersal is efficient in moving seeds great distances, but it is unpredictable. Once released, plants can't guarantee that their seed will land in suitable places for growing. Plants that rely on the wind for dispersal generally make up for this by producing a lot of seeds—picture the innumerable tiny cottonwood or willow seeds floating on early-spring breezes. This overabundance increases the odds that a few will find appropriate conditions.

Including the structures and casings that help them to fly on the wind, wind-dispersed seeds can be dustlike, as with orchids; many inches long, as with maple samaras; and even several feet wide as in tumbleweeds (common name for plants that detach at their bases from their root systems and blow across the ground, dispersing their seeds as they go).

Water Dispersal: Hydrochory

When you consider the expanse of water and the network of waterways on our planet historically and currently, it's no surprise that many seed-bearing plants evolved to take advantage of water in transporting their seeds to new territory. In the modern plant age, plants that live in intertidal or littoral zones along salt or fresh water, or small-island plants, have adapted seed structures that work with water. Think coconuts, a fruit (technically a drupe) that can float for great lengths of time and great distances, safely holding the coconut seed in one of its three soft so-called eyes.

Ocean currents and tides, rivers and streams, rising and falling seasonal pools, even raindrops and rainwash are all potential vehicles for dispersing and transporting seeds. Water is instrumental in moving seeds away from the competition of parent plants and depositing them in environments likely akin to their place of origin.

Water-dispersed seeds have developed a number of characteristics and strategies for protecting themselves from water damage in their surroundings until it's a prime time to germinate. A hydrophobic (water-repellent) seed coat, for instance, allows a seed to remain dry, and these rainjacket-like seed coats often allow for flotation as well. Other flotation devices include a thick covering of fine hairs, air pockets surrounding a seed, or a waterproof pod, rind, or skin.

In some cases, water-dispersed seeds have evolved to sink and germinate in the watery bottom ground of their wetland habitat. In most of these cases, currents will take them beyond the immediate competition of their parent plant before they absorb enough water and sink.

Finally, some seeds—generally species of low-growing herbaceous genera such as *Gentiana* and *Sedum*—have evolved to take advantage of raindrops. The force of a single drop on the ripe seed structure (often a small cup) bounces the seed out into the surrounding water or otherwise wet environment.

Wildlife Dispersal: Zoochory

Soon after seeds appeared in plants, insects became interested in those seeds. Birds and mammals followed. Just as flowering plants and insects and birds were coevolving mutualistic relationships of food (nectar and pollen) in return for pollination, so too were seed-bearing plants coevolving with animals in surprisingly specific ways.

Often colorful and flavorful, seeds attracted and rewarded animals with sugar, carbohydrates, and protein. In the process of collecting and often eating seed, animals simultaneously dispersed these seeds far and wide.

Animals (including humans) are important, as they transport seeds by eating them, by collecting and caching (hiding) them to eat later, and by unknowingly transporting "hitchhiker" seeds, like burrs and other "stickers," on their fur, feathers, hair, or clothing and equipment.

While many animals eat fruits and seeds as part of their wider diet, some animals, like the migratory cedar waxwing (mentioned earlier), are adapted to eat only fruit and are known as frugivores. Others, known as granivores, like sparrows, doves, and quail, eat only dry, hard seeds.

There are three mutualistic adaptations of zoochory: Epizoochory, which refers to dispersal on an animal. Endozoochory, referring to seeds that can germinate only after they pass through the acidic digestive system of an animal, or seeds that have coevolved with a specific bird whose beak has adapted to crack open that very seed (such as the Clark's nutcracker and the white bark pine). These processes open and scarify (strip or scar) the seed coat, allowing water and air to penetrate the coat more readily, thereby preparing the seed inside for successful germination. Finally, synzoochory refers to dispersal of a propagule by an animal "purposely" picking it up by hands or teeth and moving it somewhere else.

Ant Dispersal: Myrmecochory

Seeds and insects, specifically ants, around the world have also developed mutualistic exchanges, such as the elaisome and ant connection noted above. Seed dispersal by ants is known as myrmecochory.

Gravity Dispersal: Abscission

Many seeds rely on gravity for dispersal, a method known as abscission. Eespecially larger, heavier nuts and cones, but even many smaller seeds have gravity as their primary dispersal method.

While the danger in this strategy might be seedlings establishing too closely to the parent plant and increasing competition and possibly propagating disease or attracting predators, most gravity-dispersed seed plants have evolved to have at least some of their ripened fruits and seeds develop at the outer edges of the parent plant—at the ends of stems or branches that will, when the seed is ripe and at its heaviest, arch out and down, pulling the seeds away from the parent's trunk or stem. Once fallen, they are then moved even farther away by animals, heavy rain or wind, or other means.

At first, it would seem logical that gravity-dispersed seeds would eventually end up at the lowest point in their environment, having all rolled downhill. But consider again a tall or widely canopied tree, or an herbaceous plant with arching stalks—if growing on a slope, the branches or stalks on the uphill side would very likely drop or present their seeds uphill from the parent's main trunk or crown, thereby potentially incrementally expanding its range uphill as well as downhill with each generation.

Ballistic Dispersal: Ballochory

Perhaps the most amazing (and sometimes downright entertaining) of the seed dispersal strategies is that of ballistics (or ballochory), wherein seeds are propelled away from the parent plant with surprising force. Snap. Crackle. *Pop!*

You can hear them, you can see them explode and their seeds fly out, you can feel them tap against your legs as you hike, or squirt or tic against your hands and arms as you work among them in the garden.

In most cases, the energy harnessed to force a seed from its seed pod, or capsule or silique, comes from changing humidity levels inside the seed casing. As the seed pod warms in the sun, dries, matures, and ages, it contracts. This contraction places tension on the seams of the casing, which in time is great enough to split these seed vessels open (a process called *dehiscence*). In some seeds, the drying tension curls pods up or inward, and they essentially sling-shot their seeds away when the outer edges of the casing finally break. In many legumes, the drying tension causes pods to corkscrew (the side facing the sun dries more quickly than the underside of the pod) as they contract. This pressure creates a twisting torque, ultimately causing the seams to split and resulting in an audible pop when they do. The force of the split can send the seeds many feet from the parent. Geranium species have a carpel and style arrangement that literally sling-shots the mature seeds up to 10 feet away from the parent plant.

Contracting Dispersal: Herpochory

In another phenomenon, known as herpochory, long, slender, almost hairlike appendages on seeds (e.g., the awns of grass or erodium diaspores) are so sensitive to changes in humidity that they expand and contract repeatedly—lengthening then curling up a little with each increase or decrease in humidity. This can wiggle—or auger—them right off their parent, and when they are on the ground, it can allow them to "crawl" away from home, and drill themselves into soft surroundings, like soil, fur, or socks.

DECEMBER 25: CHRISTMAS DAY (CELTIC CHRISTIAN CALENDAR)
In this season of gifts, I'm reflecting on seeds and their often extravagant dispersal pathways as among the most important gifts this planet gives us.

Joe Joe Clark is a native plant enthusiast and California naturalist for the Napa County Open Space District. His career is focused on native plant interpretation, public engagement, and education. He credits getting out in California's native plant habitats, especially oak woodlands, with helping him convalesce following a nearly fatal health crisis in his twenties. Clark is now dedicated to helping others appreciate and preserve remaining native plant habitats.

Joe Joe has become a particular lover of true lilies (flowering plants in the genus *Lilium*) and the rugged wild spaces where they grow. And their seed. Joe Joe has studied and now teaches cultivation of the nearly twenty California native *Lilium* species in a garden setting—it's a multiyear commitment.

Lilies are remarkable once in flower, of course—all bold and brave, colorful, and calling to us with form and fragrance—but their seed capsules and seeds themselves are equally remarkable. Pendent flowers (facing down) with bell-shaped petals shielding the all-important pollen—from sun, wind, rain, or all of the above? The fleshy orange or red or pure white to pink-tinged-white petals recurve with age and maturity to reveal the pollen-laden anthers and invite pollinating visitors. But the seed capsule has different needs, and as the ovules ripen postpollination, the swelling ovary rises and ultimately faces the sun, the moon, the stars—offering its ripe seed to the very mayhem the flower had protected against: wind, rain, foraging animals.

But the seed is not offered all at once! No, no.

The ripening and ripened capsule dries, contracts, and dehisces slowly—opening from the top center. Each of the distinct sides of the capsule pull away from one another more slowly still. As this happens, there appear between each capsule segment delicate crisscrossing strands of the capsule's fibrous material: laces binding the sides together. They undo themselves as the capsule opens down—like the slow unlacing of a bodice, or dress, or shirt ...

It is a sensuous process to be sure, and one that is a study in patience and restraint: not all of the treasure is offered out at the first go; time, physical maturation, and relaxation are key. As the capsule's opening moves ever downward, the many, many golden bronzy iridescent gems of flat seeds stacked in each section of the capsule topple out one or two or a few at each breeze, each knock by a passerby, each rattle of a seed-eating bird landing on the dry stalk and surveying the sought-after food: golden bits of a lily life.

❖

DECEMBER 30: FULL MOON

It is the final full moon of the year: known variously as the full cold moon, the long nights moon, and according to the Celtic Ogham calendar, the birch moon.

John is cutting wood, and I'm washing dishes. "Come out!" he calls. We've just finished tending a burn pile of cleared windfall or pruned plant biomass. We are partway through the so-called twelve days of Christmas, and per Celtic and Christian tradition after twelfth night on January 5 or 6, when the seasonal and ritual adornments should be taken down, the little fir tree we cut in the forest earlier this month and then decorated will be ritually undecorated and the tree chipped or laid on another such burn pile. The light is falling fast, the chill coming on. I grab a vest and go back out. We stand together to watch what he called me out for: the rising of the full moon, that bright, bright celestial body, who tomorrow will begin to wane. The day, the month, and the calendar year are all coming to a close.

Does such a witnessing ever get old? Affecting us, affecting tide, affecting water-based plants and growth.

No, it never loses its magic and portent.

This marks the last full year of my fertile self, the end of the seeds of me.

SEED BEDS

JANUARY

Seed Life Linking Us

NEW MOON, JANUARY 13
FULL MOON, JANUARY 28

JANUARY 1: NEW YEAR'S DAY
Woke to the just-rising light at 6:50 a.m., a frosty feel to the air coming in the window, and a light layer of ice on the birdbath. Thirty-one degrees Fahrenheit this morning.

Today's daylight will last 7 hours and 21 minutes, up from the 7 hours and 13 minutes on the shortest day—the solstice. And while the days are lighter, they are still short, and the feel of winter—even on sunny days—is still present and still welcome.

Living in this so-called Mediterranean climate, USDA plant hardiness zone 8b, every year I have the distinct sensation (fantasy?) that once January arrives, so too should spring. Some of the plant community seem to mirror my desire in their coloring and early growing season activity: the buckeyes and acorns on moist open grassland sending out thick, white, succulent radicles probing for dirt and opportunity to secure themselves and dive deep while the ground is cool, moist, softly workable.

A green flush of so-called miner's lettuce (*Claytonia perfoliata*) covers the ground beneath the oaks in the canyon. According to native plant ecologists, the presence of this edible, reseeding annual is a sign of a healthy oak woodland, and Indigenous peoples, and later gold rush miners, ate *Claytonia* as a welcome winter green. It is fresh and a little sharp with the taste of minerals; you feel self-congratulatory and morally upright somehow as a human eating it. Proud and resourceful. We snack on it when we're out, and we add it to winter salads when we remember to pick enough as we walk up the hill to the house. Miner's lettuce greens are a symbol of winter abundance to me now, and depending on rain, they could be fresh for a couple of months; later in the season, their five-petaled starry-white flowers, held above circular minty-green leaves like a posy, will mature to small propulsive seed capsules, sending out next year's generation of nourishment.

The creek-side alders are also quick to drape themselves with many clusters of fresh green male catkins at this time of year, mahogany-hued scaled patterns etched across their surfaces. They are not yet ripe; the clouds of pollen that will come from them are a few weeks off. These reproductive parts are "promiscuous," meaning they develop well before the leaves emerge. The sheer number of them creates a green tinsel effect in the creek's canopy, especially in the last light of evening or on mornings when the tule fog sticks around into midday.

We've had very little tule fog here the past three to four years—perhaps due to the record drought conditions or high winter temperatures. When it does form, we appreciate it. Like frosty green mornings, and bare deciduous tree silhouettes, the tule fog speaks of winter and dormancy. The fog is so named for the way it appears to form from or hunker down in tule-rich marsh or wetland areas of the northern Sacramento Valley— "tule" is the common name for a native bulrush—and from which the fog seems to radiate out, blanketing the lowest land and creeping upslope to us in the canyon.

Northern California's extreme summer heat and normal seasonal drought means we experience two dormant seasons—one in winter, as expected in most seasonal climates, and one in summer, when many plants have evolved to know better than to try to maintain all-systems-go in the heat and drought. These—like the buckeye and the native grasses and spring wildflowers—routinely go summer dormant, dry, brown, deciduous.

Dormancy, a state of significantly reduced metabolic activity, is one of the greatest adaptations and survival mechanisms for many living organisms, and in seed it is one of the most mysterious. Around 70 percent of plant species have some form of seed dormancy, varying according to habitat. Seeds that have evolved in climates with extreme fluctuations in conditions are more likely to need and therefore use dormancy; in tropical regions, where temperatures and precipitation are consistent and high most of the year, dormancy is less helpful, and so less frequently an adaptation in seeds of these regions. But seeds that have evolved some period or type of dormancy are more flexible in where they can live and therefore have an advantage for survival in varying conditions.

Over their long evolution, seeds have developed individual and precise receptivity to cues—not only cues of daylight, moisture, and temperature but also, in some cases, of progression or frequency and intensity of all three of these environmental variables. This receptivity lets them know when to go into dormancy and when to break dormancy. The seed coat is one such receptor.

We as humans have throughout time learned how to break individual seeds' encoded rules of dormancy to our advantage. Those of us who soak our sweet pea seeds prior to planting will recognize one of the "triggers" or tricks to break dormancy. Diane Wilson, plantswoman and American Indian food sovereignty advocate, crafted a wonderful scene in her novel *The Seed Keeper*, in which elder women seed keepers hold seed in their mouth as they are planting in spring in order to break down the seed coats with their saliva—which is both moist and acidic.

Once dormancy has been broken, seeds become highly receptive to environmental cues regarding actual germination. For instance, once a seed coat does begin to break down and allow water (and light and warmth) to get to the embryo itself, some decomposing seed coats provide germination-stimulating enzymes for the seed they've been protecting. Other seeds have light receptors letting them know if they are too deep or not deep enough in the soil for germination. If seeds are not in a good location, and the correct cues are not received, they often stay dormant until the right conditions occur: think of all the seeds that sprout when soil is disturbed and they were brought up to or closer to the soil surface from positions that were too deep.

Some seeds have a multistep process for germinating—in all likelihood for a variety of reasons. Consider how well seeds have evolved to respond or not, for example, when the first good fall rain in this summer-dry climate is just that—the first fall rain, which may or may not be followed by more rain right away. For some annual grasses and seeds, that one rain may be enough to get going; for others, it may just be the first hint that the time is approaching, not the cue to come out.

In wildfire-adapted regions, fire, smoke, and even smoky water (like smoke-infused dew or pooled rain) can help trigger some seed germination, perhaps signaling that vegetative cover has been removed by a fire, and that there will be less competition for light and root space. This in part accounts for the many plants known as fire followers, plants like native California bush poppy (*Dendromecon*), whose seeds germinate far more successfully following a fire, as well as those plants that do not germinate at all without the scarification (abrading of the seed coat) of fire.

Similarly, multiple species of pine, including western lodge-pole pine (*Pinus contorta*) have developed cones sealed with resin, known as serotinous cones. Only when the heat of fire softens the resin do the cones open, allowing the seeds to be dispersed by wind, gravity, or wildlife. In areas of managed fire suppression, this can mean mature seeds have to wait for a long time between dispersal and germination events—longer than might be desirable for keeping the pine population healthy. Beyond protective serotinous cones, plants like chaparral-dwelling native ceanothus and coffeeberry (*Ceanothus* sp. and *Frangula californica*) bear seeds that break dormancy best with the help of an actual fire, so they can wait years for the correct heat or chemistry conditions to have a peak germination event.

This all reminds me of the aftereffects of the Camp Fire in November 2018. It was emotionally and environmentally devastating, but it was also—as fires are—clearing. With the fire reaching the creek's riparia here, a good number of old and beloved trees were burned, including a magnificent willow shading a natural swimming hole, and another very large, mature, native bay tree (*Umbellularia californica*), as well as a host of oaks and pines. However, the fire also cleared overgrown and pernicious, invasive, nonnative perennial vines and shrubs including Himalayan blackberry (*Rubus armeniacus*) and Scotch broom (*Cytisus scoparius*). While we were incredibly happy at the removal of the invasives, we worried about erosion along the creek, and visually the whole of the creekfront that burned hard left us with a visceral gut-punch sensation from the charred scar.

Within weeks, of course, green lives started to show themselves across the burn, which they almost always will do following a fire. Shoots of grasses and annuals brightened the char within six weeks, by early December. By January of 2019 we knew we were going to have a spectacular bulb year. We saw more emerging green leaves from soaproot (*Chlorogalum pomeridianum*) and triteleia and brodiaea corms than ever, profoundly reinforcing our understanding of the fortitude of geophytes (bulbs, tubers, corms, all propagules in their own right, akin to seed, these plants that we so often think of as "ephemeral") had survived heat, drought, cold, and nine months of annual dormancy.

By February following the Camp Fire, we had the bright surprise of the creek sides being lit up by swathes of white milkmaids (*Cardamine californica*) in full bloom across the entire area where invasive black-berry had been. The milkmaids seemed to appear from nowhere. In his decades with this land, John said he had never seen such a show. The naturally occurring and aggregating native seed bank (the viable seed lying dormant in any soil) came to life, stimulated perhaps by several environmental triggers: increased light, increased warmth, the disturbed soil fed by smoke and ash, and, of course, significantly reduced competi-tion—above and below ground.

JANUARY 3
Here in the canyon, it sometimes seems as though you can see a seed's radicle growing right in front of your eyes, popping out of a winter-moistened acorn shell or buckeye seed coat not long after (before even?) they hit the ground. They are eager to start growing.

For both wild and cultivated seed, dormancy and viability are related.

A seed's ability to germinate and successfully establish a new plant is known as its viability. Every living seed has a set range of time during which it is viable: some mere days, some for many years—even hundreds—depending on how ideal the storage con-ditions are and the type of seed.

Viability and dormancy are important to any gardener—they help us understand how to best save seed, when to best plant seed, weed seed management, and wildland restoration that includes reseeding. Understanding viability and dormancy can also help us manage a natural seed bank in any area, to encourage wanted plants and discourage unwanted plants.

Viability in any seed depends on set conditions. For example, how much food tissue (generally endosperm or cotyledons) the seed carries with it for its embryo to live on. An orchid seed has little or no extra food for the germinated seed; wheat grains, acorns, and buckeyes have quite a lot proportionally to the embryo itself. Viability also depends on how protective (thick and waterproof) its seed coat is, and perhaps most important, viability depends on the temperature, light, and humidity to which it is exposed while dormant (or in storage).

Viability is "tested" by gardeners, seed growers, and national seed bank managers by growing out a sample percentage of any same type, same harvest site, same date of seed collection on hand. The "float test" for viability is fairly popular, wherein you place a collection of seed in water, and the seed that floats is determined to be dead, the seed that sinks, viable (although the float test is of contested accuracy for many seed groups). Finally, seed labs have long employed a chemical test using tetrazolium salt compounds to determine viability, and also now use several spectroscopic and imaging technologies. Hyperspectral imaging is used to classify and grade seed as well as for "viability and vigor detection, damage (defect and fungus) detection, cleanness detection, and seed composition determination." At agro-industry scale, these are important controls and guarantees, as seed is—often by law—evaluated both for planting and for eating.

Well-known gardener, writer, creator, and host of the public radio-based *A Way to Garden* program and podcast, and garden columnist for the *New York Times*, Margaret Roach reminds us in one of her many pieces dedicated to seed science and seed in gardening that viability is one thing, but vigor—the strength of the seedling once it germinates—is another. How we keep and treat our seed is directly related to how and what type of offspring that seed produces.

"Germination tests," she writes, "predict viability (the ability to germinate), but they don't accurately predict vigor—the seeds' potential for uniform, fast germination and subsequent development in outdoor conditions, not the cozier, controlled conditions of a germination test. Life in the field isn't the same as life wrapped in a piece of paper toweling in a plastic bag indoors on the kitchen counter, or in the special refrigerator unit of a seed-company testing lab."

But no matter what we think we know or understand about the "rules" of dormancy and viability, we are also always being surprised—by milkmaids and by the outside boundaries of nature's tenacity for life.

In February of 2020, the *Atlantic*, the *New Scientist*, and *Smithsonian* magazines all featured headlines reporting on a seed germination breakthrough: a team led by Sarah Sallon of the Louis L. Borick Natural Medicine Research Center in Jerusalem sprouted six new trees from 2000-year-old seeds of Judean date palms discovered at various archaeological sites including the ancient and important historical and cultural sites of Masada and Qumran Caves, where the Dead Sea Scrolls were found.

While there have long been stories of ancient plants being germinated from 3,300-year-old fruits, nuts, and seeds collected in 1922 from the Egyptian tomb of Tutankhamun and held in

England's Royal Botanic Gardens, Kew (Kew Gardens) and in the Egyptian Museum in Cairo, the accuracy of the germination and the age of the seeds has been questioned.

In the case of the Judean date palm seeds, no such doubt existed. Sallon's team used sound collection methods, documented sources of collection, and radiocarbon-dated the seeds. Of 32 viable seeds that Sallon gathered from various archaeological collections after she successfully sprouted one, 6 more sprouted, some male and some female (date palms being *dioecious*, having male and female parts on separate trees, and so needing both for successful sexual reproduction). Sallon's results allow for the hope of generating mature trees that could be pollinated and yield a new, modern generation of ancients. The first of Sallon's sprouts, named Methuselah after the biblical elder, produced pollen used to fertilize a modern female date palm, which has developed fruit.

Oscar Alejandro Pérez-Escobar, who studies ancient dates at Kew, points out that "the fact that the team has done it not just once but now seven times suggests that ancient seeds could be used to resurrect genes that disappeared after thousands of years of breeding. These ancient seeds might represent lost genetic diversity we don't see anymore." As of initial analyses, the seven ancient seed sprouts revealed very different ancient genetics, genetics that represented a wide geographic range of parent plants, which highlights several very interesting ideas about the art of ancient cultivation, especially given that modern-day breeding is often siloed into homogeny as a result of technology and lab-driven production. "A highly sophisticated domestication culture existed in ancient Judea, and farmers with an interest in maintaining genetic" strength and diversity across their plantations must have purposefully used complex and far-reaching crossbreeding.

In our day and age of life with the constant tragedy and specter of biodiversity loss, this hopeful story represents one example of biodiversity restored.

Dormancy and viability are certainly aspects of us as living organisms as well, and us collectively as cultures. How do we cultivate and evolve the best uses of these useful adaptations? How do we get to the best expressions of self and society? Numbing injustice, apathy, and distractedness as less generative but more escapist versions seem like one expression of humanity's dormancy. When and how will this break? Or maybe, as so many hope and support, this is a "dark night of a hard labor" for many—seeds and humans alike.

JANUARY 5: CHRISTIAN EVE OF THE EPIPHANY (TWELFTH NIGHT)

Friend, fellow gardener, and emeritus professor of biological sciences from California State University, Chico, Robert Schlising, PhD, sends me a voluminous bouquet of dried love-in-a-mist (*Nigella damascena*) seed head stalks via John. *Nigella* has ancient and present uses as food and medicine and is valued for its ornamental flowers and seed pods. These inflated purple-striped greenish seed capsules are crowned by signature spiky styles just opening and upright. The bouquet of seed rattles when John hands it to me, and he jokes that the back of his car will green up with germinating love-in-a-mist seed next spring. Schlising grows a wide variety of native and nonnative annuals and perennials—most from seed—for the purposes of studying the diversity of native bees attracted to and sustained by these flowering plants. His is a seedy, seedling-rich suburban garden.

One of Schlising's recently completed research projects, which stretched almost a decade, was on the biology of a native, early-spring ephemeral geophyte known as steer's head (*Dicentra uniflora*), and its relationship as a larval food source to the native Parnassian butterfly (*Parnassius clodius*). Schlising and co-researcher Halkard Mackey describe how the steer's head blooms just as the snow melts on gravelly slopes of the southern Cascade mountains. According to their observations, these tenacious geophytes emerge at around 4500 feet, send out foliage, bloom, and set fruit within three weeks. Then they dry up and return to underground dormancy in less than seven weeks. The researchers have found that germination can occur in winter, below the snow, with seedlings bearing only a single cotyledon emerging from the ground in spring. The seedling quickly produces a tiny below-ground bulblet before disappearing with the seasonal summer drought of the Mediterranean-type climate. The second-year plant produces a new bulblet and sometimes a tiny tuber, but only a single leaf, and research suggests that it may take up to 10 years or more before an individual reaches flowering maturity. While fruit-producing plants demonstrated high seed set, with a good quantity of seed (between 40 and 80 per plant) being produced, the two men also observed that the rate of fruit production on flowering plants was a lot less reliable, and in one year of data only 27–43 percent of the flowers produced mature fruits with seeds. Further, once seeds were mature, dispersal of those seeds was not very high. The two researchers suspect that ants help with dispersal of some seeds.

The point? Producing seed takes a plant a whole lot of energy and time, and yet even the seed set of this one small, short-season ephemeral plant has a radiating and exponentially important role in the network of this ecosystem—nurturing species from butterflies to ants. What don't we know about it? What can we not foresee about the consequences of the disappearance or extinction of any particular seed-bearing plant?

For now, my gifted stalks of love-in-a-mist—ripened, shared, and dispersed—will be displayed architecturally in a vase in my office until I can sow some of the seed in my garden in spring.

JANUARY 6: CHRISTIAN FEAST OF THE EPIPHANY

I head to the garden. It is misting—not really raining. We should be in our rainy season, which should have started in late October, and yet we are well below normal rainfall. A "normal year" can bring up to 27 inches of rain here in the northern end of California's Sacramento Valley, and we are very dry. How long will winter's green last?

The mist, the prospect of real rain in the short-term forecast, and the need to get out of the house and away from the daily crisis-driven news feed, the need to lean into something solidly forward-looking, inspire me to sow some annual flower seeds: 'Hungarian Blue' breadseed poppy (*Papaver somniferum*) from Redwood Seeds. I broadcast the tiny things in the back garden of my house in town, among roses and lavender, pinks and spring bulbs. I also spread the seeds of a small, pale pink native, chaparral wild buckwheat (*Eriogonum dasyanthemum*), which are accustomed to wintering over in these conditions. The *Eriogonum* seeds were collected by friend and gardener Sandi Martin from her garden south of Santa Cruz, and cleaned and packed by Ginny Hunt, who runs the specialty and hard-to-find native and annual seed company Seed Hunt. Dispersing the many tiny seeds in the front parking median—the so-called hellstrip—my fingers are crossed that the delicate and airy, low, branching pink-flowering plants germinate and take hold there, calling in the tiniest of native bees and syrphid flies with their pollen and nectar come summer.

Not a measurable offset to the car-centric suburban neighborhood dominated by overwatered, overfed, overmown-and-blown, and polluting monoculture of turf grass and therefore wildlife desert, but it's something.

JANUARY 8
A friend sends me an article from *Jacobin* magazine (a publication of the political far left and described as an "American socialist" platform) from December 2020, written by South African journalist Jan Urhahn. The article reminds me just how deep the monoculture threatens to go.

"The Bill and Melinda Gates Foundation foment and fund a new Green Revolution in Africa, not having learned anything from the last Green Revolution and the damage it wrought on people, soil, seed, water, food systems. Over the last five years, the number of people around the world suffering from hunger has been on the rise. Against this backdrop, a decades-old debate continues to rage, asking which agricultural approaches [local diversified small farms or multinational industrial-scale agribusiness, now highly integrated with the petrochemical industry] can provide everyone with sufficient healthy food."

Larger and wealthier industrialized countries claim that "international agribusiness could end global hunger if only it had the means to do so, boosting agricultural productivity through the use of pesticides, hybrid seeds," and other technological external inputs. But many experts on the ground disagree, holding that hunger isn't a problem of production—rather, it's "rooted in the unequal distribution of power resources and control over agricultural inputs such as land and seeds ... Governments in the Global South, especially in Africa, are regularly pressured to modify their agricultural sectors with new laws or projects that favor international agribusiness."

Since 2006, when the Gates Foundation began, the Alliance for a Green Revolution in Africa (AGRA), along with the US-based Rockefeller Foundation, has been "deploying high-yield commercial seeds, synthetic fertilizers, and pesticides as its main weapons in an endeavor meant to help Africa unleash its own Green Revolution in agriculture to fight hunger and poverty."

But in this time period, statistics indicate that "hunger actually increased by 30 percent in the AGRA focus countries," meaning that thirty million more people are going hungry than before AGRA began its interventions, while the opportunity for small-scale farmers in these same countries was significantly undercut, outpriced, and outcompeted by AGRA projects requiring "expensive inputs such as hybrid seeds and synthetic fertilizers via agrochemical companies." The AGRA interventions increased the likelihood of small farmers getting caught in an indebtedness cycle, while AGRA-supported seed and fertilizer companies saw revenue soar. Finally, the reporting noted, self-determination and local land-based knowledge and biodiversity (and with it the ecological health of soil and the broader ecosystems) were severely restricted, damaged, or destroyed altogether: "In AGRA projects in Kenya, small-scale farmers are not allowed to decide for themselves which corn seed they plant and which fertilizers and pesticides they use on their fields. The managers of AGRA projects assume that participating agrochemical companies make the best decisions for the farmers. AGRA's focus is on a few food crops such as corn or soy, causing traditional nutrient-rich foods to be neglected and even displaced ... All in all, AGRA reduces the diversity in farmers' fields and thus also the variety of seeds being used."

To me, this entire scenario, a repeat of the original Green Revolution in the mid-1950s, undoubtedly endangers ecological agriculture, which is interdependent with and beneficial for healthy local economies and communities, and makes them even more vulnerable to the consequences of the climate crisis, to say nothing of increasingly vulnerable to the casualties of the profit-over-people-and-place predatory "nature" of the post-World-War-II-military-industrial-petrochemical-laced-agribusiness world we now face. These are seeds of increasing biological devastation.

JANUARY 12: NEW MOON
The seed catalogs are all here—some seed orders made. Already a lot of seed John and I are interested in for his garden in the canyon and mine in town is sold out again. Particular basils, watermelons, zucchini, yellow squashes, large, colorful zinnias. We have the pumpkin we want, 'Winter Luxury,' and we decide to forgo growing our own tomatoes from seed. This year, we will leave this task to our good local growers. Focus on our strengths.

Now we wait—for our annual summer-season seeds to arrive and for the right time to plant them.

JANUARY 18
The Pleiades or Seven Sisters constellation is high in the winter sky right now. We can see them each evening from the deck. On clear, cold nights, very dark after the new moon on the twelfth, the stars in the canyon spangle the oak tree silhouettes, seeming to wink at us.

For Dave Smoke-McCluskey, the Pleiades high in the sky marks his people's traditional New Year season. Smoke-McCluskey is a chef of Kanien'kéha ("people of the flint land," referred to in English as Mohawk or Iroquois) descent. Although his ancestors' traditional homelands were in the Mohawk Valley of upstate New York and into Canada, Smoke-McCluskey is today based in the Southeast. As a chef and an Indigenous person, he is inspired by his ancestral foodways, which are often portrayed as bland—a portrayal he rejects based on his own understanding of the diversity of seasonal and place-based ingredients he knows were used, and the many methods of cooking and preserving. He is dedicated to identifying, tracing, and reintroducing as much of this knowledge as he can, starting with varieties of corn, beans, and other wild foraged plants and seeds, and heritage breeds of livestock. His business, Corn Mafia, grows or sources heritage Indigenous corn, beans, squashes, and gourds. Smoke-McCluskey describes himself as a "Three Sisters evangelist" (referring to the Indigenous and mutualistic planting of corn, beans, and squash together) and uses traditional small-batch smoking, lyeing (acidifying corn kernels with lye or wood ash to prepare them for making masa flour and dried hominy), and milling methods.

Recently, Smoke-McCluskey has focused on isolating the genetics for Tuscarora Red and Tuscarora White (or Iroquois White) flour corns, Catawba corn, and Cherokee Gourdseed corn, among others. According to studies, Glenn Roberts, a grain and corn expert, and co-owner of Anson Mills in North Carolina, reports that at the time of European contact with the Americas, there were more than 100,000 distinct varieties of native maize, which have been systematically diminished to less than 20,000, and only a few of those are still used widely. For instance, the notably nondescript hybrid number two dent corn is the primary corn in most commercial cornmeal, corn chips, corn cereals, etc. In his own efforts to re-create or re-imagine and re-diversify the "exciting, adventuresome, and complex" ingredients, methods, and flavors of Indigenous foodways, Smoke-McCluskey works with many tribal individuals and groups around the country, including with North Carolina's Davidson College and the Catawba Nation, and he serves on the Southeastern regional board of Slow Foods Ark of Taste.

At this New Year for Kanien'kéha, I can't help but think about and hope that Smoke-McCluskey and his generation of Indigenous seed and food keepers mark a new year—a new era of many generations—of knowledge reclaimed, seen, and seeded forward.

Like so many more visible stars in our skies.

JANUARY 21
Seeds arrive—including a specialty salvia seed John ordered from far away, thankfully not seized by customs as my dryland heirloom wheat seed from Palestine was. John will start the salvia in the potting shed seed box soon, a few seeds at a time to experiment with which starting techniques result in best germination—looking specifically at media, temperature, humidity.

Botanist friend Julie Kierstead also sends along a packet of native *Agastache* (horsemint) seed, which John and I had been hoping to collect up north, but never did. We saw this fabulous aromatic and bumble bee–supporting plant in the meadows on the slopes of Mount Ashland in southern Oregon. John will start these seeds too.

Excitement is growing for the coming season.

JANUARY 22
Today is National Seed Swap Day, a collective day celebrating our human history of seed sharing, bartering, and swapping.

The day was formally founded in 2006 by Kathy Jentz, a gardener and writer based in Washington, D.C. In honor of the ancient and enduring practice of seed swapping, Jentz writes that she hopes the day will "reinvigorate our love for gardening by swapping seeds with our neighbors. It is a great day to remember that nature is our ultimate currency. The food we eat represents the lives we live. And when communities come together to exchange this valuable gift, we reaffirm our promises of mutual belonging and self-sustenance."

I attend a virtual lecture given by the Ecological Landscape Alliance based in Massachusetts, on wild seed and the Wild Seed Project, founded by Heather McCargo, a former propagator for Garden in the Woods, the display garden of the Native Plant Trust (formerly the New England Wild Flower Society).

McCargo's general ethos resonates deeply: "I am not interested in people protecting the seeds and saving them, I am interested in having them sow them. And know them."

Read: Become an effective native seed sower, only then consider collecting or learning how to collect them. Seeds are abundant but also precious—don't waste them.

JANUARY 23
I encounter new, different, and more intense and intentional ways seed is on a lot of gardener's minds, everywhere, which feels empowering for us all.

On Dig Delve, the online magazine of well-known gardener and garden designer Dan Pearson and his husband, garden writer and photographer Huw Morgan, in the United Kingdom, Morgan shares this:

"With the vegetable garden either too frosty or wet to work I finally got round to sorting out my boxes of vegetable seed this week, with a view to being as organized as possible for the coming season. Yesterday was the last day of the [U.K.'s] fourth annual Seed Week, an initiative started in 2017 by The Gaia Foundation, encouraging British gardeners and growers to buy seed from local, organic and small-scale producers. The aim, to establish seed sovereignty in the U.K. and Ireland by increasing the number and diversity of locally produced crops, since these are culturally adapted to local growing conditions and so are more resilient than seed produced on an industrial scale available from the larger suppliers. The majority of commercially available seed are also F1 hybrids, which are sterile and so require you to buy new seed year on year as opposed to saving your own open-pollinated seed."

"I must admit to having always bought our vegetable seed to date, albeit from smaller, independent producers including The Real Seed Company, Tamar Organics, and Brown Envelope Seed. However, last year the pandemic caused a rush on seed from new, locked down gardeners and the smaller suppliers quickly found themselves unable to keep up with demand. If you have tried ordering seed yourself in the past couple of weeks you will have found that, once again, the smaller producers (those mentioned above included) have had to pause sales on their websites due to overwhelming demand. Add to this the new import regulations imposed following Brexit, and we suddenly find ourselves in a position where European-raised onion sets, seed potatoes and seed are either not getting through customs or suppliers have decided it is too much hassle to bother shipping here. This makes it more important than ever to relearn the old ways of seed saving so that we can become more self-sufficient."

I am struck by how similar their experience has been to ours. Morgan goes on to share that he and his surrounding community created a seed and seedling sharing network for people's surplus of both and he describes how as the season progressed in 2020, not only would he and Pearson routinely see seedlings and plugs left by driveways and gates for others to pick up, there also came to be extra produce shared in the same manner. He writes: "There was something very connective about this, despite the distance we all had to keep and the clandestine nature of the exchanges.

A way of binding our little community together at a time when we were all reeling from the isolation of our first lockdown."

In finding and learning more about each gardener and seed steward in my work and exploration thus far, I feel what Morgan describes—a binding and connective interstitial tissue being laid down from one to the other to the other. A different and generative kind of seed interdependence.

Finally, Morgan tells the story of finding his stash of the runner bean 'Enorma' seed, saved by his great-aunt Megan (who was still happily and actively gardening at the age of 95) in 2011. He writes: "Megan had been a Land Girl during the Second World War and was the most impressive kitchen gardener I have ever known ... This year, almost eight years after Megan died at the age of 98, I intend to plant her home-collected seed. A way of connecting me to the Welsh family that has gradually dwindled over the years and, perhaps, some of Megan's skill and stamina will rub off on me along the way. Saving and sharing creates these connections between family, friends and strangers. It feels like nothing is quite as important as that right now."

None of us are alone—Morgan, Jentz, Smoke-McCluskey, McCargo —in being pulled by the call and connection of seed going back, going forward. Seed is shared in flowers, in food, in feeling—across friends, families, and other fault lines.

JANUARY 27
California native pipevine (*Aristolochia californica*) is starting to bloom.

The little gray-green-mauve striped teapot or pipe-shaped flowers start so very small they are sometimes hard to see on the dormant-seeming vines. Running throughout the creek-side shrubs and trees, the foliage of the pipevine is the only larval food source for the also-endemic pipevine swallowtail butterfly (*Battus philenor*). When the leaves appear on the vine, the adult butterflies will generally lay their small reddish-orange dots of eggs on the backs of the pale green and lightly fuzzy heart-shaped leaves. When the eggs hatch, the larva and later the mature caterpillars will almost defoliate the section of the pipevine they are on, then pupate into their chrysalis form and start the journey again. As the larva and caterpillars are eating away in their stages of growth, the fading teapot flowers, pollinated by fungus gnats, are forming their own new architecture of life: a winged, fibrous seed capsule, pendent and fleshy green with lengthwise ribs. Woody and tough, a golden wheat color in maturity, the seed capsule dries and opens along its seams into a lantern-like form from which the seeds disperse, and the capsule remains hanging—gathering light, and swaying in later summer and even winter breezes.

John and I deadhead the bank of hybrid shrub Iceberg roses in the front dry (mostly otherwise native) garden at my house in town. Rose hips brighten the intertwining winter-skeletal hedge. Plump red and burgundy hips.

You can grow a rose from a rose hip—it is the fruit and holds the seeds of the plant. Being a hybrid, however, an Iceberg rose hip would not produce an Iceberg rose—but it would produce some kind of rose.

For now, I will just be content with placing the hips from the pruning pile in a vase on the kitchen counter. Bright winter flashes of life.

FEBRUARY

Seed Shares and Seed Laws

NEW MOON, FEBRUARY 11
FULL MOON, FEBRUARY 27

FEBRUARY 1: CELTIC FESTIVAL OF IMBOLC

We are now at Imbolc—that magic moment noted in the Celtic calendar when we reach halfway between the winter solstice and the vernal equinox. A time of no-going-back-now. That lovely sense of spring will grow weekly—with the moon and with our proximity and angle to the sun assuring this eventuality.

These patterns and rhythms so ancient and ever present—even when we are wildly divorced from them in front of fluorescent flickering screens and behind desks, they still reach us . . . but how quickly we have shifted in the course of our human history, from basing every movement on them to ignoring them completely, busily inventing mechanisms to separate us from them. Are we better off for it?

Now, at least here in our zone 8b, it is time to plant some of our summer seeds—some direct, some in pots under cover in the canyon.

John finds a box of old mail-order seed and plant catalogs in the basement, hundreds of thick and thin colorful pages from sellers and growers around the country from the 1930s, 1950s, and 1970s. He compiled them from his years as head grower for Lamb Nursery in Spokane, Washington, in the 1980s. We both note our feeling that there is perhaps a great germination of small seed companies and growers around the country right now, assisted by the accessibility and ease of the internet and online shopping, but also overwhelmed by demand following COVID-19. This great germination reflects similar urgencies felt by households during the Great Depression, post–World War II, with the oil crisis and back-to-the-land movement of the 1970s, and following the Great Recession of 2007–2008.

The long history and the many types of seed growers, sharers, swappers, suppliers, and distributors lie behind our ability to source and plant seed well beyond our individual ability to save seed. But sometimes we are so deeply indoctrinated and entwined in one economic or social system, one mindset or way of life, that we cannot see the structure itself let alone see beyond it to what came before or what could possibly be imagined after.

I've always saved certain seeds from one season to the next, just as my mother did. Easy seeds—annual flowers mostly, like sweet peas and nasturtiums. Otherwise, I (as she before me) mostly order seeds or starts for the plants I want to grow. After Wes Dempsey illuminated for me the wonder in a pine nut, I dabbled in collecting ripe seed from abundant wildflowers to try sowing. But in 2015, when *Cultivating Place* was in its early pre-production phase and I was still producing a local version of it called *In a North State Garden,* I had another seed epiphany that opened my eyes and heart to a far greater continuum of seed than I had ever known or considered.

It was fall pledge drive at NSPR, the public radio station that co-produces *Cultivating Place*, and I was scheduled to work several pledge drive shifts with one of the evening jazz program hosts, Daniel Atkinson. We had never met, but, chatting as you do between drive messaging, we got to talking.

Besides studying African American history through the lens of jazz and sharing that forward as a musician and jazz program host, Atkinson was an enthusiastic gardener, and he loved my program, so when he heard it was growing up and out into the nationally focused *Cultivating Place*, he was excited. He shared a story of having gone with his mother to clean out his recently passed great-aunt's house in the southeastern United States, and he and his mother's shared joy on finding a selection of glass baby-food jars holding a selection of bean seeds. Bean seed lines that had been in the family since his mother could remember. Her mother, her grandparents, everyone of at least four generations had grown, cooked with, saved, and passed on these seeds.

Waiting for me the next day at the station was a wax paper sandwich bag with a colorful selection of beans. Atkinson's note on a half sheet of yellow steno pad paper read: "A few heirloom seeds from ancestors in Louisiana, which include speckled butter beans, red zippers, black crowders, and field peas, all fresh from this growing season! The zippers are prolific, the butter beans come in late and the black crowders don't produce much, but they're pretty!"

Like the jazz music that Atkinson studied for the history and stories it held, these seeds held, as he reverently shared with me, not only his family's history, but aspects of the whole history of his African heritage and the African diaspora.

Notice the etymological relationship between diaspore, the structure
for seed dispersal on a plant, and diaspora, the dispersion of any people
from their original homeland. The repeating feedback loop of seed and
human reflection …

❖

Daniel gave me the perspective to see that beyond the structure of
our current seed supply chain lie other forms and natures of supply and exchange—akin to the gift economy Robin Wall Kimmerer
elucidates in *Braiding Sweetgrass*; as illustrated by Huw Morgan's
outlining the community seed, plant, and produce exchange that
sprouted during the pandemic lockdowns; and more important,
as modeled on how plants offer themselves into the systems of
the natural world.

These insights begin to illuminate seed demand, its supply,
and its mechanisms for distribution. So when I read about the
work of the Organic Seed Alliance (OSA) protecting and strengthening small, localized, organic seed networks and suppliers in an
agricultural newsletter, I pay attention. When I read about the
work of Dr. Elizabeth Hoover (at the time at Brown University)
to reconnect Indigenous garden and seed with the larger Indigenous community, I pay attention.

From these conversations, I begin to connect with a com-
munity of keepers of culture, keepers of seed: Ira Wallace of the
Southern Exposure Seed Exchange; Leah Penniman of Soul Fire
Farm, tracing and growing out seeds of the African diaspora; Win-
ona LaDuke of Honor the Earth Heritage Farms in Minnesota;
Diane Wilson, emeritus executive director of both Dream of Wild
Health in Minnesota and the Native American Food Sovereignty

Alliance in Arizona; Rowen White of Sierra Seeds and the Indigenous Seed Keepers Network. All of these women are tracing, preserving, and, as White says, "rehydrating" the relationships between seeds of North American native food plants and their traditional people and cultures. Similarly, Kitazawa Seed; Kristyn Leach, of Namu Farm and Second Generation Seeds; and Kellee Matsushita-Tseng of Second Generation Seeds, among many others, are doing the same work for seeds, stories, and history of the Asian diaspora.

What these cultural seed keepers make clear is that there was, is, and will always be a seed community outside of the industrialized, commercial one that many understand as *the* seed supply chain.

The Organic Seed Alliance takes us a little deeper into the history of the "supply chain" of commercial seed in the United States. OSA cofounder Matthew Dillon notes that in 2005, among the many large and small seed company mergers of the past decade, the then-Monsanto Corporation bought a smaller US-based seed supplier, Seminis. The announcement, to his annoyance, got very little attention in the press. "Why should it get attention? Have *you* ever heard of Seminis?" He answers his own question with a quote from the company's public relations rep, Gary Koppenjan: "If you've had a salad, you've had a Seminis product." "Product" refers to the living green plant we all eat: lettuce.

Seminis' hybrids claim to improve nutrition, boost crop yields, limit spoilage, and reduce the need for chemicals. Their retail line includes over 3500 seed varieties, including a whole lot of lettuce seed. Small and mid-sized seed suppliers specifically working with organic and ecologically focused growers had long depended on the reliable and beloved hybrids and varietal seeds offered by Seminis, which had—until this point—not been involved in genetically modified (GM) or engineered (GE) seed. Many of these same smaller industry suppliers and growers had no interest in supporting Monsanto even by association, and there was (and remains) a lot of concern over the merger. Why? Speculation that if Monsanto could slowly start building the GMO (genetically modified organism) vegetable and fruit market, then the debate over GMOs becomes a moot point, as they will have made their way onto the majority of households' dinner plates and thus gained acceptance (or at least acquiescence).

But why, you might wonder, would a notorious petrochemical company and then a pharmaceutical company (that being Bayer, who later bought Monsanto) be interested in seed at all? The shortest distance between two points is often a straight line: because seed is very, very big financial business—*especially* when tied to the petrochemical fortunes of fertilizer, pesticides, herbicides, and patented commodity seed that has to be purchased new every year by large-scale farmers around the world.

As of 2020, according to Food & Power, an online food policy forum, "the seed business is one of the most concentrated industries in American agriculture. Today, about 80% of corn and over 90% of soybeans grown in the United States feature Monsanto seed traits, either sold by Monsanto or by its licensees. In 2011, the top ten seed companies in the world totaled about $25 billion in sales, comprising 75% of the overall market. In 2020, the top four corporations, Bayer (including what was formerly Monsanto), Corteva (including what was formerly DuPont), Syngenta (part of ChemChina), and Limagrain together controlled 50% of the global seed market, with Bayer and Corteva alone claiming roughly 40%."

Using data compiled by Farm Action, a fair practice food and agriculture system advocacy network, Food & Power goes on to point out that "when it comes to genetic traits, this control is even more pronounced: Bayer controls 98% of trait markers for herbicide-resistant soybeans, and 79% of trait markers for herbicide-resistant corn."

Today, the vast majority of lettuce, soybean, and corn production and soil-destroying, carcinogenic pesticides and herbicides are owned by multinational corporations.

What gardener, grower, eater, or thinker wouldn't think these were really, really unsettling—and just plain yucky—salad bowl mates?

The history of chemicals in and on our food and our food-growing land, becomes clear by looking back along a simple timeline.

The historic global "trade" of plants by land and sea often meant "forcibly extracted" and is documented by the earliest recorded Egyptian, Mesopotamian, Aztec, Mayan, Roman, Greek, Chinese, Japanese, generally European, and other "empire" civilizations. Even in the name of "science" and research. Think how Thomas Jefferson supported the Lewis and Clark expedition, which set off to collect plants from the western territories in 1804. Think of the beneficiaries of Darwin's botanical voyage and collections of plants and observations in the 1830s.

As Dillon notes, "Consolidations in the seed world are nothing new ... A century and a half ago there was only one mega-distributor of seeds in this country. Lobbying and activism brought about its demise. That distributor was the United States government, and the rabble rousers who broke that monopoly were none other than the American Seed Trade Association whose largest modern financial benefactor is none other than Monsanto."

Before the 1850s, seeds were generally sourced in the time-honored ways of land-based people the world over: by seed saving, seed swapping and sharing, communal granges, cooperatives. They were sourced as well through state-sponsored seed collecting and often appropriation (stealing?) of variety selections made over the centuries by humans observing plant traits and collecting seed specifically with all manner of desired things in mind: color, flavor, size, how well they kept, climate adaptation, etc.

Beginning in the 1850s in the United States, however, according to Dillon's timeline, seed was also distributed "through the beneficence of the United States government." The US Patent and Trade Office (PTO) and congressional representatives "saw to the collection, propagation, and distribution of varieties to their constituents. By 1861, the PTO annually distributed more than 2.4 million packages of seed (containing five packets each of different varieties). The flow of seed reached its highest volume in 1897 (under USDA management) with more than 1.1 billion packets of seed distributed." Why? Simply due to the government's recognition that "feeding an expanding continent would require a diversification of foods."

Wheat, rye, oats, peas, cabbage, and many other vegetable crops were critical to a growing nation's food security. Using the best arable land to "plant European-preferred foods also purposefully disrupted the land-and-ecosystems-based food supply of the

Indigenous cultures on these lands, as did the new population's new methods of growing corn, beans, and squash." Immigrants were encouraged to bring seed from the Old World. "By 1819 the US Treasury Department issued a directive to its overseas consultants and Navy officers to systematically collect plant materials [wherever they were]."

In 1866, cabbage seed became the first commercial seed crop. The organization of the American Seed Trade Association in 1883 was followed by the still-young group lobbying to end government programs, supposedly in order to improve the competitive seed market and to bolster the fledgling industry.

If the government continued to distribute seed, the ASTA argued, it was in direct competition with the private seed trade. But the government seed distribution program was very popular with would-be farmers and their westward-heading families and communities, and so it was good for politicians. Therefore it continued for the time being. The USDA's seed budget at one point counted for a full 10 percent of the agency's overall annual expenditures.

As summarized by Netherlands-based Niels Louwaars, comparing different open seed source conditions in Europe and the United States, this was pivotal. "Farmer breeding had been going on for millennia; commercial seed production had started a century before, but systematic breeding of field crops was a new development during the latter part of the 19th century. Only after 1900, with the rediscovery of Mendel's laws on heredity, breeding developed into a science."

Mendelian genetics and laws of heredity allowed for the science of creating stable hybrid F1 seed for market, and in the early part of the twentieth century, hybrid seed began to provide seed companies with a potential increase in product profitability, because if farmers had success with those hybrids, growers and buyers would now need to return to the hybrid's owner or distributor each year.

In the United States, most of the hybrid development was occurring at land-grant universities (LGUs), and these publicly supported universities [for some time] refused to give individual companies exclusive rights to the seed because their research was intended for open source benefit. However, in 1924, after more than 40 years of lobbying, the ASTA succeeded in convincing Congress to cut the USDA seed distribution programs. Subsequently, the USDA still supported breeding at the state agricultural schools, but in time and with pressure, these tax-dollar-funded public programs were convinced "that their appropriate role was in training plant breeders, performing fundamental research, and creating raw materials and technologies for private industry to capitalize on." And so the LGUs developed inbred (hybrid) parental lines and breeding stock that the seed trade could use to create proprietary hybrid varieties. This was a major step toward the privatization and commodification of seed, and a boon for the industrialized, for-profit seed industry.

In 1930, Congress passed the Plant Patent Act. This federal act gave breeders some property-rights protection, but it also maintained protections for the concept of natural genetic heritage. Because of this, as noted by Kiki Hubbard, longtime seed policy reporter and the director of advocacy and communications for the Organic Seed Alliance, the Plant Patent Act excluded sexually reproducing plants as patentable subject matter and applied only to asexual reproduction such as vegetative reproduction by grafting and cuttings , tissue culture, and, more recently introduced, gene editing and other developing technologies.

More consumer protection and seed industry oversight regulation went into effect with the Federal Seed Act, passed in 1939 and put into effect in 1940. The enforcement authority for these regulations was held by the Agricultural Marketing Service (AMS) of the USDA. The AMS is obliged to provide testing of seed for sellers to remain in compliance. In an effort to promote uniformity between seed sellers and buyers across state lines and fair and healthy competition within the seed trade, the Seed Act also required that seed shipped in interstate commerce be labeled with certain consistent and verifiable information (such as quantity, quality, etc.). In theory, this allowed individual and commercial seed buyers to make informed choices.

Following World War II, the seed industry was still remarkably diversified, as was food production. "Monocropping and large-scale corporate agriculture" was still a nascent trend, ticking up a bit with some consolidation in the 1960s as seed companies owning good hybrid stock started to come together.

With the Plant Variety Protection Act of 1970, though, breeders gained the exclusive right to propagate and market a new variety for 20 years. The law did provide important exemptions to this exclusivity, a nod toward not stifling innovation: (1) other plant breeders could use protected varieties for breeding and research, and (2) farmers could save seed from protected varieties to replant on their own farms.

On a different but interestingly parallel plane in the seed sharing and growing world, in 1975, Seed Savers Exchange (SSE) was founded in Missouri by Diane Ott Whealy and Kent Whealy. Ott Whealy's grandfather had entrusted to the couple the seeds of just two garden plants. These seeds, brought by Grandpa Ott's parents from Bavaria when they immigrated to Iowa in 1884, became the first two varieties in the SSE collection. The Whealys went on to form a "network of gardeners interested in preserving heirloom varieties and sharing seeds." More on SSE soon.

Access to and control of seed breeding, supply, and distribution channels on the broad public and commercial levels changed dramatically when the Supreme Court ruled 5 to 4 in the case of Diamond v. Chakrabarty on June 16, 1980, and cleared the patenting of life forms on the basis of their genetic coding. Prior to the Chakrabarty decision, a plant (or animal) could be owned, but their genetics could not. The PTO granted more than 1800 genetic patents following the ruling. It was at this key moment that companies with no historical seed interest began purchasing seed companies as promising associates for otherwise unassociated fields: the buyers were primarily and overwhelmingly chemical and pharmaceutical companies.

Within a few short years, mergers and acquisitions with transaction prices in the billions put a majority ownership of plant genetics into the hands of a few multinational companies. Dillon notes that "no other natural resource (marine, timber, minerals) has ever shifted from public to private hands with such rapidity, such intensity of concentration, and so little oversight."

Hubbard summarizes this emblematic cultural paradigm and ethics shift: "The expansion of intellectual property (IP) rights associated with seed has transformed our relationship with these living organisms in ways that were previously unimaginable."

But many farmers and growers, particularly those associated with and dedicated to the expanding individual seed-saving and organic-food movements, were not only unhappy and existentially uncomfortable with this new paradigm, they were catalyzed by it.

The energy among small and organic growers to protect and support open-source natural and organic seed supply chains, seed saving, seed breeding and genetics manifested in real actions in the late 1990s.

In 1999, High Mowing Organic Seeds of northern Vermont introduced the Safe Seed Pledge initiative. The small, independent seed grower "guided a coalition of 9 other seed companies in drafting a statement about the signers' stance on genetic engineering. To date the Pledge has been signed by over 370 seed companies worldwide."

The Safe Seed Pledge, which is now administered by the Council for Responsible Genetics, reads: "Agriculture and seeds provide the basis upon which our lives depend. We must protect this foundation as a safe and genetically stable source for future generations. For the benefit of all farmers, gardeners and consumers who want an alternative, we pledge that we do not knowingly buy or sell genetically engineered seeds or plants. The mechanical transfer of genetic material outside of natural reproductive methods and between genera, families or kingdoms poses great biological risks, as well as economic, political and cultural threats. We feel that genetically engineered varieties have been insufficiently tested prior to public release. More research and testing is necessary to further assess the potential risks of genetically engineered seeds. Further, we wish to support agricultural progress that leads to healthier soils, genetically diverse agricultural ecosystems and ultimately healthy people and communities."

While Monsanto's purchasing of Seminis may not have gotten a lot of mainstream media attention, it got a lot of attention within the smaller, local seed breeding, growing, and supply community—many of whom saw a direct threat to a strong, independent food system with integrity as well as human and environmental health in mind.

Longtime organic vegetable breeder Frank Morton of Shoulder to Shoulder Farm and Wild Garden Seed based in Philomath, Oregon, sums it up: "There is a direct threat to our food system when we have a preponderance of genetic resources controlled by institutions whose only goal is profit. ... When these services [breeding and production] were diffused amongst many individuals and groups with diverse motives, we had a much more diverse and healthy food system."

As has been widely shown across any number of other industries, diversity *and* competition have historically made for healthier economies. Diversity without true competition, not so much.

This leaves small, independent seed companies and farmers with the heaviest lifting in the task of raising public awareness about the pitfalls inherent in the large-corporate-conglomerate-owned seed model.

While the organic food and farming sector had been growing nicely since the 1980s and 1990s, it was not until 2002, when the National Organic Program required that certified organic growers use organic seed "when commercially available," that the organic seed-growing industry was finally financially incentivized.

While this was a long-fought-for standard important for transparency and integrity in organic markets and in the seed industry, it also landed in a seed supply network that was not quite ready, and this caused some unintended consequences. For example, as noted by organic seed expert and advocate C. R. Lawn of the Maine-based seed cooperative Fedco Seeds, organic seed was not yet up to speed in quantity or in quality, trialing, and testing, leaving a lot of wiggle room in the potential loophole "when commercially available."

Into this intensifying landscape of the seed industry, its growth, oversight, and control, the first decade-plus of the 2000s saw solid additions to the open-source, diversified-seed side of things, as well as further consolidation on the industrialized side.

The Organic Seed Alliance formed in Oregon in 2003 from the open-seed-source advocacy work of the Abundant Life Seed Foundation. In 2005, more than 70 university breeders, representatives from farmer-based nongovernmental organizations (NGOs), and policy specialists met at the Summit for Seeds and Breeds for the 21st Century in Washington, D.C. These breeders represented a diverse set of crops and came from university-based programs that had traditionally served clients of large-scale, industrialized, Green Revolution–style agriculture. Attendee stakeholders called on each other to "reinvigorate public breeding" to meet the needs of organic and sustainable agriculture.

In 2008, Monsanto went on to buy a major Canadian seed grower and supplier, De Ruiter—further consolidating the proprietary and diversified seed genetics now held by Bayer (not just the large so-called commodity crop seed).

In 2012, the Open Source Seed Initiative (OSSI) was launched in the United States by a handful of plant and seed people committed to ensuring as much seed as possible be held in the commons in perpetuity—freely and openly available to all (including all "derivatives" or new breeding from these varieties). Notable seed experts, breeders, and advocates, including C. R. Lawn who sat on the OSSI board, called on all levels of breeders specifically to pledge some of the results of their breeding to this end.

By 2014, "37 varieties of 14 species were released by various public and private breeders under the OSSI Pledge. Breeding of new hybrid lines takes years—how successful OSSI will be in securing a large quantity of seed outside of the patent and exclusive ownership range is yet to be seen—but with the inclusion of the 'derivatives' clause, every introduction pledged to OSSI is potentially exponential. Several plant breeders, notably those operating in the organic sector, and some in US research universities, have followed suit and pledged their new breeding results to the OSSI collection."

In early 2022, I interviewed Dave Melhorn, executive director of Johnny's Selected Seeds, and Lauren Giroux, director of product selection and trialing research at Johnny's. Johnny's is a midlevel organic, non-GMO seed grower and supplier based in Maine. In our conversation, Melhorn noted his feeling that in the last 10–20 years there has been an overall relaxing of people's concerns about GMOs and GE seed in our general home garden seed supply.

Why? According to Melhorn, while there had been understandable fears at the time of the Monsanto purchase of Seminis that GE and GMO seed would soon dominate our seed supply, "the open market" had in large part answered that fear by not supporting such a shift in ethos, and by the FDA's essentially rejecting GMO wheat approval in the United States after testing between the late 1990s and the early 2000s. This decision to not approve the GMO wheat, which is primarily a human food grain rather than a livestock food crop or a crop used for its derivatives in other foods, essentially limited GMO technology to large international industrial-scale commodity crops: corn, soy, and canola. Additionally, Melhorn and Giroux both point out that fears about loss of diverse seed offerings or access to the full range of seed as a result of seed company consolidations has not happened. On the contrary, says Melhorn, when a larger company buys a smaller company, you often see the smaller company enjoy greater diversity due to increased financial and infrastructure support. As a case in point, he offered historic W. Atlee Burpee—founded in Philadelphia, Pennsylvania, in 1876, bought by General Foods in 1970, and then consolidated under George Ball Inc.—thriving and still qualifying as a "diversified family horticultural business."

A larger parent company with more resources certainly does not always result in greater vigor for a smaller endeavor consolidated into it. To cite an example of how one consolidation affects many, take Trisler Seeds, Inc., based in Fairmount, Illinois, with a 70-year history in seed corn, on which Kiki Hubbard of the OSA reported. In 2006, Monsanto's holding company, American Seeds, Inc. (ASI), purchased Trisler, after which Trisler's diversity in seed options decreased dramatically. Postacquisition, Trisler's "conventional (non-GE) corn options were cut by an amazing 91%—even in light of a major resurgence in demand for non-GE corn and soybean varieties. This demand was in part driven by increased cost of GE seed and herbicides, the emergence of glyphosate-resistant weeds, and premium prices paid for non-GE grain."

Monsanto purchased Heritage Seeds, based in Indiana, the same year, and eventually stopped selling its non-GE varieties altogether. Lewis Hybrids, an Illinois family business established in 1946, "underwent similar shifts in catalog offerings after it was acquired alongside Trisler and Heritage."

An instance of a smaller seed grower and supplier benefiting from the resources that consolidation can offer them would be the 2007 merger of NE Seed and D. Palmer Seed into a "sister" company, DP Seeds LLC. Their stated goal was "to create a line of high quality, chemical-free seed products at a reasonable price." The 2007 announcement makes a special note of the fact that "we are dedicated to bringing you products that our growers and independent breeders have as their vision, not ours." Furthermore, NE Seed, who built their reputation on chemical-free and GMO-free, often organic seed, now owned the proprietary hybrid offerings of DP Seeds genetics. Because DP Seeds genetics were available as untreated seeds, and these were notably often without "organic equivalent," they were good market bets because they were accessible to certified organic growers needing to stay in compliance with the standards of the National Organic Program.

Johnny's Selected Seeds, founded in 1973 by young farmer and seed grower Rob Johnston Jr., is a seed grower, supplier, and trial research leader sourcing from growers all around the world (in our 2021 interview, Melhorn notes that about 75 percent of their seed is grown "overseas"). Johnny's carries organic, conventional, hybrid selections, as well as hundreds of open-pollinated heirloom seeds. They do not "knowingly" sell or source GMO seeds, but they do continue to carry Seminis seed varieties that have proven to be invaluable to them and their farming customers.

Melhorn's thinking is largely corroborated by a 2021 USDA wheat market update: "Specifically, the 1996 Farm Act strengthened the market orientation of crop planting by eliminating the requirement that farmers maintain base acreage of a [single] crop to qualify for Government payments. In addition, wheat sowings have lost ground to coarse grains and oilseeds due to technological innovations [read: genetic engineering] that have improved production prospects for corn and soybeans. Genetic improvement [read: genetic engineering] has been slower for wheat due to the food grain's significantly more complex genetics and lower potential returns from research investments. Farmers grow wheat primarily for human food use, and US food processors are wary of consumers' reactions to products containing genetically modified (GM) wheat. No GM wheat is commercially grown in the United States."

Some of this is reassuring, but only to a small degree. Because while no GM wheat is legally or knowingly grown in the United States, even by 2013, Bayer-Monsanto's GM wheat genetics had been identified in samples of wheat being grown in Oregon. Additionally, with the 2018 merger of Bayer and Monsanto and with both De Ruiter and Seminis under the big-pharma/agro-industrial umbrella, despite large numbers of individuals and many small groups of people working for the continued diversification of seed, for the protection of open-source seed and seed genetics, and for organic seed, the fact remains that the largest markets for the largest commercial crops on the largest number of acres have and continue to increase disproportionate power and control over our food supply with just a relative handful of kinds of seed by a relative handful of controllers. The dollar value of the genetically modified seed market is also forecast to go from $20 billion to $30 billion by the late 2020s. The sheer magnitude of what is controlled and managed by Bayer-Monsanto is astounding. The century-long trek that takes us from government-led seed distribution for a growing country to the American Seed Trade Association being funded by Monsanto, is convoluted—and worrying.

Staple grain and food seed, further consolidated.

Not coincidentally, these staple seeds and foods are held sacred by land-based cultures around the world: corn, soy, rice, wheat, potato. At the great and fully acknowledged risk of sounding like a conspiracy theorist, the phrase "control the food, control the people" does come to mind.

The Food and Drug Administration lays out the chance of ingesting these consolidated seeds most simply: "It is very likely you are eating foods and food products that are made with ingredients that come from GMO crops. Many GMO crops are used to make ingredients that Americans eat such as cornstarch, corn syrup, corn oil, soybean oil, canola oil, or granulated sugar. A few fresh fruits and vegetables are available in GMO varieties, including potatoes, summer squash, apples, and papayas. Although GMOs are in a lot of the foods we eat, most of the GMO crops grown in the United States are used for animal food." Animals *we* then go on to eat the meat, dairy, or eggs from ...

To make it easier for consumers to know if the foods they eat contain GMO ingredients, the US Department of Agriculture maintains a list of bioengineered foods available throughout the world. Additionally, you will start seeing the "bioengineered" label on some of the foods we eat because of the new National Bioengineered Food Disclosure Standard (NBFDS). The NBFDS was announced in 2018, after the National Bioengineered Food Disclosure Law passed Congress in July of 2016, directing the USDA to establish a national, mandatory standard for disclosing foods that are or may be bioengineered. As the USDA outlines, "the Standard defines bioengineered foods as those that contain detectable genetic material that has been modified through certain lab techniques and cannot be created through conventional breeding or found in nature. The implementation date of the Standard is January 1, 2020, except for small food manufacturers, whose implementation date is January 1, 2021. The mandatory compliance date is January 1, 2022."

While I am personally not a fan of the idea of eating engineered or modified food, nor am I convinced that it will be what helps humans to combat hunger in a rapidly expanding world population, I am not actually anti-GMO or technological advances. Many persuasive and compelling arguments, posed by people I trust and admire, fall on the side of closed-source seed breeding wherein breeders' intellectual property rights are protected. These advocates believe that innovation, ambition, and long, hard years of work coming up with and refining great new hybrids or genetics are incentivized by these protections and a breeder's ability to make money that results from these property rights.

For me the sticking point lies here: it's putting at risk the sacredness, immeasurable value, and precariousness of the genetics this generous planet has naturally evolved (often along with us humans). Who are we, after all, to diminish, gamble with, and compromise that miraculous gift every growing season with acres and acres of GMO corn, canola, cotton, and soy?

The seed from these crops and acres is not able to be saved and grown out, and yet the preponderance of GMO crops are wind- or self-pollinated, putting similar crops within pollinating distance at risk of contamination and thereby rendering an unwittingly contaminated farm in violation of seed utility patent laws. But far more important, the contamination scenarios stand the chance of altering the genetics of these farm crops for the foreseeable future.

The sheer number of acres of large monocropping, chemical fertilizer-pesticide-herbicide treated facilities continues to add to the erosion of plant, soil, and wildlife ecosystem biodiversity in all directions. This is compounded, of course, by the increasing urbanization of land.

According to reports between 2018 and 2020 from the American Farmland Trust, since 2009 the United States has lost 11 million acres of farmland to urbanization—roughly the area of Massachusetts and New Jersey combined. We've lost 31 million acres of farmland since 1992, from both local farmers' and larger agricultural systems' land.

This system of patented GMO seed continues to exponentially consolidate the dollars and decision-making power over our seed, land, and food into the hands of the few (with profit in mind) over the many. In large part many of the latter group are more or equally concerned with community health than they are with exorbitant shareholder profits.

This same trend is apparent in the GE soybean market. Within a matter of several years after their introduction in the late 1990s, GE soybeans resistant to Dicamba, a selective herbicide, made up close to three-quarters of the commercial market. As Hubbard notes: "One interpretation of rapid adoption is demand. Another is lack of choice."

Or fear and intimidation?

Once Dicamba-resistant soybeans began to edge out nonresistant varieties, any farmer not growing them risked the possibility that their entire crop could be lost to Dicamba drift (which would likely kill or severely damage a nonresistant planting) or genetic cross-pollination contamination, for which farmers could be held responsible as having "stolen."

Hubbard also notes that a class-action lawsuit being brought by farmers who feel they have no choice but to grow GE soybean or risk losing their crops, seemed well supported by the data: "Dicamba drift allegedly affected approximately 3.6 million acres of soybeans in 2017. More than 1000 farmers are currently suing Bayer for damage caused by Dicamba drift on account of this new chemical-seed package. And, as if organic and other non-GE grain growers didn't have enough to worry about: Bayer is currently applying for government approval of Dicamba-resistant corn."

Lauren Giroux of Johnny's Selected Seeds emphasized her response to GMO and consolidation concerns in our seed supply and distribution systems during our 2021 *Cultivating Place* interview: "Where there is consolidation, there is also energy to counter that with diversity. I don't see diversity or open-pollinated seed going anywhere. If anything, I see renewed energy around some seed stewardship, and keeping some of those genetics available for gardeners, for small growers, for all growers to [continue to] have an option to be more independent and have greater seed security." And for her it comes back to both "celebrating the diversity of all sources of where seed comes from, and to the growers' and buyers' awareness [about] type of seed, and understanding the benefits of each," such as open-pollinated, or hybrid, so that the "market growers and ultimate buyers and eaters have what they need."

But, of course, the megaconglomerates have a few things the smaller seed growers do not: seemingly endless bank accounts to direct at massive advertising campaign and relentless lobbyists (you've likely seen the commercials during Sunday afternoon football making Roundup look like a healthy choice for your whole family—dogs and small children included—in achieving the perfect lush green turf lawn).

Battling these odds seems like an overwhelming burden to be carried by fewer and fewer acres of "untouched" farmland and diversity and by ecologically inclined small growers, gardeners, and thinkers with less and less market share.

How can an ordinary, nongrowing, nongardening member of the public be expected to hold attentive awareness about this one issue, especially with so many other social and political and health issues affecting us in front-page ways over the past few years?

Melhorn and Giroux do not openly profess to be worried.

But I do.

Can we count on multinational corporations to suspend the protections—and billions in profits—afforded them by intellectual property rights on the argument that we "should" protect the rhythms the earth has spent 4.5 billion years developing? Can we keep our eyes, priorities, and values on what's best for seed, or the planet, or for us as humans in the long term all at the same time, when we can't even keep track of the natural markers of seasonal shifts (suns, moons, weather) we've used for millennia to measure time itself? Does our own nature matter to us at all anymore, or are we as a species so confident of our dominance over it?

Imbolc is an ancient festival of spring, a celebration of the season's lushness, freshness, fertility, and abundant diversity of everything—smells, tastes, colors, sensations.

Just 60 years ago Rachel Carson sounded an alarm by offering out the terrifying specter of a silent spring: "They should not be called pesticides, they should be called biocides." We as a society did prevail over DDT, the environmental chemical of greatest concern in Carson's era. But in the single ensuing generation, our global chemical and genetic engineering efforts have proliferated, while our planet's own biodiversity has plummeted.

Are we headed toward a silencing of spring monumentally farther reaching than Carson forewarned?

FEBRUARY 7

We hike to the top of the flat, expansive ridge above the canyon today. We try to make the hike to the top once a week to see the changing bloom, seed, seasonal details. It is sunny and clear, hot even, as we walk. We need rain, of course, and remain in a record-breaking drought, but it is a nice time of year to hike here as the rattlesnakes are still sleeping, the grass is not yet so high or dry as to make the hike tedious with bush whacking and stickers, and the poison oak (*Toxicodendrun diversilobum*) is easily spotted and avoided with the grass still low. The very upright, glossy, reddish-brown stems of colonies are mostly hip high or taller and still bare, just the very tips and buds starting to swell or show the first ruffly edges of soon-to-emerge foliage. An occasional cluster of last year's waxy, cream-colored, now-puckered and leathery-with-age fruits (technically drupes and each about the size of a small raisin) can be seen hanging on in some stands. Delicate burgundy to black striations run from top to bottom on this food source beloved and relied on by overwintering and winter-migrating birds, including the resident California towhee.

At the top, all along the rocky escarpments at the edges of the plateau, we are amazed by last season's extravagant seed stalks of California bee plant (*Scrophularia californica*) and the seed set on them. John has never seen it in such abundance. The result of last year's (and the year before that's) big spring blooms after the Camp Fire cleaned the area? Is this a fire-following plant? Or simply a seed bank stalwart now released from dormancy and a chance at the sunlight?

We would never have otherwise noticed them had the area not been cleared—so slender, airy, and unassuming are the arching stalks—but their large, leafy basal growth catches our attention. The mounds of soft, broad, bright green leaves stand out as unusually large and fleshy compared to other plants growing on this exposed slope and dry, flat ridge.

If the stalks almost disappear against the background of tall, dried grass above the fresh green growth below, the fairly tiny seed capsules are harder still to pick out, and John holds his hand behind a cluster for me to try to get a picture. Each dry and cracked (dehisced) capsule is maybe one-tenth inch across. They are so small and recessive, how do the bees find their likewise tiny flowers preceding these seeds? But by sight or scent, they do find the creamy-mauve potbellied flowers—less than .15 of an inch wide or high—resulting in this abundant seed. In their open state, the seed capsules are essentially perpendicular to the ground, and the tiny black seed inside rattles out with disturbance by wind and wildlife. The pepper-shaker approach again. Who, if anyone, eats them?

The toyon shrubs are still loaded with red berries and the robins are having a time of it—perhaps the cold spells of December and January sweetened the berries?

We also come across a mass of the Dr. Seuss–esque whirligig-pom-pom seed heads of foothill clematis (*Clematis lasiantha*) deep inside the armature of a deciduous woody buckbrush shrub (*Ceanothus cuneatus*), which until now has protected the heads of twirly, feathery styles—each style attached to a seed—from the winter winds and few rains.

Maybe the next rains, the spring winds, or the first nesting birds plucking at their silky plumes will send them on their way …

The variation on seed form, even in this one prescribed place, is incalculable. So too their reach and reason for being on land and in life.

FEBRUARY 11 AND 12: NEW MOON AND LUNAR NEW YEAR
Cultures following a lunar or lunisolar calendar mark time not only by the sun's position in relation to Earth, but also by the cycle and phases of the moon—the new moon being the first day of a new moon(th) cycle. Asian cultures and calendars, Jewish and Buddhist calendars are all lunisolar. Traditionally the second new moon following the winter solstice marks the Lunar New Year, which not coincidentally is considered the beginning of spring for the lunar-observant cultures.

Here the buckeyes (*Aesculus californica*) are pushing out their earliest leaves following their many-months-long summer and then winter-to-now deciduous state. Little green bunches push up and out from the growing tip of each pale white-to-gray stem. The stems arch out from the tree or shrub and then curve back up just at this growing tip, giving the impression that they are offering their young, unfurling, almost fleur-de-lis-shaped foliage bouquets out to the world.

The nonnative mustards (brought to California by the Spanish in the sixteenth century) are in full primary-color yellow bloom all up and down the canyon, up and down the fields and verges from town to the canyon. A pervasive and persistent annual flowering reminder of human cultivation and distribution of seeds and plants: an invasive, which like many invasive plants, comes with confusing messaging. For instance, the Oregon State University Agricultural Extension office lauds how much European honeybees (also native to that continent, of course) love the mustards, while the *LA Times* environmental writers bemoan how much ready fuel—by growing to six feet in some seasons—these same mustards create in fire-prone areas. The California Invasive Plant Council lists *Brassica nigra* (black mustard) as a moderately severe plant pest in California: "Like other mustards, Brasssica nigra grows profusely and produces allelopathic chemicals that prevent germination of native plants. The spread of black mustard can increase the frequency of fires in chaparral and coastal sage scrub, changing these habitats to annual grassland." But this is just one view on this historied plant.

Kristyn Leach, a farmer of Korean descent, is a seed grower and seed keeper tracing and preserving the great diversity of seed and food—and the rich history held therein—of the Asian diaspora, which would include black mustard, a valuable food and spice (from its seed) in its native regions of Africa and Asia. Leach provides a resonant description of the calculus of what this plant is capable of doing: "With one mustard seed you can grow one mustard plant, each flowering stem produces upwards of fifty flowers, each producing one seed pod in which there may be more than fifty seeds. Each plant can produce tens of thousands of seeds."

And in an interview on the Civil Eats website, Leach shares this: "There is just no greater resource for us to think about in terms of food security and food sovereignty than acknowledging the role seeds play in that ... every seed contains this vast and continuing story, to be able to feel a sense of a place within that story is fairly incredible." And powerful.

On the one hand the mustard, as with many so-deemed invasive plants, is a bounty; on the other hand it is a bane—both legacies of our collective ancestors, traditionally honored at the Lunar New Year. Finding a potential balance might be the best legacy for us to grow forward as ancestors ourselves—balance opportunities to control the bane and maximize the bounty.

FEBRUARY 14

With what winter moisture we have in the soil and with spring growth just getting started on summer-blooming weeds, we spend the day in the canyon pulling, piling, and then burning stem after stem of Scotch broom—one section at a time. Once the plants are past a certain age (three years?), and the soil has reached concrete-like hardness in summer, their depth-seeking tap roots are not possible to hand pull. John is at it for days, I chip in when I can. We clear a nice big square of it—it feels satisfying and as though we made a little headway. We try not to look at the unmanaged populations upstream and downstream. Or even at the patches we can't get to right now, today.

Scotch broom (*Cytisus scoparius*) is native to the British Isles and central and southern Europe. It was introduced to the United States as an ornamental in the mid-1800s. (*Yes, I see the parallels between this colonizing plant and my own Scot-Irish-Anglo ancestry.*) Initially introduced as an ornamental, and later to control erosion and stabilize coastal dunes, it spread without check from there. Established infestations are difficult to eliminate because the plant creates large, long-lived seed banks. Brooms of several varieties are estimated to infest more than 60,000 acres in California, and the plants spread by abundant seeding (each flower in a cluster forms a seed pod, and each seed pod bears between 5 and 20 shiny, black seeds which, like most pea species, disperse loudly and forcefully when the pod pops open), and by vegetative runners. Prolific seed set and assertive runners eventually help broom to form dense colonies where they are happy. Both the bright yellow flowers and the innumerable seeds are toxic to people and animals because of their active quinolizidine alkaloids. The life cycle of broom is such that after a few years' growth, they often become woody and degenerate into acres of standing dry tinder, and because the younger green growth is loaded with resin, both old and young are highly flammable. The seeds are viable for up to 80 years.

These adaptations were advantageous in the plants' native regions, but this strength and resilience is environmentally devastating in broom's new regions, which are devoid of coevolutionary control mechanisms like native wildlife who can make use of the plant or its seeds. Here, we never see insects or birds nectaring or collecting pollen from the blooms, nor birds snacking on the seed in fall. The plant's growth and spread is somewhat checked in the Southern California and Central Valley portions of the state by the extreme dryness and at higher elevations of the Sierra and other mountain ranges by winter cold. In the 1960s the Scotch broom seed beetle, which coevolved to lay its eggs and have its larva feed on broom seed, was introduced from the United Kingdom as one possible control. If the beetle is somewhat helpful, it has not stopped the expansion of broom here.

That said, it's noteworthy logic: if you're having a problem with seed, getting someone to eat that seed in a way that destroys rather than aids its viability seems like a good control mechanism bet.

FEBRUARY 15
When we hike to the top of the ridge this week, we see that the spring procession of bloom is building steam. We are treated to views of many happy colonies of white shooting stars (*Primula clevelandii*). In UC Berkeley's online Jepson eFlora database, shooting star fruit is described as *circumscissile*, meaning it has a dehiscent opening like a pot you take

the lid off, opening latitudinally rather than from top to bottom, or along a side (and again the descriptor for the seed type and behavior, just as plant names do, has linguistic echoes we recognize, think circumscribe, circumspect, circumnavigate, circumcise). I have never noticed their seed pods or fruit; I make a mental note to pay attention as they mature.

Another bloom we are excited to see, especially John for the forage the plants offer the early bumble bee queens and their first worker offspring as they build their colonies, is one of our native solanums—maybe *Solanum parishii*? Maybe *Solanum umbelliferum*? In the nightshade family (like potatoes, tomatoes, and peppers), the deep to pale purple flowers with their sharply peaked bright yellow downward-pointing stamens, look just like the flowers of our common garden nightshades, and similarly, are particularly suited to the vibrating buzz pollination (sonication) provided by bumble bees. The small berries of this solanum are like little clusters of mottled-green cherry tomatoes. Like many plants in the nightshade family, all parts of the plant are poisonous, especially the fruit.

Back down on the canyon floor, the milkmaids continue to bloom—bright white flashes in the understory … in forgotten places laid bare by the fire. We make a note to watch for their seed set in coming weeks.

FEBRUARY 28: FULL SNOW MOON/ASH (TREE) MOON/ BALD EAGLE MOON

John and I are visiting family in Colorado's Fraser Valley on the Front Range of the Rocky Mountains. Despite our own summer arid climate, we are not used to the extreme dryness here. We can feel it on our skin, in our eyes, in our sinuses. We are not used to the 8500 foot elevation, or the minus 11 degree morning.

Snowshoeing behind the property's barn, I notice what looks like grit on a low ridge of snow beside the snowshoeing track. When I look closely, I see wheat-colored stems of four or five relict seed heads, with small conical domes maybe a quarter centimeter across. Delicate-looking but clearly rugged and persistent calyces surround the central dome. Maybe five of them are bent down. The "grit" is actually the last of the seeds, dispersed across the snow. *Eriophyllum* maybe? *Grindelia*? Definitely in Asteraceae given the conical central seed cluster. The black flecks of seed against the snow in the cold-to-me sun are absorbing the sun's heat and melting the snow beneath them, some already having created their own tunnel right to the ground below. Perhaps the snow provides needed cold stratification and, with each night's freeze, insulation until spring begins her earliest advance, when germination might be possible.

Pretty stinking ingenious—miraculous even?

A lesson on endurance, fortitude, persistence, patience, and resourcefulness.

Seed Commerce

NEW MOON, MARCH 13
FULL MOON, MARCH 28

MARCH 1

We wake to the sound of the turkeys gobbling, clucking, chortling, and fanning in the season. The toms and the hens dig together for seed and grubs in the soil, flying awkwardly to the top of the olive tree to pick the last of the wrinkly purple fruit—the great birds always looking and sounding like they could topple off or through at any second.

It is not a melodious sound, their gobbling and strutting, and yet it is a joyous sound of spring and life.

The canyon is over the top in its fertility this time of year. Green, on green, on green, the cool and relative dampness of the dryish winter still results in the oaks unfurling their pale green canopies, below them the spring annual wildflowers—clovers, fringepods, saxifrage, California poppies, and chick lupine line the road and color up the hillsides. Geophytes, too, accent the fields of greening grasses—triteliea, brodiaea, iris, calachortus—and plenty of other herbaceous perennials, Douglas violets and yampah among them, all beneath the last of the rollout of spring flowering shrubs.

Someone driving in the canyon for the first time might be very tempted, as I was, to assume all this is relatively "pristine." At first glance it might look as though it has been altered very little by human hand despite the modest to rustic 40- to 100-year-old houses that sit back in the tree cover along its two-mile length.

But like just about anywhere in North America, this canyon shows the evidence, and scars, of human relationship with seeds and plants and the landscape going back hundreds if not thousands of years.

The canyon walls are divoted with caves and several Maidu grinding stones—large flat stones sculpted with sometimes one, sometimes many rounded "bowls" ground into their surface. Some of these ground-out bowls are shallow, some as deep as a few inches, and they can be seen both inside and outside of these caves. These time-worn work surfaces were used to grind acorns and other seeds into flours and pastes. The caves also show evidence of old hearth fires, and the most recent Mechoopda use of these sites likely dates back to contact with European trappers as early as the 1820s. By 1849, a year after gold was found on John Sutter's land and kicked off the California gold rush, General John Bidwell used earnings from his gold-mining work for Sutter to purchase a nearby land grant, Rancho Arroyo Chico, along a steady tributary of the Sacramento River. This would eventually become the city of Chico, California, due north and west of this canyon. In time, some portion of Bidwell's land grant would become a campus in the California State University system, another portion of the grant a state park.

By 1850, the closest town (which is no longer) to the canyon was established as housing and a "dump" site for a lumber company operating 30 miles east. According to a written history by an early white woman settler in the canyon, whose family relocated here from Vermont in 1878 following the Homestead Act of 1869, "the [logging] Company had a V flume, and floated the lumber from east of them, down the flume. I can remember the flume well and all the large buildings and piles of lumber." However, as she recounted, "the Company cut all their best pine and used it to build the flume and then their best lumber was gone and the Company went broke and sold the buildings and what lumber there was left and so ended the lumber industry" of the canyon's vicinity. This history also explains why there are far fewer gray pines in the canyon than it seems there should or could be.

This little onetime community is within 20 miles of many historic American Indian villages that were thriving at the time of first European contact in the early 1800s. From the top of the canyon's ridges, it is in visible proximity of the region's devastating malaria outbreak (brought by white settlers) in 1833. It is within a day's walk of the 1844 land grant creating the Rancho Arroyo Chico; of the historic commercial wheat growing of the mid- and late-1800s; of the "mother orange," a Mediterranean sweet orange planted in the town of Oroville in 1856, helping to kick off the Northern California citrus industry. This little canyon is in view of the epicenter for commercial rice growing here, beginning with Chinese gold and railway laborers growing rice for their own use throughout the gold rush years, and then increasing exponentially in the 1910s, with large-scale production.

In the last few decades, a small family-owned citrus orchard was established at the mouth of the canyon by a retired couple, and they sell seasonal mandarins, navel oranges, improved Meyer and Eureka lemons, and oroblanco grapefruit at an honor-system stand. Maybe 30 years ago, a large landowner at the top of the canyon attempted to establish a gold mine with the financial backing of foreign investors, but the operation was defeated by residents fighting for the quality and integrity of the creek and riparian habitat. Several iterations of pot growers have since leased the land of the abandoned mine site.

John and his family started his specialty perennial plant mail-order business here in 1986 on the site of a house that had burned to the ground in a 1985 fire.

Now, each spring, the vegetable gardeners and fruit growers along the road plant their gardens, sometimes sharing seed, seedlings, onion and garlic sets, even making group orders from the nearest nursery. They share excess produce and preserves throughout the season too.

Every generation of people in the canyon have made their own growth marks representing one universal story played out over time and on land on our globe: care, cultivation, displacement, extraction, abandonment, repeat.

MARCH 3
The winter-blooming flowers are of course the first to go to seed in spring.

The earliest blooming, common manzanita (*Arctostaphylos manzanita*) are already forming dangling clusters of green pomes. They have plump, sweetish, flesh around several stonelike seeds that are sometimes fused together. The earlier blooms fed the overwintering hummingbirds from late December to late January. Among these blooms the hummingbirds nectared alongside the earliest waking bumble bees, whose buzz pollination helped release the tiny bell-shaped bloom's pollen and move it one step closer to successful seed set. The later blooming whiteleaf manzanita (*A. viscida*) is just in bloom now. Up to 55 different insects are thought to be pollen, nectar, or larval associates of the many species of manzanita that coexist with the oak and conifer forests and the chaparral of California. The whiteleaf manzanita will form fruit in its turn.

Between the nectar and pollen of the flowers, leaves for larva, and the fruit which will persist from now to next winter, manzanita support a wide array of life across the full year. The floral buds for next year form alongside the berries, which can take 3 to 7 months to fully ripen, but then these seeds will feed a wide variety of berry-eating birds, rodents (whose caches of seed help ensure the next generation of manzanita), raccoons, foxes, coyotes, deer, and bears (and humans, if the berries are cooked to break down the tannins) through fall and early winter.

In an interesting twist, manzanita are long-lived in the absence of fire, but highly flammable and resinous as mature shrubs. Those that have not formed or do not form a crown burl, from which resprouting is fairly reliable, are generally killed by even low-intensity fires. This is especially true of whiteleaf manzanita. However, a large number of the hard-coated seeds will wait dormant in the soil (often in those rodent caches) for fire's scarification to kick-start germination.

What kills the parents brings the offspring to life. A competition control mechanism for both generations maybe, but also perhaps a failsafe adaptation to ensure the continuity of the species across any and all conditions.

Does it sometimes take a near apocalypse to reignite an encoded ferocity for life?

MARCH 5

I am cutting back the front garden at my house in town this week—
the three-foot-tall and equally wide dried fountains of native deergrass
(*Muhlenbergia rigens*) whose inflorescences of flowering and then
grain-producing spikelets are now done.

I am also cutting back what are now acutely arching fortified stalks—
sword-like—from the several clumps of *Hesperaloe parviflora*, native
to the Chihuahuan Desert. Planted in the "hellstrip" between the sidewalk and the street, each *Hesperaloe* flowering stalk is now topped by
progressions of almost tulip-shaped seed capsules cracking open along
seams delineating the capsules' three chambers. Each chamber is full of
thin, flat black, teardrop-shaped seeds—big seeds, maybe one-eighth
inch long? *Hesperaloe*'s subfamily, Agavoideae, derives its name from
the Greek for "imposing stature." My neighbors on the way to the
mailboxes can relate to the imposing descriptor. They will be glad I am
cutting the spiky stalks back.

The *Hesperaloe* seed capsules individually are described as
"beaked" and held upright and open at the top, with the peak of
the "beaks" curving out and away from the opening to allow birds
or water or light in and to let the seeds out.

These perfectly formed capsules remind me again how incredible the range of seed "vessels" are. Evolved to grow, hold, and
then release their many varied seed treasures, they are nature's
creativity and ingenuity at work over millennia. They are the
original single-use storage containers, of more intelligent, durable
yet compostable materials—plastic zippered baggies have little on
them. Studying these particularly sturdy, shapely, squat, potbellied forms with recurving beaks, it's evident there's an elegance
to their opening lines and the plunge of the opening edges.

It's easy to think that civilizations ancient and contemporary—from Mesopotamian to Aztec, first people of North America to those of Australia and Africa—could well have derived their ceramic and carved and woven vessel forms from the seedy natural world around them.

Nothing is new under the old, old sun. With their seeds and fruits (to say nothing of flowers and roots), plants have evolved almost every form humans have reproduced for their own utility and artistry: in seeds and their associated vessels, there are cups and saucers, vases and candelabras, augurs, screws, cranes, oceangoing vessels, airliners, and cathedral archways. Seed forms and diaspores writ large offer seemingly everything from which to craft beautiful and productively engineered civilizations.

They are pulley and lever, catapult, and brick shithouse, protecting, holding, and eventually encouraging the life inside them toward posterity.

MARCH 7

The ides of March, a traditional day for Europeans to sow pea seeds in the garden, given that they like cold germination, is just over a week away. John already has seed going in the open-ended but covered potting shed, along with cuttings of native and cultivated garden plants he wants to propagate, and we are still enjoying harvesting a lot of fall-sown winter spinach, lettuces, and seriously sweet little carrots. I sowed my (pre-soaked) sweet pea seeds in the late fall and once up, they will tolerate most of the cold nights we will continue to get till April or so. With all of this in mind, the vegetable garden comes into focus.

We sort through our seed collection deciding what we want to plant this year, trying to determine the oldest from the newest of the seed—was it this carrot we liked? Was it this basil or that one?

Seed catalogs inform and delight us as they arrive in our mailboxes seasonally. Gardeners (John among them), horticultural libraries, societies, and even universities, especially those with an agricultural history or ag school or college, keep collections of seed and trade catalogs for the history, artistry, and knowledge they hold. They are a record of our horticultural past.

In John's personal archive of catalogs and nursery correspondence, we find a 1941 Garden Guide, the full-color seed catalog from F. Lagomarsino & Sons, Seedsmen of Sacramento. Black-and-white photography alternates with hand-colored imagery; native and nonnative flower seeds are offered. "Novelty" introductions of the time include "Tithonia, Fireball; Columbine, Crimson Star," and "Aster, Early Giant Wilt-Resistant, light blue" alongside "Aster, Improved New Giant California Sunshine." And Unwin's Dwarf Hybrids of native *Clarkia elegans*. A southwestern native, *Heuchera sanguinea*, is among the perennials.

Throughout the catalog are little graphic callouts offering such advice as "Use Bearmor Fertilizer for Annuals and Perennials."

Under the fruit and vegetable seeds, an announcement of "Klondike University Strain" watermelon includes this information: "This excellent new strain was developed at University Farm at Davis, California. It is the most outstanding strain of this popular melon. By careful breeding and selection, the desired qualities of uniformity in size, shape, color and quality have been stabilized. The seeds are small, fewer number and uniformly dark color throughout. Due to the uniformity in size, shape and strength of rind, this variety is one of the best for shipping, and there's also none equaled for the home and market garden." A packet is listed for five cents; ten pounds is listed for eleven dollars.

The cover design strikes me as especially indicative of how a seed catalog, at first glance an apolitical document, has the power to compress fraught historical relationships into a compact visual package. The "Garden Guide" title overlays a large red disk, a reference to the Japanese flag, in which the white numbers 1941 curve. The back of the catalog is a photo of perfect green turf lawn, alongside ad boxes for "RHO-ZA-LIA essential plant food for Azaleas, Rhododendrons and Camellias." California was the epicenter for Asian plant introductions and Asian nurseries in the United States—a point of celebration and pride in 1941 that would change sharply (with civil-rights-destroying results for American citizens of Japanese birth or ancestry) in 1942 with Japanese internment mandates.

Oregon State University in Corvallis has a collection of some 2000 seed and nursery catalogs dating between 1832 and 1966. The Smithsonian Institution Libraries Trade Literature Collection, held at the National Museum of American History Library, includes more than 10,000 dating from 1830 to the present, including the collection belonging to W. Atlee Burpee. The Atlanta History Center's Cherokee Garden Library, overseen by director Staci Catron, has a "unique seed and nursery catalog collection" pertinent especially to the Southeast, "representing over 500 seed, nursery, and supply companies dating from 1827 to the present." The collection includes the entire catalog history of the H. G. Hastings seed and garden company, established in Florida in 1889. The collection curators note that "the study of older seed and nursery catalogs makes it possible to trace how and when specific developments occurred in the seed and garden industry in response to available technology and the demands of gardeners in changing times."

The OSU collection's historical overview points out that "the earliest" seed and nursery trade catalogs "have historical links to much older 'herbals,' books of plants made for the study of medicine and botany. Starting in the late 16th century, it became fashionable for kings and wealthy aristocrats to outdo one another in amassing large collections of exotic plants. To add to the prestige of these collections, some owners had them cataloged in elaborately illustrated books called *Florilegia*," making for lofty ancestry to our seed catalogs of today.

The oldest catalog in the OSU collection dates to 1832 and is from G. Thorburn & Sons, Thorburn being a Scottish-born immigrant who came to New York in the 1790s. According to the

mid-nineteenth century notes on OSU's collection, as a comple-
ment to his grocery business, Thorburn began selling "flower
pots" and from there "flowering plants and seeds." This eventually led to his own seed catalog, in which he included "sowing
times and cultural information." In his autobiography, Thorburn
documented that he "first saw a seed catalog in late 1805 when a
man from London sold him a packet of seeds containing a catalog
from William Malcolm and Company, London."

Based on Thorburn's catalog (and others), the OSU curators can date the tomato becoming popular for home gardeners
around 1810, and have found that "in the 1830s, patent medi-
cines were only just beginning to replace medicinal herbs." This
is reflected in the reduction of herb offerings in the catalogs of
the time, as large herb gardens meant only for pleasure did not
become common until the twentieth century.

Per OSU's collection curators, after 1840, the seed and nursery
trade in the United States expanded exponentially along with the
railway, improved mail service, and annually published seed and
nursery catalogs. Post–Civil War, mail order became much more
common due to "improved transportation networks and postal
reforms in the 1860s that made it cheaper to ship seeds and plant
material as well as catalogs." The larger US market also meant
more competition, with the result that catalogs became showier:
illustrations and photographs became richer and more colorful,
plant names became elaborate and descriptive selling points, with
big and *better* often part of variety names.

Around this era, again according to OSU's interpretive
research, growing for markets took off as small enterprise. "As
truck farming increased in scale there was a great demand for

reliable commercial varieties, and some market gardeners began producing seeds for this purpose. Improvements in food preservation also led to the need for varieties suitable for canning and pickling; in 1875, the refrigerated railway car was brought into use leading to an even larger scale commercial vegetable and fruit trade."

These seed catalog collections also show how home-based and commercial seed production increased dramatically around both world wars, when the US market was isolated from trade with England and Europe. An enormous investment of time, dollars, and acres went into making American markets less reliant on imported seed and other goods, and simultaneously, specific seed began to be offered with disease resistance or selected traits for specific regions and conditions in the United States—like the Pacific Northwest, which remains a seed-growing center today.

Despite noticeable austerity within catalogs of the time, the Depression era saw a significant uptick in printed catalogs in the United States—OSU librarians note that "gardening was popular during the Depression both as a means of increasing the food supply and as an inexpensive leisure activity."

Technology and its impacts on gardening is also apparent, OSU notes: "The Chase Brothers catalog of 1940" discussed how cars and good roads had decreased privacy in front yards and porches, leading gardeners to divert more resources to beautifying back yard "outdoor living rooms," a term that first came into use in 1928. In contrast, "front yards became less elaborate, with lawns and evergreen shrubs ... Horses no longer appeared in catalog photographs of the 1930s, and Unwin's 1932 catalog discusses the difficulties of maintaining soil fertility since manure was in short supply. The company carried an organic fertilizer as a superior alternative to chemical preparations."

All of this history leads in one way or another to the landscape of the seed growers, sellers, and catalogs we have in the 2020s. According to a 2012 Center for Food Safety report, citing data collected by journalist Matthew Wilde and published in Iowa's *Waterloo-Cedar Falls Courier* in 2012, "The number of small, independent seed companies has rapidly declined: In 1996, there were 300 independent seed companies in the United States; by 2009, there were fewer than 100."

An educated guess puts small, independent, and open-source-supporting seed companies in the United States somewhere below 500 in 2021. Perhaps an indication of a responsive uptick? A great new germination?

Even when characterized as "small and independent," seed sellers rarely grow 100 percent of the seed they sell, and some of them do not grow any of their own seed. Many seed companies list the percentage of the seed they grow themselves somewhere in their informational materials (catalog, website, etc.). The percentages range from 25 percent to 85 percent own grown. Just because they are smaller in size or sales, and just because they are not owned by a larger corporation, does not predetermine their stance on organic, on open source, on consolidation, on chemical fertilizers, pesticides, and herbicides, or on the use or inclusion of GMO or GE.

For example, earlier this growing season, John and I visit Pyramid Farms, a local organic vegetable and flower farm, to rehome John's many lengths of shade cloth, which the farm will put to good use and keep it out of the landfill. Matthew Martin and Lisa Carle, who run Pyramid, are locally famous for their sweet, sweet carrots and their advocacy for slow food, organic ecological methods, reasonable working conditions for their farmer crew, and their support of local public-school gardens and school garden education.

Martin shares that there were large carrot-seed crop failures in 2019, that there were big blocks in the carrot-seed market in 2020. He had just ordered all of his seed for 2021 that very morning. Most of the commercial seed in the world is now grown in China, he tells us, and grown under cover at that, which strikes me as really interesting.

It also strikes me as crazy that Martin's best source for production-level seed is China.

And more crazy: even when I buy my own home garden seed from what I deem reliable sources, I am not at all clear on where those companies source their seeds. Do they grow some of them themselves? Do they grow *any* of them themselves? Who actually grows what—and does it matter to me? To us collectively? Should it matter more?

In the "independent" seed *grower* category, there is no correlation with philosophical stance. Take for example the "independent" animal-forage-seed grower in Elkhorn, Nebraska, Rob-See-Co, which announced a 2021 acquisition of another "family-owned" "independent" Midwest seed grower, Masters Choice. Although not owned by a large multinational corporation, Rob-See-Co licenses the right to use Syngenta GMO technology.

The moniker "family-owned" has the capacity to veil and greenwash all manner of obfuscations. Keep in mind the Sacklers are the "family" that owns Purdue Pharma. Just because you can claim to be a family-owned organization does not necessarily place your work on the happiest side of seed care or environmental stewardship.

While many seed companies rely on legacy names as branding, such as Burpee or Ferry-Morse (established in 1856 and claiming to be the first company to sell seeds in packets with growing season marked on them for best results), even these "folksy" companies have some interesting business associates. Ferry-Morse (a signer of the Safe Seed Pledge) was purchased by Green Garden Products (formerly Plantation Products) and then consolidated into Central Garden & Pet, which also owns big pesticide and fungicide producers such as Diacon and Sevin.

Seed growers and sellers differentiate themselves in the 2020s in a variety of ways, including by the region they represent and groups of people they serve, as well as where they stand on current economic, environmental, and social justice concerns.

If a seed company does grow their own seed, they proudly share that percentage with you; if they even partially offer organic or open-pollinated seeds, they tell you; if they are signers of the Safe Seed Pledge, or have developed or offer seed selections that are morally bound by and dedicated to the Open Source Seed Initiative, they tell you.

Of all the independent seed companies, Fedco, beginning under the leadership of C. R. Lawn in the 1970s, set a standard in seed-variety-labeling transparency in order to allow and encourage buyers (home gardeners or market growers) to know exactly where and by whom their seed was grown, and to whom any part of the profits are returned.

Maine-based Fedco has been in the seed business since 1978. They took on a well-established tree business in 1983, added fall "bulbs" the next year, "included Tom Robert's potato offerings by 1985," and added the Organic Grower Supply of the Maine

Organic Farmers and Gardeners as of 1988. Fedco had 98 orders its first year, and now completes "58,000 orders annually for a total of $6 million in revenue, and ships to all 50 states." They are a cooperative and state that "profit is not our primary goal ... Consumers own 60% of the cooperative, and worker members 40%. Consumer and worker members share proportionately in the cooperative's profits through our annual patronage dividends."

Incidentally, Fedco, in agreement with their cooperative members' majority desire, phased out all seed from Seminis after it was purchased by Monsanto.

The more underground (pun intended) seed growing, sharing, and distribution networks outside of these more conventional business models are also significant players in the independent seed world, as are hybrid models between seed catalogs, seed businesses (albeit nonprofit), seed banks, and seed commons. More on that soon.

Ultimately, our gardens and our garden seed are always about more than just what I am growing in my garden today—or you are growing in yours. It is about how we grow the world.

Every gardener should do their own research into their seed companies of choice.

Every dollar we spend on seed is a vote for how we want seed grown, cared for, and cared about. It is a vote for how we want to see and care for both our world and ourselves.

I'll take mine revered, respected, and replenished.

MARCH 11
We hiked to the top of the ridge today. We are on a good every-two-week cycle to check on our plant friends and communities. The manzanita berries continue to plump and color up.

At least three different native clovers are now in bloom. The nonnative late winter bloomers are setting seed already, but it is the luxurious healthy stands of lacepod a.k.a. fringepod (*Thysanocarpus curvipes*), named for the lacey little disk-like seed pods sequinning the stem from top to bottom that, to my eye, are the most compelling seed forms in the landscape. Wide swathes of these shimmering, translucent spikes glow in the spring light.

I hold a handful of the pink-edged, pale-green-and-cream-centered seeds to simply admire their minute and delicate, but bold, sense of style.

Thysanocarpus curvipes is of the Brassica family (think broccoli, kale, cauliflower) and their abundance and design aesthetics make me wonder about them as a possible food source. What little I can find leads me to believe the seeds are or have been eaten, parched or blanched, by the Mechoopda. But also that they might be bitter. There is a single seed inside each lacey disk, and given their eyelet wings, I ponder the wind or water flotation abilities of the little vessels.

MARCH 15: THE IDES OF MARCH
Heather McCargo, founder of Wild Seed Project in Maine, articulated something really insightful recently about seed and us as gardeners: There is a universally held image of gathering a handful of seed, and just walking across seemingly open and receptive land broadcast sowing the seed in early spring with the full belief that a vibrant and perfectly harmonious meadow will subsequently materialize.

But for anyone who has broadcast sown any seed just about anywhere, you know this is not exactly what comes to pass. Or grow.

The willow, the poppy, the cottonwood, and the pomegranate know that you must put a whole hell of a lot of seed out into the world to even hope that one or two of them will find fertile ground; that one or two of them will get past the beady eyes, beaks, mouths, and talons of birds; will stay intact against corrupting bacteria; will grow faster than aphids and squirrels can eat them, and live to a maturity of seed-bearing age themselves.

Seeds are strategic and resilient and adaptable and adapting—but they are also fragile, precious, tender, and often very specific in their requirements.

By all means try broadcast sowing; but McCargo would admonish us to be very careful that we're not complicating native seeds' already difficult task of finding a foothold by introducing competing foreign species, no matter how they might be marketed on a cute packet promising "wild-flowers." The simple act of sowing will launch you into an apprenticeship of how seed grows, how plants grow from seed. Once you understand more about them and their individual workings, then graduate to saving your own seed (and stewarding those precious resources), perhaps you will feel ready to knowledgeably and gratefully ask the wild plants of your place if they are willing to share seed—as land-based peoples the world over teach us to do—so you may try your hand at partnering with those lives.

MARCH 20
The vernal equinox. We are halfway through this singular cycle around the sun. Fully opposite where we were at the autumnal equinox in September.

In a conversation with Kristin Perers, an American-born, London-based artist and photographer and vicar's wife, she spoke about trying rigorously to find the sacred in the everyday.

She has been exploring her lifelong impulse to ground herself into the season and the plant lives of the places in which she finds herself. She described how she and her husband over the years have had heated debates about the nature and presence of God—of the abiding layers and levels of faith and the "vestments" with which we clothe our days.

She was stranded in Florida for four months in the early part of the COVID-19 pandemic. In that forced isolation, away from immediate family and daily life, she relied upon a morning yoga practice to ground her. When she had to practice indoors, she would pick a flower from the garden and use it as the focal meditative point of her practice.

The inherent grace of the flower's life reminded her that she too had these elemental aspects of beauty, elegance, and grace.

Is for me, perhaps, the amazement of holding a seed, sowing a seed, my own form of meditation? It is life distilled down so completely that it becomes an emblem of divinity, life, eternity, reincarnation—what every

religion and thinker has striven to define in terms humans can grasp—
a universal and repeating rhythm of which we are also, but only, one part.

And if giving and supporting life is a love language, then perhaps a
seed—like a messiah, a child of God people believe was given to them—
is proof positive that love is a cosmic force, in a nutshell.

MARCH 27

My mother was diagnosed with fairly aggressive breast cancer at the
age of 38, in the late 1970s, when she was in the thick of establishing two
home-based, bootstrap small businesses. In the face of a harsh diagnosis and very unsure prognosis, she—a lifelong gardener—did not take
to her bed for any longer than therapy dictated or any more than she
had always done. Each morning she drank her first cup of sweet, milky
coffee in bed, she smoked her first cigarette, and she made her lists for
the day, her green felt-tip pen working methodically across her yellow
legal-sized ruled notepad. Lists of what needed doing in the garden—
planting, transplanting, dividing, trimming, watering, feeding, harvesting.
Reminders to cut flowers for the table, the mantel, for any arriving guests.
Tasks for the produce garden; what needed seeding and what seed
needed collecting.

My very earliest memories are of playing in an earthy potting-soil mix
beneath a simple plywood potting table, wooden post legs marking
my space. Women's voices intermingled melodically—a small group of
them, including my mother, would be seeding trays, pricking out, potting
on, and potting up those seedlings ready for a salable-size container—
a four-inch pot, a one-gallon pot, whatever it might be. They were propagating all kinds of plants in the warm humidity of a poly-sided greenhouse in winter in Berthoud, Colorado, preparing for the spring season
of vegetable starts, hanging baskets, and bedding plants. The scent of
a potting shed, and the sound of such intermingling female voices are
ones I still associate with safety and nurture.

My mother—I realize many years after her death—prepared a fertile seed
bed on which she hoped her daughters would grow. This is what most
parents try to do: provide what their children need to grow and set their
own seeds; not just seeds that are the next generation of children, but
"seeds" of words, thoughts, deeds to grow new worlds dendritic and

branching out from them. Parents and children are related, but also coevolving in their own ways.

MARCH 28
Not all seeds or seed systems are a simple equation of more is more.

Judith Larner Lowry, founder and owner of Larner Seeds, based in Bolinas, California, told me that when she started her work in the late 1970s, less than 1 percent of California's native bunch-grass ecosystems remained intact. By the 2020s, this canyon's native grass species have dipped to a fraction somewhere below 1 percent.

As is true across much of California, 99 percent of the grasses we see throughout the canyon are nonnative, mostly invasive. And while not all nonnative plants have invasive tendencies, those that do cause astounding environmental chaos, outcompeting native plants for resources—water, sun, shade, soil, soil-borne nutrients—and choking forests, fields, waterways. They decrease overall plant diversity, which in most scenarios also seriously decreases wildlife habitat and food, affecting entire ecosystems and broader ecoregions.

Lowry notes that 85 percent of all invasive species we struggle with in North America were introductions from home gardens. The canyon riparia reflects this. We see fig, privet, olive, erodium, euphorbia, star thistle, and so many nonnative grasses, John and I have to admit they've established themselves so convincingly they now blend in as part of a scenery that almost looks "right" even to our trained eyes.

I want to believe that garden escapees are an inadvertent evil, but many nurseries and catalogs are still selling known invasives—grasses, shrubs, and perennials, as seed and as plants—simply because they're deemed attractive. In some cases, these are marketed as "sterile" varieties that will not reproduce and escape the garden fence, but no mention is made of how few generations it could take for them to revert back to a fertile variety, once again produce seed, and someday overwhelm ecosystems ill-equipped to control them.

Take the feather grass *Nassella tenuissima*, billed as a fantastic low-water western garden plant selection—but simultaneously listed as invasive in many western states. Here, all it takes is one view of a previously botanically diverse drainage or slope covered in this invasive you know through observation over years is not providing food or habitat, or the realization that it's a huge fire hazard, for these plants to go from looking attractive to looking nothing but *un*attractive.

Human-seed relationships are as enduring in their potentially negative impacts as they are in their positive, adaptive, and resilient impacts.

Any power like that with two such divergent probabilities should be approached with as much respect as perhaps fear, and with best intentions and as much knowledge as possible.

The seeds my mother would have been using in her first nursery job in USDA zone 4b at 5030 feet on the Front Range of Colorado, and the seed packets John and I have been reading all month, now beginning to sow as conditions seem right here in 8b and less than 1000 feet in interior Northern California, have a lot in common, even 50 years later. This is thanks in part to that Federal Seed Act first outlined and enforced in 1940, with amendments made regularly ever since.

In theory, the Seed Act was meant to protect the still-young seed trade, the buyers of seed, and the land (and crops) on which and for which those buyers would sow that seed.

Since its inception in 1939, the Seed Act has required that seed shipped between states or outside of the United States be labeled with certain information, with different regulations based on seed volume, human food crops versus ornamental crops, and for forage crops versus restoration or ecosystem crops.

The Agricultural Marketing Service of the USDA oversees and enforces the Seed Act, but each state has its own seed regulatory and administrative structures.

In California, the Seed Advisory Board, an 11-person team appointed by the secretary of agriculture, oversees state seed law. The Seed Services Program, nested under the Plant Health and Pest Prevention Services Division, is administered by the California Department of Food and Agriculture (CDFA) from offices in five different districts across the state.

I caught Jillian Hagenston, an environmental scientist working for the CDFA in their Fresno district, by phone one day as she was in the field sampling seed from a warehouse. When I began to ask specific questions on seed-labeling laws, she cheerfully made her way to her truck to pull out her California and federal seed law manuals.

She clarifies that while the state, and seed sellers working across state lines from within California, comply with federal regulations, the California Seed Law is concerned solely with vegetable and agricultural seed. Ergo, California does not regulate flower, ornamental shrub, or tree seed. In California historically, the vegetable and agricultural seed industries requested state regulation, and Hagenston's understanding is that "the ornamental seed trade is confident they can self-regulate." It's complicated to trace, even for those working within it.

Further, for all the labeling requirements at federal and state levels, about lot numbers, addresses, germination rates, disclosures about whether seeds have been treated and with what, there is still *no* requirement to list the country of origin for vegetable or flower seed intended for home garden use. Which is "mildly interesting," Hagenston noted with a touch of irony.

But isn't food security intimately related to seed security? Where does our food come from, if not from seeds? A basic understanding of the invisible but incredibly far-reaching industry that produced the seed packets on my kitchen counter, the vegetables in the crisper, and grains in the pantry, is integral to this literacy of seed sense.

If we knew where our seed was cultivated, would we advocate for good living conditions and wages for the workers there as we have for tech products and sneakers? Would we be more careful about seed's impacts on the land on which it is grown? Or vice versa—would we wonder what might be in the soil to begin with? Collectively, we have only recently had to face just how dependent we are on international supply chains—and only because they became immediately visible in our most recent moments of greatest need.

I think about my handful of beautiful lacepod seeds, hand picked. It occurs to me that in obscuring the line of connectivity between seed origins and consumer, we're abdicating both relationship and responsibility: to the places, to the people, to the plant beings, to the economies, and to the benefits or negative fallout from these relationships—seen and unseen. Now multiply that times every seed in every packet I've ever sown. I'm also complicit.

Isn't all of this the living and viable germ at the heart of "seed security"?

MARCH 30

The moon is now two days past full but is still brightly lighting the canyon at night. Last night, it threw shadows of the bare winter trees' branching canopies on the ground below—like a camera obscura in the night sky illuminating the landscape plan of the universe in overview. The oaks and the pines each distilled down to a different graphic representation of the essence of their habit and form—their simplest shapes.

Some records of Celtic tradition indicate that this full moon is known as the full windy moon. The last of last season's seeds rattle on their stalks and branches, along with the very first of this season's seeds.

SEED READING

APRIL

Seed's Human Banking History

NEW MOON, APRIL 12
FULL MOON, APRIL 27

APRIL 1

John and I join Elena Gregg, a botanist, for a field monitoring session on a piece of state-approved "preserve" land. The preserve is situated within the densely developed and developing southern edge of a nearby city. At the site, we help record the bloom of the endangered Butte County meadowfoam (*Limnanthes floccosa* subsp. *californica*). This is one of its last known populations, but also one of its densest. We wade into hundreds and hundreds of the low-growing soft-white open-faced flowers in all phases of bloom.

Gregg works in the private sector, but is also acting president of the Friends of the Ahart Herbarium at California State University, Chico. She is an expert at conducting rare plant surveys and is particularly interested in documenting what insects help to pollinate these diminutive, white annual wildflower cups in this spring moment.

The Butte County meadowfoam rings the edges and outskirts of vernal pools here—in the company of other colorful annual herbaceous wildflowers: johnny-tuck (*Triphysaria eriantha*), yellow carpet (*Blennosperma nanum* var. *nanum*), and goldfields (*Lasthenia californica*). John shows me how you can tell the difference between these two similar-looking small and low-growing spring yellow ray flowers: "Look under the tiny petals. If they are brownish on the back, those are the 'yellow carpets' showing the dust that's been swept under them." This made me laugh.

We see three different clovers (*Trifolium* spp.), small groups of frying pan poppies (*Eschscholzia lobbii*), and large gatherings of pink checkerbloom (*Sidalcea calycosa* ssp. *calycosa*) and alliums (*Allium* sp.) in foliage and bud about to steal the floral show away from these earlier bloomers.

According to Gregg, who has been monitoring this site for six years, the array and quantity of bloom this year is good, and she feels optimistic about the overall seed set and the soil and site's natural seed bank. The monitoring is part of ongoing potential mitigation for a large development adjacent to and further afield from the increasingly isolated "preserve" acreage. The idea of mitigation is that if a development endangers or harms a plant or animal life in the course of the development, that loss is offset by "preserving" this same species at another site. Don't envision this "mitigation preserve" as a welcoming green space—it's behind high fences topped by double strands of barbed wire, more of a prison than a park. As spring ephemerals, meadowfoam have a very short window of total bloom time in which they are open for insect pollination. If the right insects do not arrive during that window, meadowfoam turns to self-pollination, a not-too-uncommon failsafe response in the plant world. But, while it gets the seed setting job done, self-pollination too many seasons in a row can also lead to inbreeding and therefore inbreeding depression and the weakening of the species. Cross-pollination by insects results in vigor from better genetic variety.

Mitigation protocols for endangered plant species do not typically require saving individuals from the site before or as it's destroyed, nor do they typically include saving and redistributing their seed. Botanists, ecologists, regulatory agencies, and land managers are too concerned with changing or damaging the genetics of one restricted population with the genetics from another group. For instance, there's another population of meadowfoam less than a half mile away, where a large-house, urban-sprawl development is angling to win zoning approval—but the population facing the bulldozer is not able to be relocated to the preserve site. That officially sanctioned mitigation protocols do not include any kind of rescue or assisted migration strikes me as a strangely painful limbo position for a botanist to have to operate in—watching a plant population die, be turned under and over, without intervening out of fear of inadvertently making things worse.

During our three-and-a-half-hour monitoring session, we covered the entire site. In the earliest hours, the three of us observed four or five small native bees on open flowers, all seemingly the same species of bee. Gregg collected two of these bees to send to a certified lab for species identification. Later, we observed a different, larger bee. We guessed at it being a different genus perhaps, one that began flying later in the day as temperatures rose.

Overall, we were acutely aware of how few flying insects we saw. For such a floriferous spring site, it seemed shocking. Were we viewing the insect apocalypse in real time? Could we hope it was merely that we saw so few insects because it is still early in the bloom and bug season? Because we were there too early in the day, from 11:00 a.m. to 1:30 p.m., while it was still cool? Because the city had already begun mosquito abatement and this had affected other insect species? Of all of the different plant species in bloom, only a few of them have coevolved for insect pollination, the others relying on wind or self-pollination, so perhaps the lack of pollinating insects here and now is "normal" for this type of meadow mix? Some combination of all of the above?

It feels unsettling not to have a better grasp on answers.

APRIL 3

The flowers of the shooting star are all but spent. Their faces, once held down perhaps for best approach by bumble bees and other pollinators, have rotated skyward so that as the seed pod forms and ripens, the seed does not simply spill out on the ground directly below. Their rosy recurved petals dry and fall away around a rising dome of the maybe one-tenth inch green, fleshy seed pod. The pod is translucent and inside the still closed pod you can see little drops of water—in the warming days and nights, perhaps this functions like a tiny greenhouse for the forming seed, before the lid of the greenhouse pops open?

Once you start to "see" seed, you will see them seemingly everywhere. It can feel overwhelming to go from seeing nothing to feeling within the multitude of everything.

As we walk through the berm gardens now, a little weedy cress, which was flowering prolifically above its many green basal-foliage rosettes in late January has set seed. It pops and disperses as you move through, or by, or near—leaving your ankles with the sensation of being peppered, the sensation of very light tapping on your wrists as you weed. That soft tik tiki tik itik tik shhhing sound—the next generation blanketing the ground efficiently.

The oaks, cottonwoods, and willows are in tassel—meaning the pollen-producing flowers of the oak are out, and the green seed-producing catkins are out on the cottonwood (*Populus fremontii*) trees. The drapey green fringe is highlighted against the spring-soft just-emerging leaves along their branches. In this season, pollen from oak, pine, and cotton-wood swirls in any breeze, creates a yellow film across little eddies in the creeks, pooled water in swales and puddles. It leaves a yellow layer of dust across all surfaces in the house. For those who suffer from allergies, it is a miserable season. But it is also a sensuous season—it's not often life announces itself with such vibrant pigmentation, saturation.

The wild seed bank is actively recruiting deposits.

The wild seed bank in any region is one leg of the framework on which any concept of human-based "seed security" must stand—we're reliant on it.

Another leg is the ongoing flow of information, in the form of DNA, between people, places, and plants—natural pollination, seed formation, and dispersal, as well as human seed saving, selecting, and casual sharing between neighbors or at organized community swaps, government distribution, seed catalogs, commercial growing and trade markets.

The last of these legs that form a stable tripod of security is specifically conservation-minded human efforts. Efforts made not just for the next meal or next season of meals, but for the longest, farthest horizons: posterity, the Indigenous worldview of the "next seven generations," the "future" and its many unknowns.

Human seed banks are curated collections of seed, from a place or of a specific type, saved (generally in long-term dry, cold storage) in order to preserve their genetics. This is known as *ex situ* (off-site) genetic conservation. Dr. John Dickie, senior research leader under science operations at the United Kingdom's Royal Botanic Gardens, Kew (Kew), shared that as formal undertakings, ex situ seed banks started out as a way for the agricultural community interested in crop science in the late nineteenth and early to mid-twentieth centuries to keep track of and have on hand all of the genetics they were working with as they began to develop new breeds, crosses, and eventually hybrids.

The oldest such agricultural seed bank, the Vavilov Institute, was started in 1894 in Russia. Prior to this time, most academic botany in Russia had been focused on wild species, not cultivated crops. Booming growth and, Dickie says, "the intensive development of agriculture in the 1870s and 1880s promoted an increased interest in agronomy and agricultural science in general in the Russian empire." An empire intent on expanding and thus needing secure, steady, and self-produced food to fuel this growth and to protect its food sources from any other empire's attempted encroachment.

Professor A. F. Batalin was the first scientist on record in Russia to study local cultivated plants there. He encountered materials of "immense richness" and repeatedly stressed the need to establish a laboratory for applied botany that would concentrate on studying the flora of Russia. This idea was supported by other researchers, leading to the organization of the Russian Bureau of Applied Botany in 1894 under the Ministry of Land Cultivation and State Property. Batalin was the first director of the bureau, and its only staff member. A taxonomist, he also acted as director of the Imperial Botanical Gardens of Saint Petersburg (now known as the Saint Petersburg Botanical Garden), founded by Peter the Great in 1714, and where Batalin was also the director of their Seed Testing Station. It was there, according to historical reports, that Batalin "on his own initiative started collecting and researching varietal diversity of rye, spelt, millet, rice, buckwheat, legumes, common onion, oil bearing cruciferous and other crops." Today, the center he started is known as N. I. Vavilov All-Russian Institute of Plant Genetic Resources (VIR), after another of the world's most important crop scientists and seed collectors.

Gary Nabhan, ethnobotanist, biologist, ecologist, and cofounder of the Native Seeds/SEARCH seed banking and conservation organization outside of Tucson, Arizona, writes of Vavilov, "All of our notions about biological diversity and needing a diversity of foods on our plates to keep us healthy sprung from his work. He was one of the first scientists to really listen to farmers—traditional farmers, peasant farmers around the world—when they said they felt seed diversity was important in their fields."

The institute is famous as well for the dedication of the scientists working with Vavilov during the Siege of Leningrad (now Saint Petersburg) by Nazi Germany from 1941 to 1944. When the siege began, Vavilov was away on one of his many seed collecting trips. At the institute, the handful of scientists there barricaded themselves into the seed vault in order to protect the collection they knew was key to food production and therefore survival. As many others have noted, including Nabhan and Dr. Stephanie Greene of the USDA in my different conversations with them both, these Russian scientists died of starvation while safeguarding "food" all around them in the form of bags of the collected wheat and rice, etc. That is how profoundly important they understood the collection was to the future of the world. Vavilov himself was later detained by Stalin's army as an enemy of the state for his beliefs on the best ways to improve agricultural yield and died of starvation in a Russian gulag. In time, Vavilov's methods were proven to be accurate.

This idea of storing agriculturally significant collections and records accelerated in most industrialized countries in the mid-twentieth century as agricultural crop breeding expanded, encouraged by governments looking to feed their growing populations and increase their agricultural trade. "Breeders were," as Dickie explained, "doing some really clever stuff to produce new high-yielding varieties, but they were also homogenous and of single genotypes [from one genetic line]. The breeders worried about losing the diversity of the old varieties and landraces [varieties of locally adapted seed selected with resistances to locally specific factors like drought, soil conditions, other climate conditions, and/or diseases]." While the new breeds were good, as single genotypes they were also susceptible to being wiped out "by one large problem like a new disease, new pest, new climatic condition. Breeders wanted to hang on to all of this original diversity of traits they were working with so that they could go back to them and re-breed if needed—at that time by traditional breeding methods, but now with the additional opportunities of genetic engineering."

And so began a widespread global push to "bank" all of the genetic diversity humans could. This included the wild progenitors of commercial crop plants, some known, many more being researched all the time, in order to "rapidly," per Dickie, reintroduce lost traits back into crop genetics as needed to address new diseases, pests, or resistance loss.

International networks of "crop gene banks," as they are also known, popped up, often associated with the largest plant breeding institutes—government-based and commercial-industry-based. This includes the USDA's National Laboratory for Genetic Resources Preservation (NLGRP, often referred to as the US Seed Bank) based in Fort Collins, Colorado, and founded in 1959. "It's essentially the backup reserves seed bank for US agriculture and the world," says Dr. Christina Walters, its lead scientist.

The USDA's collection, one of if not the largest seed and gene bank in the world, includes 19 regional germplasm conservation collections around the country. It focuses "on plants that are considered to be valuable resources, crops that we eat every day, those we use to build houses or clothe ourselves," says Dr. Stephanie Greene, the supervisory plant physiologist (commonly referred to as the plant and seed curator) for the USDA's Fort Collins collection.

"Germplasm is a funny word," admits Walters. "It is not germ, and it is not plasma; it's little bits of cells or tissue that you can use to grow a whole new individual. But you can store it and put it in what we call suspended animation." Using germplasm of any kind, like the seeds such collections were all initially based on, "is an incredibly efficient way of creating and maintaining a very large collection in a relatively small space."

Where Walters is in charge of testing and ongoing seed storage science research for the collection at the Fort Collins center, Greene oversees the actual accessioning, documenting, and curating of the collection's holdings—incoming and outgoing.

In addition, the facility in Fort Collins "is sort of the mother ship and holds a secure backup copy of every seed or germplasm (like vegetative cells or cuttings) in the collections at the other 19 facilities." They do the same for other collections of significant crop species from geographic regions around the world, including the Canadian collection, as well as backup collections for botanic gardens across the country. If this careful curation was inspired by any biological process, it would be the process of setting seed itself. Redundancy is a good and elegantly intelligent idea.

The agricultural gene banking world has grown exponentially since the 1950s, well beyond the collection of the Vavilov Institute and the USDA. It is integral to global food security in the face of climate change as well as sociopolitical upheaval. As such, global international networks have organized around very large, shared goals.

Dickie points out that many of these goals and organizing networks stem from the 1992 Rio Earth Summit where a Convention on Biodiversity (CBD) was signed by 153 nations committing to "undertake to conserve all of their own regional biodiversity *in situ* [in the existing native environments], which is best, but also *ex situ* [off-site, such as in a seed bank], for redundancy."

The CBD treaty has three goals: the conservation of biological diversity, the sustainable use of biological diversity, and the fair sharing of products made from genestocks. To advance these goals, the signatories are sworn to "develop plans for protecting habitat and species; provide funds and technology to help developing countries provide such protection; ensure commercial access to biological resources for development and share revenues fairly among source countries and developers; and establish safety regulations and accept liability for risks associated with biotechnology development." After a lot of debate and negotiation, and although 30 ratifications were needed for it to ultimately move forward, 153 nations signed on.

Notably, the United States was not one of them. This was due to several concerns including "that the benefit-sharing provisions were incompatible with existing international regimes for intellectual property rights; and that the requirement to regulate the biotechnology industry would needlessly stifle innovation."

In other words, the United States, under President George H. W. Bush, did not sign the 1992 biodiversity treaty because it felt business and profit interests trumped planetary health and biodiversity interests.

This was not a huge surprise, as the United States had been thinking in a self-interested, strategic way about the potential of agricultural-commercial crossovers for decades. Early precursors to globally focused gene banking can be seen in the 1940s era Office of Special Studies, created by the US-based Rockefeller Foundation and the government of Mexico's department of agriculture, looking to "improve" crop varieties and yields, specifically wheat and maize. This led to the formation of early agribusiness research centers such as the International Rice Research Institute (IRRI) established in 1960 by the vast business interests of not only the Rockefeller Foundation but also the US-based Ford Foundation in collaboration with the government of the Philippines. In 1966 the Centro Internacional de Mejoramiento de Maíz y Trigo (International Maize and Wheat Improvement Center, CIMMYT) was officially established in El Batán, Mexico, an outgrowth of the work of the earlier Office of Special Studies. And in 1975, the International Center for Agricultural Research in the Dry Areas (ICARDA) was opened in Aleppo, Syria. All such centers amassed remarkable seed banks specific to their research areas. In 1971, as an umbrella organization for protective research and agricultural development, the Consultative Group on International Agricultural Research (CGIAR) formed "as an informal organization of countries, international development agencies and private foundations that cooperate in underwriting a network of more than a dozen independent, international agricultural research institutes."

The funders and participating entities included the World Bank, the Food and Agriculture Organization of the U.N. (FAO), the United Nations Development Programme, and the International Fund for Agricultural Development.

Note the focus on diverse, culturally tended, evolved, and associated staple food crops of the planet: wheat, rice, maize, corn.

The results of such research centers' work, in concert with the emerging synthetic chemical fertilizer, insecticide, and herbicide industries born of postwar excess munitions materials and research at the time, was the so-called Green Revolution. The Global North introduced (deployed?) new proprietary hybrid seed varieties (which had to be repurchased annually from the business that created them), and new field management techniques, tools, and technologies based on these mechanizations and chemical inputs to the land and growers in the Global South.

The Green Revolution was declared to be the "solution" to poverty and world hunger. It also, of course, ensured the dependence of farmers worldwide on the agribusinesses who sold them seed and chemical products to maintain that seed.

In hindsight, the methods, plants, and tools (seed and mechanical tools) born of the Green Revolution have been linked by many to the global loss of traditional seed-saving skills and deterioration of hubs of localized farming. This same externally determined industrialization is also linked to the degradation of soil, water, air, and ecosystem health in countries on which the so-called revolution was imposed, or those the so-called revolution exploited.

In 1996, following up from the Rio Summit and the CBD, 150 countries adopted the first Global Plan of Action for conserving and using crop diversity. In June of 2004, the International Treaty on Plant Genetic Resources for Food and Agriculture came into effect, including a mandate for an "effective, efficient global system at the core of its efforts to conserve and use crop diversity for food security." This was the basis for the Global Crop Diversity Trust (Crop Trust), officially formed in October of 2004 by the FAO and Bioversity International on behalf of the CGIAR to help support this global system in a sustainable way.

By 2007, the Crop Trust had developed the framework for its signature project, encapsulated (literally) in the 2008 opening of perhaps the world's most famous agricultural-based seed bank, the Svalbard Global Seed Vault (SGSV, or, depressingly, the Doomsday Vault). A partnership between the Norwegian government, the nonprofit Nordic Genetic Research Center (NordGen), and the Crop Trust, which administers the facility, the SGSV is insulated by permafrost "deep inside a mountain on a remote island of the Svalbard archipelago, halfway between mainland Norway and the North Pole." It is "built to stand the test of time" against both natural and manmade disasters—from earthquakes to rising temperatures and sea levels to nuclear war. Although the unpredicted and accelerated effects of climate change being seen in the Arctic as of 2016–2020 is testing those assumptions with melting permafrost and some vault flooding, none of this had endangered the seed vaults themselves as of 2022.

Since it began accepting accessions from partner nations and groups in 2008, SGSV has become one of the largest collections of crop diversity in the world, as contributors believe in its security. "Worldwide, more than 1700 gene banks hold collections of food crops for safekeeping, yet many of these are vulnerable, exposed not only to natural catastrophes and war, but also to avoidable disasters, such as lack of funding or poor management. Something as mundane as a poorly functioning freezer can ruin an entire collection. And the loss of a crop variety is as irreversible as the extinction of a dinosaur, [contemporary] animal or any form of life," states the Crop Trust. As of the early 2020s, it reported that the top 10 crops conserved are rice, wheat, barley, sorghum, bean, corn, soybean, chickpea, millet, and cowpeas. The top depositors include the earlier-formed global research centers such as ICARDA, IRRI, and CIMMYT.

SGSV, with three separate seed vaults within the mountain facility, has the capacity to store 4.5 million varieties of crops, for a maximum of 2.5 billion seeds: "The Vault holds more than 983,500 seed varieties, originating from almost every country in the world. Ranging from unique varieties of major African and Asian food staples ... to European and South American varieties of eggplant, lettuce, barley, and potato."

It is of note that *no* GM or GE seed, or other germplasm, are allowed to be stored in the SGSV, based on the "wishes and priorities" of the Norwegian government and people.

Unlike most large, government-based, agricultural seed or gene banks, from which interested, vetted, and approved researchers or breeders can request samples of seed or germplasm to work with (provided the collection has the supply to distribute), SGSV allows for secure withdrawals only *by the groups that deposited*. And each contributor can only withdraw their own deposits. Not even the SGSV staff have the authority to open the accessions.

As of early 2022, only two withdrawals had been made from SGSV, both by ICARDA. After increasing military conflict in the ongoing civil war that began in 2011, in 2014 the scientists at the ICARDA center in Aleppo, Syria, had to abandon their facility with no means of safeguarding or taking the seed or plants (or animals) with them. The Aleppo center, under the directorship of seed and plant conservationist Ali Shehadeh, who had made a large number of the seed collections himself, had made regular backup deposits of collections to SGSV from 2008 to 2014, and had backed up about 80 percent of their total collection.

When the Aleppo center was lost, two new centers were created, one in Morocco and the other in Lebanon's Bekaa Valley. Aleppo's work was largely regenerated at the two new centers using withdrawals in 2015 and 2017 from their earlier SGSV deposits, and by 2021, the new centers were able to begin returning to SGSV some percentage of the withdrawn seed. According to a 2021 report, the rebuilding of the gene bank in Lebanon, still under the leadership of a 60-something Shehadeh, and its backup in Norway, was expected to take until at least 2030.

Based on numbers from 2017, "ICARDA's entire collection houses seeds that have sustained the people of the Middle East for centuries, including some 14,700 varieties of bread wheat, 32,000 varieties of barley, and nearly 16,000 varieties of chickpea, the key component of falafel. The Lebanon seed bank houses about 39,000 accessions, and [the center in] Morocco, another 32,000."

In another interplay between past, present, and future, Dr. Christina Walters works on what she calls a "collaboration with a famous plant physiologist" and botanist, Frits Warmolt Went (1903–1990). In 1947 and 1948, Went, while at the California

Institute of Technology, worked with Dr. Philip Munz, director of Rancho Santa Ana Botanic Garden (RSABG, now California Botanic Garden, CalBG), to create a seed longevity experiment designed to last 360 years. Went compiled sets of seed partially vacuum sealed in glass tubes from 91 California native plants (from varying families and habitats) provided by RSABG staff.

To gather data and answer questions about traits, taxonomy, and habitat conditions as they relate to seed longevity and therefore best long-term storage protocols, the plan was for one set of the seed to be germinated and grown out after the first year, then every ten years for a period, and finally, every 20 years through 2307. Initial germination tests were conducted in 1948, 1957, and 1967 as planned. After a physical move of the RSBGA in 1990, with Went's approval before he died that same year, the experiment was transferred to the US Seed Bank (NLGRP) in Fort Collins in 1990.

Under Walters's lead, seed from the experiment was germinated again in 1997. Although recommended seed storage protocols have evolved to use low-humidity, low-temperature conditions since Went recommended vacuum-sealed glass containers in the 1940s, the results of the germinations over time have provided new questions, and new lenses on old questions, using new tools.

As the Center for Plant Conservation notes, "whether or not this groundbreaking study continues for the full 360 years, the foresight of Went and Munz has already proven immensely useful to increasing our understanding of seed and seed storage."

Walters loves that not only is she collaborating with this remarkable plantsperson before her, but that he too was enthralled with the same questions that motivate her: What is life, what is death, how is a seed in its dormancy on the living edge of both, and what can that teach us?

"It's really confirming," she adds, "that when you are doing good science you are often asking the same questions." And those questions, like seeds and seed science, involve "math, mystery, and magic."

The political and economic winds shift regularly around these various worldwide collections. Their caretakers—Dickie, Walters, Greene, Shehadeh, their staffs, the staff at SGSV, and so on—guard knowledge, but they cannot make policy based on that knowledge even though their specific vein of research, findings, and feelings might make them the best writers of it. That notwithstanding, as "public policy" is made and remade over the decades, these guardians must abide by the rules of others and tend to lives whose worth they may gauge by different metrics.

These large government- or business-funded seed banks have developed specific protocols for what comes into and what goes out of the collections—often with the stated priorities of food security and innovative breeding as their basis. As a result, and not surprisingly, these regulations and protocols come under a great deal of scrutiny and receive a great deal of criticism. They are often seen as representing government and big-business agendas, which may or may not be, and have not always played out to be in the best interests of the environment, biodiversity, or the bulk of humanity.

❖

APRIL 9

While reading Diane Wilson's novel *The Seed Keeper*, I consider the history of seed banks and banking in a different way.

In the story, Wilson drills down through the history within her community and within individual families. The book's main character is Rosalie Iron Wing, a woman of American Indian (Dakhóta) and European descent, working her way back to a relationship with and understanding of her native ancestry from almost complete assimilation into mainstream white European culture.

Another voice in the book is Rosalie's great-great-grandmother, Marie, a Dakhóta girl living in what would become Minnesota in the mid-to-late 1800s when the Dakhóta were being killed or forcibly removed from their traditional lands as European settlement increased. In one scene, a young Marie and her mother are leaving their land and region in front of soldiers in late fall/early winter. As they travel, Marie's mother leads them to their hidden underground cache of seeds and dried food from the previous year's growing season, stored in case of a poor harvest in the current season. She takes all the dry food she and Marie can carry as well as some of the seeds to grow out wherever they end up, and she firmly tells young Marie to remember this place and this cache in case she can get back to it, which she later does.

While fiction, the novel is based on real people, events, and oral histories of Wilson's community. Wilson is the emeritus director of two nonprofit organizations focused on American Indian food history and sovereignty: Dream of Wild Health and the Native American Food Sovereignty Alliance, under which the Indigenous Seed Keepers Network operates. She was inspired to write the book "while participating in the Dakhóta Commemorative March, a 150-mile walk to honor the Dakhóta people who were forcibly removed from Minnesota in 1863, in the aftermath of the US-Dakhóta War." During the march, elders passed down stories of many Dakhóta women (being the designated and sacred seed keepers) who, even in the traumatic and terrifying upheaval of evacuating, had instinctively gathered what seeds they could and sewn or otherwise hidden them in their clothing in order to save them for establishing a life sometime in an envisioned future. Wilson, in plumbing the history of her people, buried by colonialism, brings back up to light traditional seed ways as integral to her story. Like other seed keepers, she is re-codifying seed knowledge back into the larger cultural narrative.

Similarly, histories are documented by descendants of African women braiding seeds into their hair prior to their enslavement and forcible removal from their homes to the United States, Great Britain, and elsewhere.

These in-clothing and in-hair seeds are also seed banks, no less valuable for being clandestine, whose techniques for preservation date back unknown thousands of years as humans have battled with and some-times overcome unseen catastrophes: climatic, seasonal, imperialistic.

APRIL 11: NEW MOON
John and I spend the morning taking cuttings of favorite herbaceous plants: California fuchsia (*Epilobium canum*), calamintha, and several salvia species and varieties. Cuttings are another reproduction method for the plants we love, but the new plants will be clones, genetically iden-tical to the "mother" plant, not the result of the great genetic shake-up of sexually reproduced seed.

I am in charge of prepping and potting the cuttings. I trim the lowest leaves on the stem, then cut the upper leaves in half or more to reduce evapotranspiration but still allow enough of the leaves' green surface for photosynthesis while the cutting is putting on roots. The work is focused and rhythmic, standing at an old plywood counter with the dark honey-colored veneer of decades of such cutting or seeding or potting activity ingrained into its worn surface.

The far end of the bench is covered with seeded plug trays, maybe 14 x 20 inches, 3 inches deep. Like Chia Pets, some are now lush with lettuce and spinach seedlings started weeks ago and now ready to be pricked out and planted; others, started maybe 10 days ago, have just a few little green shoots making their way up here and there in the half-inch-across cells.

It is a sunny, lightly breezy day, and the open-ended, plastic-roofed potting shed is snug and earthy, the sound of my little snips accompa-nied by spring's generation of fat, glossy carpenter bees—30 or more of them—buzzing in and out of their many years' worth of entrances in the shed's plywood walls. They hover, and sometimes tumble together to the potting soil.

Their vibration matches the vibration of seeds sprouting, the aromatic emission of disturbed foliage, the frequencies of the midday sunlight, the fast-slow revolution of the planet on her axis.

Potting seedlings on is as delicate and tender an activity as sowing seeds themselves. Working with tiny, soft seedlings of zucchini, zinnia, spinach, allium, and marigold, I am reminded that they are called seedlings because you are in fact still working with the seed itself—it's just fattened up, unfurled, and stretched out with hydration. I like to imagine that if you had sharper ears, you could hear a seed thirstily drinking in its first real water once the seed coat lets down its guard. The endosperm is still thick, the radicle now fleshy and pushing down, the greening stem rising, the seed leaves—the cotyledons—emerged. These features were all present in the seed itself.

Something I had to learn the hard way was that all seedlings, like seeds, have their own distinct appearance. It took me almost four years of living in Northern California to realize that what I was hand weeding in the early spring beneath the native oaks in my garden were not the seedlings of olive or privet, or some other unwanted nonnative invasive, but rather the very potent seedlings of our native poison oak, that healthy resident and companion of the oak woodlands, whose waxy berries feed the winter birds.

Four springs in a row, I took myself to the emergency room for a cortisone shot to stop the swelling across my forehead and eyes where I had pushed stray hair back with a contaminated hand. The swelling once came close to sealing my left eye. Four springs in a row! I thought I was possibly allergic to something in the air—poison oak pollen maybe? But of course I was allergic to the very thing I was rubbing across my own face.

Know your seedlings, just as you know your seeds, and you will know your plants better. Each one is different, and if you learn each one's unique personality, you will recognize them, be able to call them by name, and treat them with their due respect.

APRIL 14

Down in the creek, tall, reddish, and thick—maybe one-third inch—
flowering stems have shot up from the still-dormant basal crowns of
the native umbrella plant (*Darmera peltata*). These plants dot the water's
edge along both sides of the creek—lush and large with their rhubarb-like
circular leaves in summer. These visibly hairy (hirsute) two-to-three-foot
stems are immediately visible just now without the leaves to hide them,
and each stem is topped by a domed many-flowered white-to-pale-pink
cluster (corymb). Each individual five-petaled *Darmera* flower—less than
a half an inch across—in the cluster sports a ring of stamens capped by
creamy white anthers all sort of dancing around two plump, deeper pink
pistils with even deeper pink nectar wells (nectaries) below.

Darmera mother plants and seeds have an amazing next phase,
when the leaves are out and the fertilized flower clusters have
set seeds just above the leaves. The superior ovaries, once pollinated, swell into twin seed-holding follicles, each a gently faded,
papery, magenta-pink version of the once lustrous pink pistil (and
ovaries) they had been. As they swell with ripening seed, the follicles lean away from each other but still touch at the base. Once
mature, they each split open slowly along the inner seams—from
the top to the bottom. As they open, the rotund follicles release
seed with each big wind, with small rises in creek water or current strength lapping at the spent flowering stems, with creatures
flying by or scrambling over the generous, open-faced leaves and
knocking the stems. As the many small cinnamon-colored seeds
disperse, they are caught and held on the large landing pads of
leaves below, giving them a second chance at dispersal by blow-
ing, knocking, lapping and launching from there.

The leaves act like large, loving hands or aproned laps, offering and even nudging or shooing the legions of little seeds into the current, as though encouraging them to get out beyond their mama's shadow and the competition of her roots and drip line.

Landscape architect Julie Moir Messervy first articulated in a way I could absorb how our first landscapes are of course our own mother's physical bodies. And founder of the Palestine Heirloom Seed Library Vivien Sansour first articulated in a way I could hear that we are all seeds and this planet is our greater landscape.

Twenty-three years ago today my mother passed from this gardened world to the next.

She died on April 14, and had been born on April 28. In her honor, I try to complete a garden project, to plant or seed something in her honor between those two dates every year. I have planted heavily scented roses (her favorite), winter pansies, spring lilies of the valley (her wedding bouquet). With each season of my own life, I wonder what flowers, garden fragrances, or homegrown foods my daughters will someday associate with me.

What seeds do the children of our world want and deserve from all adults?

APRIL 19

One expression of conservation through genetic seed banking is based on a more grassroots backyard operation sometimes referred to as "participatory conservation." This grew in popularity across the United States in the twentieth century, and its inspiration is the passed-along, passed-down, and swapped-seed genetics of garden variety seed savers within families, towns, cultural, and other related communities of gardeners throughout time.

A poster child for this level of conservation of, by, and for the people is Seed Savers Exchange (SSE), founded in 1975, eight years before the USDA outlined and began to form an official research group to study seed banking.

SSE's mission is to "steward America's culturally diverse and endangered garden and food crop legacy for present and future generations, educating and connecting people through collecting, regenerating, and sharing heirloom seeds, plants, and stories." As noted earlier, SSE was founded by Kent Whealy and Diane Ott Whealy, and the collection was founded with the seeds of two heritage plant varieties (a morning glory and a tomato) passed down by Ott Whealy's Bavarian grandfather.

Ott Whealy grew up within a farming family, just down the road from her grandparents' dairy farm, hearing seed stories and sharing seeds. As Whealy and Ott Whealy began their own working and family lives, they were witness to a major shift in farming practices. Ott Whealy's grandparents' way of life was becoming eclipsed by corporate and technological farming methods, and like many in their generation, Whealy and Ott Whealy were worried. With the death of her grandparents could also go the stories, knowledge, and quite possibly their seeds. Whealy and Ott Whealy determined to not let that happen. Whealy wrote to a few "back-to-the-land" magazines in 1975 proposing seed swaps, and soon a group of gardeners from across the United States and Canada were exchanging seeds through the mail, with the group growing exponentially each year, reflecting collective—and growing—concerns and interests in the gardening world.

After the seed exchange collection outgrew their house, in 1985, the Whealys planted a display garden on five acres outside of Decorah, Iowa, to showcase the diversity they had amassed. In 1986, the organization purchased more land, and in 1987 it moved to what would become the 890-acre Heritage Farm, a public-access resource center including display gardens, growing grounds, orchards, a horticultural library, native plant and faunal habitat, and their own underground freezer vault seed bank.

The SSE collection as of the early 2020s includes seeds, tissue culture, and orchards, and the group stewards over 20,000 accessions, over 700 in vitro potato varieties, and over 900 apple tree varieties. Over 13,000 members contribute—gardeners, orchardists, chefs, and plant collectors—all dedicated to the preservation and distribution of heirloom varieties of vegetables, fruits, grains, flowers, and herbs. From those members, SSE annually offers over 13,000 unique seed exchange listings.

When I speak with Tim Johnson, SSE's head of preservation from 2012 to 2017 and currently director of the Botanic Garden of Smith College, he offers some interesting insights into the vulnerabilities of a community-based seed saving/sharing endeavor. Following in the path of his predecessor (Shanyn Siegel) and with long-term goals of SSE in mind, working with staff, "so many wonderful people," Johnson strove to professionalize, prioritize, strategize, and stabilize SSE's seed banking realities, goals, and dreams. Interestingly, he notes that SSE got started during the Cold War (1942–1989), and in some way he feels that the culture-wide fears of that time added to the zeal around the need for seed saving. "Among the seed people, there was a deep fear that a lot of cold-tolerant seed stock and selections were rapidly being lost in Russia. SSE sponsored field collecting trips to many Soviet-bloc regions to help offset that," and as with other

groups of the time "they had an urgency mindset to collect everything they could and sort it out later." Seeds were also constantly
being sent in by the general public and being accessioned from
other vernacular collections. The SSE collection swelled.

The early 2000s was "sort it out later" time, when SSE was
going through the growing pains of trying to organize their collection, to establish protocols for storing, testing, documenting,
and growing out. "On the land SSE has, with the collection we
had even then, and the isolation distances needed for some of
the crops like corn or squash," Johnson says, "the math did not
lie" as to how many varieties of any one crop they could plant
out in one year to care for their seed responsibly. "Even though
it's possible to store properly grown and dried squash seeds for
a hundred years or more, we figured out that given demand for
seeds and relatively small growing populations, it was more real-
istic to assume a variety would need to be regrown every twenty
years. We knew that we could grow about ten to twelve varieties of squash each year, which meant that we could realistically
maintain a collection of about two hundred to two hundred and
forty varieties of squash in perpetuity. But we had about twelve
hundred varieties in the collection." Also, the record for each
sample of collected seed was sometimes incomplete, of dubi-
ous accuracy, or just clearly wrong. Johnson relates how they
would grow out a sample labeled one thing and they would get,
for example, three different phenotypes from it. SSE invested a
lot of planning, money, and effort in this phase of professionaliz-
ing their sorting approach. They hired new seed historians, and
they digitized all the information they had, including stories connected to the donated seed. "The difference between any sample

being an heirloom or just germplasm was the history, the story," acknowledges Johnson.

At the same time, SSE was working to really increase the quality of the seeds they were producing. "We realized," he shares, "that there were seeds that had come to us in too poor of shape to do anything about. Or accessions in which there was such little viable seed or the seed was so crossed that they were not salvageable." As a result, they had to let go of some collections. They began documenting much more comprehensive information: history, provenance, and sometimes even cultivation methodology for managing collected samples, allowing for true preservation long term. Johnson says, "We realized that we were a biological organization running like an antique mall, and you just can't be that low-key especially with low-longevity seed, like leeks or seeds from plants in the Apiaceae or Brassicaceae, which are characteristically short-lived [scientists are not exactly sure why this is true], you don't have time to waste in growing them out and replenishing the seed in storage."

When Johnson started, around 30,000 accessions were being sorted, and by the time he left, "the accessions being managed were closer to 20,000," partially due to the consolidation of many, many duplicates. He points out the parallels between this consolidation and the losses noted in our cultivated food seed over the last 150 years. Seeds marketed in 1918 could be named anything you wanted, as naming was not regulated. Thus, a given species or variety might have had four or more names between sellers, catalogs, or lists; believed "losses" in food seed in this time period also reflect the same consolidation of duplicates under one name.

While SSE may have outgrown its homey, backyard, grassroots origins, it remains the largest public-access gene and seed bank of its kind. And it is still based on, as Johnson describes, the fact that the power of gardening persists as a "folk and oral tradition" based on people working together, sharing information and seed in person.

As of 2009, SSE's collection became one of the early depositors to the Svalbard seed vault, to some fanfare thanks to the involvement of heirloom seed and food activist and billionaire heiress Amy Goldman, board member at SSE since 1990. She made the deposit next to Cary Fowler, a career-long researcher into and outspoken advocate for genetic preservation who served as executive director of the Crop Trust from 2007 to 2012. Goldman and Fowler were married in 2012; she remains a special adviser to SSE's board as of early 2022.

APRIL 20

Thinking again about which native plants and seeds now growing so profusely around me the Indigenous peoples here may still use—perhaps especially as food—I begin to research how, in 1983, another kind of community-based seed bank and seed-sharing endeavor also got underway. The nonprofit Native Seeds/Southwestern Endangered Aridland Resource Clearing House (Native Seeds/SEARCH or NS/S) was founded in the Tucson area by Gary Nabhan, Karen Reichhardt, Barney Burns, and Mahina Drees as an outgrowth of a Meals for Millions (now Freedom from Hunger) project supporting the Tohono O'odham Nation. The tribal elders and participants in the project to establish gardens came away from it indicating what they really wanted was not merely access to anyone else's food, but access to and knowledge of seeds of their own traditional foods, the varieties grown by their ancestors. They wanted seed and food sovereignty.

When you consider the large economic and cultural shifts the United States went through in the twentieth century (predicated on the nearly complete destruction of land-based peoples managing the continent), especially with the United States fully settled and with the rise of a suburban and urban middle class post–World War II through the 1970s, the disconnection of people from their seeds and land-based lives is among our most unpleasant cultural connect-the-dots: from the erosion of the Tohono O'odham Nation tribal elders (among all American Indian groups) physically possessing and remaining culturally connected to their own heritage seeds, to the loss of an entire family-farming way of life as illustrated by Diane Ott Whealy's grandparents and their passed-down Bavarian seed, to the majority of the United States living in urban or suburban settings hardly able to identify seed on most plants.

The farther we get from this cause-and-effect timeline, the harder it is to follow, and in many cases the cause-and-effect was purposefully obscured and erased because of the many human transgressions it included. These disconnections trace the history of settler expansion and the taking of land through intimidation, deceit, and theft, the forced displacement and removal of Native peoples, accompanied by outlawing their religions and prohibiting the use of their languages through the euphemistically named "boarding school era," and culminates in the nearly complete replacement/destruction of native landscapes into farmland focusing on European or other nonnative food crops in the name of nation building and "national" food security. The systematic destruction of American Indian foods and seeds, eradication of the ecosystems from which these seeds and foods originated, and the separation of these peoples from their seed and its places is one of the bloody genocides in which US history is steeped.

The mission of NS/S is to "conserve and promote the rich, arid-adapted crop diversity of the Southwest in support of sustainable farming and food security. NS/S seeks to find, protect, and preserve the seeds of the people of the Greater Southwest so that these arid-adapted crops may benefit all peoples and nourish a changing world."

The NS/S seed bank as of early 2022 held 2000 varieties of crops adapted to arid landscapes extending from southern Colorado to central Mexico, many of them rare or endangered. The collection represents the cultural heritage and farming knowledge of over 50 Indigenous communities, as well as recent immigrants like Spanish missionaries and Mormon homesteaders, and conserves a number of the wild progenitors of these crops.

These seeds and the [historic traditional] knowledge of how to grow them are quite literally the result of hundreds of years of human kinship with the plants of this place. Humans observing which plants were edible, and which taste best in which season. Which plants—with sun-reflecting foliage; predator-deterring spines; water-storing bodies; fine, soft hairs to hold humidity; or dramatic seasonal dormancy—survive months and months of bone-dry heat, of cold, wind, and snow, and can still withstand the flash floods and heavy soils of winter and monsoon season. Humans observing which plants bore edible seed, and which seeds stored well and in what ways—cold, dry, hot, dark.

Some of these plants—native wild teosinte corn, or wild peppers, or squash—were also adapted via human cultivation, with techniques including being grown in "waffle beds," wherein deep furrows were made to best catch and percolate what little rainwater or dew there was directly to seedling root systems. Each seed is a testament to endurance, to a constant action/reaction relationship between plants, humans, place over many generations of both. These plants and seeds and cultures have an epic history rich with lessons.

John and I visited NS/S's Conservation Center headquarters in Tucson in September of 2021, pandemic concerns still very high, perhaps especially high in hard-hit Indigenous communities. We walked the center's gardens with Alexandra Zamecnik, executive director, and Joel Johnson, conservation garden farmer. We toured the seed-processing and short-term storage areas with Sheryl Joy, acting seed bank manager, and got a glimpse into the deep-freeze seed bank.

This region receives an average of just under 12 inches of precipitation a year, between one-third to three-quarters of it coming in the July and August monsoon season, but this year Tucson had been blessed with frequent monsoon rains in the weeks leading up to our visit. Everything felt very green and lush for that time of year in a high desert valley at about 2400 feet in elevation. We saw the buoyant diversity of the center's sunflowers along the fence line of the property well before we arrived at the building.

As we toured the grow-out gardens, Johnson explained that NS/S was in a shift. "For most of the organization's history, the collections were grown and managed at a fifty-two-acre farm in Patagonia, Arizona [below the home of cofounder Gary

Nabhan], where high-intensity production of seed and regenerating the seed bank was undertaken by a team of twenty-plus staff and interns. In one season, the team could grow out twenty different lines of corn, keeping seed pure by hand-bagging, shoot-bagging, etc."

But the NS/S team realized that growing all of their seed at the Patagonia site meant that the seed was adapting to the conditions there. The NS/S collections represent people and places in climates and microclimates very different from Tucson, with contributions and collections from places and communities all over the Southwest and Northern Mexico these last 40-plus years. To counteract potential loss of seed diversity through site-specific adaptation, and to expand access to and agency over both seed and seed stewarding skills, as of 2021, NS/S regenerates a portion of the collection at different sites, including the Conservation Center gardens in Tucson and, perhaps most important, in partnership with (and investment in) numerous regional small farmers. Some of these farmers grow out for the regeneration collection kept in cold storage on-site at the center; others grow seed at scale to provide seed to the American Indian communities who request them for their members or for their community gardens. The NS/S annual seed listing online offers surplus seed of around 500 varieties to the public.

Today, 36 years on from its founding, the NS/S priority has shifted from collecting rare seeds to exploring the rich and varied potential of plants to provide nutrition and livelihoods to today's farmers, gardeners, and consumers. NS/S is just one example of recent acknowledgment by land and resource managers in all sectors of the United States that we have much to learn from, and much accountability to, the traditional ecological knowledge and the people who hold and steward that knowledge.

"While continuing to preserve our collection, NS/S also provides high-quality training in seed-saving and farming techniques to empower communities to use and conserve this treasure themselves," Zamecnik told me. She was chosen as the executive director of NS/S specifically for her background working on international projects, with extensive experience in Mexico and Central America focused on forestry, biodiversity conservation, and climate change from a multicultural perspective. In 2022, the NS/S board was close to 50 percent American Indian.

The challenges of a warming climate are many: increased drought, more intense and unpredictable wildfires and storms, new pests or diseases, and pests and diseases that have adapted to previously effective chemical pesticides. As these continue to plague our ecosystems and agricultural health, it is the sheer magnitude of genetic diversity and the genetics that combined and recombined over human/plant history that have resulted in the adaptive traits that met the challenges of the past and still offer the ingredients for meeting new challenges. The value of preserving the diversity of agricultural seeds at the local level, and the empowered diversity of humans working with them, seems as obvious as the importance of the availability and security of fresh local food itself.

APRIL 27

Today my mother would have been 79.

The parallels and interconnections between my mother and me; me and this place; this place, these seeds, all of us, and this planet; this planet and the largest questions of longevity, life and death, are not lost on me.

Is it inappropriate, indulgent, myopic to contextualize my understanding of seed writ large with my understanding of self and place?

How else can we empathically understand them? Value them?
And each other?

They are the verdant cycling chassis of life on which our places, our pasts, and our ancestors, communities, and individual days are held, by which they are enlivened . . . and dispersed onward.

The Wild Side of Seed Banks

NEW MOON, MAY 11
FULL MOON, MAY 26

MAY 1: MAY DAY; BELTANE

The first of May is often referred to as May Day—but also as Beltane, the Gaelic May Day festival. Festivities across the ancient (and again now the modern) Celtic world. A day of fertility rituals and celebrations, dances around ribbon-and-flower decorated maypoles (signifying trees), which some trace back to Germanic and Roman influences.

Baskets filled with flowers and stories of the "crowning of the May" were a big deal in my childhood; my mother loved May Day. My mother's father emigrated from the United Kingdom in the 1920s, coming through Ellis Island on his way to work in horse stables, riding and training polo ponies on the East Coast.

Since 1886, May Day has also been recognized internationally as honoring and continuing a global push for workers' rights to fair and humane working condition, wages, protections. On May 4, 1886, in Chicago, police killed four people at a peaceful labor rally, turning the protest into a riot that brought the labor movement worldwide attention.

In an odd turn of events, in 1923, the phrase *Mayday* became a—likewise internationally—recognized radio signal for distress. Because the written or Morse-code distress signal of SOS presented some difficulties in radio transmission—S sometimes sounding like F—the Allied forces during the first world war agreed to the new distress signal of *m'aidez*, which is French for "help me!" and is pronounced the same way as May Day in English.

I can't help thinking of the hard work done by the plants of our planet— in all of their energetic ways—this fecund May 1, and of the many distress signals they and their communities, their seeds, are also sending us.

MAY 2

In the canyon the buckeye is in full bloom—the arching-upward flowering spikes (panicles) remind me of candles on a birthday cake. For such large spikes (up to 18 inches) of such a quantity (upwards of 80) of small flowers (each less than half an inch across), the mere one or sometimes two or three to a cluster of large seeds seem unlikely somehow, each glossy chestnut-colored seed the span of my palm.

Beneath the buckeye and the oaks in full deep green leaf again, the last waves of native bulbs and corms are out: twining brodiaea (*Dichelostemma volubile*) and Ithuriel's spear (*Triteleia laxa*)—one wrapping its red stem up grasses, up shrubs, up trees; the other a stately candelabra in shades of violet and blue, like cheerful flags above the browning grasses.

Triteleia resonates with me as an instance of how my own heritage has evolved. Ithuriel was a character in John Milton's epic English poem, *Paradise Lost*, an angel sent by Gabriel to find Satan in the Garden of Eden, but as a spring-flowering plant native to most of California and the southern part of Oregon, the corms of Ithuriel's spear have long been eaten by Indigenous people across its range, where I now make my life.

I am mulling over something I heard recently on public radio from urban revitalization strategist Majora Carter: "Environmental justice [means that] no community should be saddled with more environmental burdens and less environmental benefits than any other." I cannot help but correlate the losses humans have caused as we have moved across realms of our planet, how we have named and renamed and claimed and unclaimed, and the losses we face in the very near future, and then wonder what if? What if we had listened to, learned from, respected, and celebrated one another and each distinct place and its lives as each wave of people moved from one place to the next. What if?

But that is not by and large what has happened. And so I am left wondering: What if we did that from here on?

It strikes me that every seed keeper and seed scientist I have spoken with about the work to preserve the diversity of seed evolved or selected and bred and then shared emphasized the critical importance of preserving genetic diversity—for our food or otherwise—by keeping it growing in the ecosystems, habitats, and human communities where it exists naturally, as a first and best practice, with ex situ conservation in seed and gene banks as a complementary safeguard. "Survival is dispersal over time," John Dickie at the Royal Botanic Gardens, Kew, said reflectively when we spoke.

I am reminded over and over again of the first principle in the ethics of medicine: first, do no harm.

The human harm done to the biodiversity of our generous planet as of 2022 goes far beyond tragic losses of agricultural crops.

Back at Kew, Dickie laid out for me how, while its repository of seed was growing over the past 150 years, so too was a global interest in agricultural genetics compounded by increasing concern about the loss of global biodiversity. In the early to mid-twentieth century, some of the major botanic gardens around the world were inspired to create gene banks for preserving general plant biodiversity. Kew, "along with others such as the Royal Botanic Garden of Madrid, wanted to see if it was possible to start conserving wild species in the same way that the crop gene banks were doing."

The Kew seed bank started out modestly, with seed from its own extensive gardens, many of those plants collected (pillaged?) over centuries of Great Britain's empire building and global colonization, as well as seed exchanged between botanic gardens around the world. Kew people collected throughout the United

Kingdom and the Mediterranean Basin and hosted collecting visits from collaborators outside of the country, "for instance, sugar beet breeders from the US came and made collections of the wild beet relative species found along the coast of the U.K."

In the mid-1990s, an independent committee evaluated the Kew collection and determined that for best practices and resource accountability, Kew should "either scale down and leave this work to others who could and would do it better, or they should expand significantly to make a real impact." They chose the latter.

For the proposed expansion, Kew applied to the Millennium Commission, which was offering grants from lottery ticket money to fund landmark projects. Kew won a grant that financed a brand-new, state-of-the-art facility: the Millennium Seed Bank. The ten-year grant also backed Kew's efforts to bank 10 percent of the world's wild plant species through partnerships around the world, including with the United States.

"We started with collecting in the arid US Southwest, but all of these partnerships go on even now. What we established was a network of partner institutes [originally known as the Millennium Seed Bank Project, and as of 2022 the MSBP], including botanic gardens and others around the world. Through these partnerships, often working jointly, seed and germplasm is collected and shared in an effort to conserve wild plant biodiversity within each country, helping each country to fulfill the obligations their countries made at the Convention on Biodiversity [CBD] at the 1992 Rio Earth Summit," Dickie says.

Why did it take us so long to conclude that collaboration like this was ... fruitful?

As noted earlier, the signers of the CBD had undertaken to conserve all of their biodiversity in situ but also ex situ for redundancy. Dickie explains that, as a rule, the biodiversity conservation collection goals try to account for maximum genetic diversity within a species, within a genus, across families. Finally, they are looking to collect for phylodiversity, across phylogeny, or evolutionary relationships, often determined by molecular analysis rather than how a plant looks (its morphology) to account for the different genetic information included in plants that evolved and speciated out at different times in the earth's history.

"We have built up a network of more than 97 countries and gardens over the years, and today we have something like 96,000 collections [and more than 2.4 billion seeds] down in our vaults in deep freeze, -20 degrees and air dried, representing something like 40,000 species. Another few thousand species are out in the network not duplicated at Kew. Collections are usually duplicated in-country for each partner and again at Kew for a stable backup," Dickie added. "The MSB is the largest, most diverse wild plant species genetic resource in the world, with seeds from some of the most extreme [as well as the most] familiar landscapes."

The MSB prioritizes seeds that store well, from areas that have been identified as vulnerable to climate change projections, that are useful to human livelihoods and economies, or are endemic and threatened food crops.

Interestingly, while previously much of the national-level seed banking was focused on agricultural seed banking, the MSB work and contacts over time have bolstered and helped diverse US wild-seed-banking efforts to become more cohesive and integrated: MSB partner organizations represent some of the primary organizing hubs around the seed and gene banking of native plant biodiversity across the United States.

The first known formalized US native seed bank, the Seed Bank for Rare and Endangered Species of the Pacific Northwest, was established in 1983 at Berry Botanic Garden in Portland, Oregon. After founder Rae Selling Berry's death in 1976, garden board member Molly Grothaus "pointed out that, although Kew's seed bank at Wakehurst Place had begun in the early 1970s and the United States Department of Agriculture guarded seed of agricultural interest, the United States had no seed bank of imperiled native plants." With grant funding from the Fred Meyer Foundation, the garden hired a young botanist, Julie Kierstead, to craft a best-practice seed bank, including systems and protocols for the collection: from long-term storage, to germination of the native seeds, to the intended reintroduction of these species to the wild. Kierstead's system received a Chevron Conservation Award in 1988, and was used as a template by others. In 2010, the Berry Botanic Garden was closed and the seed bank incorporated into Portland State University as the Rae Selling Berry Seed Bank and Plant Conservation Program, with 18,000 accessions consisting of packets of seed representing over 350 of the region's rarest and most vulnerable plants. These seeds constitute an "insurance policy" against the extirpation of sampled populations or species. They are held primarily for use in reintroductions to the wild and in rare plant research.

Every effort helps.

MAY 6

The arugula (*Eruca vesicaria*) and parsley (*Petroselinum crispum*) are both in lanky long-stemmed flower and forming seed. The sound around the airy, pale green parsley flower umbels and young seed heads is that of one big happy colony of insect life—large bees and butterflies, small shiny-green native bees, several wasps, ladybugs, aphids. They are all here—the herbivorous, the mate-seeking, the predatory—landing on, hovering over, tag-teaming, and lapping up the various food sources. I save seed from both these plants every year, just in case, but these are also seriously generous plants, seeding themselves in the beds below their aging stems and heads, as well as in the gravel path and even in the nearby native plant dry border. They reseed in place pretty reliably.

The greens feed me and John through winter; the flowers, seeds, stem, and decomposing plants feed everyone else the rest of the year.

It is the simplest form of seed saving: late-summer dry seed from ripe seed heads slipped into clean white envelopes and stored in my darkest, coolest front closet, in a narrow shoebox perfect for just this.

MAY 11

We have decided to try melons as well as one winter cooking pumpkin this year. The cool, sweet hydration of a late-summer melon in our dry heat—like the joy of sliding into a shady pool of the creek—makes that infernal stretch of the year more livable.

John has preferred 'Winter Luxury' pumpkin for baking ever since his daughter, Elicia, brought several to him from her work running the gardens at Green Gulch Farm, the farm for the San Francisco Zen Center. He has planted them every year since. We planted from saved seed the first year after her gift, but because squashes (Curcubitaceae) have a tendency to cross-pollinate among themselves if not well isolated, the seed did not come true to type. Since then, we have sourced new seed every other year or so.

For our melons, we research in Amy Goldman's updated *The Melon*, the descriptions at Kitazawa Seed, and the offerings from seed keeper (and scholar of seeds of the African diaspora) Ira Wallace at Southern Exposure Seed Exchange. Ultimately, we select watermelon 'Ali Baba', which we source from Baker Creek; 'Hime Kansen' hybrid Japanese icebox watermelon from Kitazawa; and, from Southern Exposure a 'Wilson Sweet'.

Deer may be a problem, so we will fence, and we are also planting in gopher cages. Fingers crossed.

Altogether the seeds of these squash and melons include one large cream-colored teardrop, one smaller, rounder wheat-colored seed, one speckled brown seed, and the smallest seed, a deep, vibrant jet black, is a teardrop a quarter the size of the largest cream-colored one. In hand, they are a mandala of nuanced variation on a theme.

MAY 15

We could have a next generation of young arugula seedlings within 4 days—a week tops, while the squash and melon seeds will take a little longer, between 7 and 14 days. This is their germination time, something that is particular to each seed. We could be harvesting good-sized arugula leaves for the kitchen within two weeks, while we will anticipate mature squash or melons in 80, 95, or 100 days. Arugula seed stored well (cool and dark) should be viable for about three years; squash and melons are generally considered viable for at least five. My own ability to successfully save seeds with more precise requirements I know is hindered by my lack of careful seed-keeping records, lack of strictly monitored storage (for example, just how hot my coolest front closet gets in summertime), and my enjoyment of ordering new and interesting seed from time to time.

No seed bank or successful seed collection of any kind can be achieved or maintained without adhering to best practices for collection, storage, record keeping, and grow out.

All the aspects of seed life and life cycles, including how and when they germinate, how and when they break dormancy, and their longevity, are subjects of ongoing research, and storage protocols change with new research. As Christina Walters at USDA remarked to me: "When I first came to the collection, I was tasked with keeping the seed alive forever. I have spent the rest of my thirty-plus year career trying to define 'forever.'"

If trying to help the planet or a seed bank by gathering or propagating some wild seed sounds appealing, know that the parameters for legal collection of seed outside of your own home garden and land varies by state, by environmental conditions, by habitat, and by plant population. In most cases it is illegal to collect seed in the wild or on government land without a permit. When collecting for yourself from your own land/garden, collect the healthiest, ripest seed, when it is close to dispersing itself. Store the viable, pure seed only (remove any chaff or pods or casings) to minimize fungal, bacterial, or even insect (and insect egg) contamination.

While seed saving might be a gardening task that connotes late summer or autumn, the fact is seed saving begins the minute plants offer their seeds, regardless of season. Some notes from the California Botanic Garden, managed by Dr. Naomi Fraga, director of conservation and Cheryl Birker, seed conservation program manager, on how to choose the most promising seeds: "Maximum germination, seedling vigor, and longest storage life is achieved when fully ripened, current season, pest-free seed is harvested. Note in the field whether the seeds that are being collected have viable embryos. Healthy, sound seed has an interior area that is filled from edge to edge with generally white and fairly moist endosperm and/or embryo tissue."

As for storage, Dickie suggests that while a lot of innovation and technological advances have been made, many of the best storage practices—kivas and earthenware seed pots, mason jars, shoe boxes and chocolate tins the world over—still apply. "Food preservationists have long taught us that to stop or slow the deterioration of anything, you clean it, you dry it, and you cool it. Within limits, the drier the seeds and the cooler they are, the longer we can keep them alive." Once dry, store in a sealed container in a cool, dark place till ready to plant again.

There is an order of magnitude leap from even the serious home-garden seed saver approach to institutional seed banks' requirements and capabilities around temperature and humidity controls. California Botanic Garden works from what's known as Harrington's rule: Each 1 percent reduction in moisture content and 10 degrees Fahrenheit reduction in temperature doubles the life of the seed. But the nuances of this are always being studied. According to Walters's findings in this area at the USDA's Fort Collins facility, the optimum seed moisture content should be based on the storage temperature, and her recommendations suggest that the optimum water content for seed storage increases with decreasing storage temperatures. And, as is somewhat intuitive, the sooner you can get any seed to optimum storage temperature, light, and humidity levels, the longer the seed will retain viability.

MAY 20

John begins work on a large native plant garden design and installation in town. His clients—a multigenerational family—want to remove about 6000 square feet of irrigated turf grass from their 12,000-square-foot suburban-development backyard. They want to add habitat for birds, and the grandmother in particular wants to introduce the flowers and seeds that remind her of her days backpacking in the Sierra. John will spend months here, smothering the turf grass with cardboard mulch and creating a native plant community of more than 220 plants of 45 species.

As the plants go in, he will start to enjoy the company of resident Anna's hummingbirds, finches, sparrows, native bees, and late-summer butterflies.

This is just one yard in one neighborhood in a county of hundreds of thousands of square feet of irrigated turf (alongside established walnut orchards, the ground beneath which is sanitized by spraying every spring, and barren because their "farmers" see no intrinsic need to court or support native pollinators for trees that are wind pollinated). This overhaul of half of a back garden might seem small, but it provides a needed link in a habitat network.

Adding nutrient-rich pollen, nectar, larval food, shelter, nesting materials, and ecosystem seeds where there were very few creates an opening. It's a small but fierce something.

MAY 21

Evolving parallel to seed banking at the global level in the second half of the twentieth century to now is a field of smaller, more localized native plant seed saving, growing, sharing, and selling in the private sector. These small place-based seed start-ups reflect an interesting trend influencing the home gardener and running somewhat counter to a garden world increasingly dominated by selling "gardening" as a lifestyle and status symbol, even as another commodity.

Two examples of this include the work of plantswomen Gail Haggard and Judith Larner Lowry, who, independent of one another in the late 1970s, founded businesses dedicated to native seeds and plants. These were based around an environmental garden ethic dedicated to working with the "essentials"—soil, water, climate, seed-grown native plants—of their locations and within the limits of each of them. Both women were also looking to keep or bring into cultivation plants not widely available at garden centers, or, later, big box stores that have come to serve as impoverished, homogenized, and contracted nursery analogs.

As of 2022, Haggard's Plants of the Southwest, with mail-order and physical locations in Santa Fe and New Mexico, still offer around 220 native plants as seed and from seed, and Lowry's Larner Seeds, based in Bolinas, California, cultivates and ethically wild-collects seeds of more than 200 California natives.

Similarly, in the early 1980s, a young back-to-the-lander, Alan Wade (whose father had been a student of Aldo Leopold's, and in whose life Leopold's 1949 *A Sand County Almanac*, with its essay "Land Ethic," was seminal), began his native plant and seed company: Prairie Moon Nursery in Winona, Minnesota. Prairie Moon's offerings come from a network of more than 70 seed producers throughout the Midwest.

Taken together, these efforts represent regionally based and ecosystem-inspired business models working to improve biodiversity conservation through lovingly maintained collections— and relations.

Together these human endeavors make at least one thing very clear: a good many people and groups are at work thinking about, trying to collect, trying to control, and manage the world's seed.

However, there is friction around defining what seed is: A living entity with rights of its own? A family member? A natural inanimate resource? This erupts at the intersection of seed, community, business and capitalism, environmental health and biodiversity, and seed and gene banking—friction around to whom seed belongs, or whether it can "belong" to anyone; and friction as to how it is best banked and stewarded for the future in a deeply disturbed and uncertain present.

Dickie at Kew sees seed-source countries and communities as sometimes "very cautious" about contributing to large public seed banks, sensing that "business interests have often used collections for profit only, at the expense of the cultures, communities, and countries of origin." In his view, this is counterbalanced by "sometimes genuine business interest in wanting to attack problems of food security by, for example, breeding better varieties. There's a very lively trade-off debate going on back and forth in the work right now."

At the highest global-network levels, the worry at the heart of these frictions led to the Nagoya Protocol being adopted in 2010 and ratified in 2014. The Nagoya Protocol on Access to Genetic Resources and the Fair and Equitable Sharing of Benefits Arising from their Utilization is a supplementary agreement to the Convention on Biological Diversity. It provides a "transparent legal framework for the effective implementation" of one of the three objectives of the CBD: the fair and equitable sharing of benefits (read: profits) arising out of the utilization of genetic resources, with a goal of contributing to the conservation and sustainable use of biodiversity.

A great deal of overlap exists between the identification of, conservation of, and research into the possible loss of or contamination of "crop plant" seeds, their many locally expressed and adapted landraces, their wild progenitors, and straight biodiversity conservation at the seed level.

A lot of seed science, seed knowledge, and seed security is at stake where people can exploit these overlaps. Which, as Dickie and I agree in our conversation, could be seen as a sign of healthy participation in how we want seed and plants cared for and handled. It shows that people, countries, industry, and organizations are paying attention and caring. "It is," Dickie adds, "not unlike the friction in a healthy and functioning democracy."

MAY 22
As reported by the Agrarian Trust, a new law banning Roundup and other glyphosate-based chemicals in all public parks citywide goes into effect in New York City today.

The Center for Biological Diversity makes a public email announcement in response: "Because they're engineered to kill living things, pesticides are a major threat to the planet's health," with study after study demonstrating that pesticides, insecticides, and fungicides remain in soil and damage soil life for years after their original use. They also show up in surface and ground water, disrupting water quality and the health of aquatic life, from invertebrates to fish to birds; directly impacting pollinator health and reproduction (and therefore correlated with catastrophic global insect and pollinator decline); and implicated as neurotoxic in humans, associated with neurological diseases, like Parkinson's disease, and neurological development disorders, placing pregnant women and children at greater risk of damage from such chemicals.

However, indications are that their use is not decreasing, but increasing. And they are not uncommonly found on seeds (like the neonicotinoids associated with pollinator declines). "Between the 1950s and the 1990s, less than 10% of soybean acres and less than 50% of corn acres were treated with insecticides. Now, EPA estimates that nearly 100% of nonorganic corn seed planted in the

United States is coated with one of two insecticides—clothianidin and thiamethoxam. Industry estimates for other crops suggest that between 2012 and 2014, approximately 76% of soybeans, 62% of cotton and 56% of wheat acres were planted to insecticide and fungicide-coated seed."

Coating allows for a quick systemic uptake of a given chemical in the seed as it develops, germinates, and grows into a plant. That pathway means that the chemical can persist in the plant parts and systems throughout its life cycle—from roots and leaves, to nectar, pollen, and the final seed/fruit.

As of 2004, more than 18,000 pesticides were licensed for use in the United States, and in the history of the Environmental Protection Agency fewer than 150 have been banned. According to the Pesticide Action Network of Europe (PAN Europe)—which has been successfully working for anti-pesticide research and legislation in the EU since 1982—and a 2019 study published in *Environmental Health*, "72 pesticides approved in the United States are banned or being phased out in the European Union (EU). That was also true for 17 pesticides in Brazil and 11 in China."

In May of 2020, the European Commission published their official Farm to Fork Strategy, described as the heart of their Green Deal agenda "for a fair, healthy and environmentally friendly food system. The strategy sets out both regulatory and nonregulatory initiatives, with the common agricultural and fisheries policies as key tools to support a just transition to sustainable food systems."

Seeds treated with pesticides, insecticides, and fungicides are extremely common in California, where a third of the fresh vegetables and two-thirds of the fresh fruits and nuts for the United States are grown. Treated seed, as designated by seed-labeling laws, are noted as such and labeled with the same warnings and precautions as other poisons and toxins—the skull and crossbones, recommendation to wear protective clothing, what to do if you ingest or get the product in your eyes. Yet the state's pesticide agency doesn't consider the seeds "pesticides" under the law, a legal loophole meaning that the use of pesticide-laced seed isn't regulated or tracked, nor is the disposal of unused treated seed. In 2021, Vermont became the first and only state to date to define and regulate treated seed as analogous to pesticides themselves.

Banning one toxic chemical when many more are simply waiting in the development-pipeline wings does us little good. The only way to regulate these "toxic seeds" is to redevelop the mindset that makes them the first and sometimes only choices in the problem-solving triage of farming and gardening—for producers large and small.

MAY 25

The wild grape vines (*Vitis californica*) are fully fleshed out in big, broadly rounded green leaves and bunches of fertilized swelling green fruits. They literally festoon the alders, willows, and bay trees, draped like party garland at head height when we walk down to the creek.

With a high of 102 today, the creek is almost warm enough for swimming. A few weeks and we will be floating with the watercress, beside the cattails, creek carex, yellow seep monkeyflower, hummingbird-calling red cardinal flowers, bumble bee–calling stachys, and oppressive but sweet-fruit-bearing (and bird-raccoon-skunk inviting) Himalayan blackberry.

As we wade around in the dappled shade of the alders, the bay that survived the Camp Fire, and the nearest oaks, we see small birds like kinglets, towhees, and bushtits come in and out of view. They sing, flit, chirp, check in on us along with a small fleet of yellow, anise, and pipevine swallowtail butterflies. The butterflies gently, almost absentmindedly, loop around in the warm air currents above the swimming hole. Meanwhile, the much more intent dragonflies are just beginning their patrol season of this same airspace, circling and hovering in search of prey.

The temperature along the creek is easily 10 degrees cooler than up in the open parts of the canyon garden or grasslands, and by midsummer the difference could run to as much as 30 degrees.

Hanging in or near the creek, folding up leaves, burrowing deep in the soil, or napping in the shade of a tree canopy—we all search out ways to cope, to adapt.

Seed Libraries and Literacy

NEW MOON, JUNE 10
FULL MOON, JUNE 24

JUNE 1

The canyon is awash in seeds. It's almost impossible now to isolate and appreciate each in its turn. The full flush of spring blooms has passed: in the grasses of the fields, in the once green hillsides, along the creek; invasive and native, everywhere you look, fruit and seed are swelling, coloring, dispersing.

The redbud (*Cercis occidentalis*) off the end of the deck is thick with dangling pea pods—translucent green with small areas of burnishing appearing across the rounded contours of the developing "pea" inside. The edible pods (best when young and tender, before they get too fibrous) will be decorative ever-changing elements through the remainder of the season. We still have months of high heat and no rain expectation to go.

The soaproot (*Chlorogalum pomeridianum*), abundant after the Camp Fire, is flowering luxuriantly on the slopes of the garden and surrounding canyon. Stalks of up to six feet or more are lit up by open, white, six-tepaled (a structure of petals and sepals that look similar) flowers, each tepal is fully recurved when in full bloom. Each flower has six bright-yellow-tipped stamens as long as the petals, standing straight up, and often hosting a bumble bee. These airy flowers form all along the top third of each of the soaproot's stem. Each pollinated flower in turn forms a spherical capsule, and when fully in seed, the stems are decoratively studded with lustrous green pearls of seed (which will mature to brown). Someone once told me that pearls symbolize wisdom born of experience, which seems exactly apt for seed as well. The soap-root takes up to 10 years to grow from seed into a flowering specimen.

These flowers open early each evening like starlight, not long before the bats emerge from the eaves of a wooden shed. They are quiet, swooping spirits protecting the property.

A feathery-leafed annual larkspur (*Delphinium variegatum*) in the front garden has proud candlestick stems of upright, narrowly rounded, vase-like seed pods still green and fleshy. The coddled specimens in the garden—*Rosa* 'Gertrude Jekyll', *R.* 'April Love', and *R.* 'Lady Emma Hamilton'—and their hardier, but more delicately flowered cousin, *R. californica*, in the hedgerows and roadside verges here are all forming their hips, succulent and globed. *Rosa californica* is leggier and wilder than the garden roses, and by August she will be covered in smallish (one-eighth inch?) pointed, bright orange hips. They visually flash at us on our daily walks, as well as to the creatures that will forage on them.

It is a sensual and abundant time of year: fruits and nuts, seeds and grains all preparing themselves for the rest of us, the seedeaters. We the seedeaters are full of hope and full of expectation. And gratitude.

JUNE 8

Winds have been up, and after two heat waves so far this spring and early summer, the California poppies (*Eschschlozia californica*) have completed their cycle. Their seed pods ripened to their plumpest, straightest greenness, and then dried into brown, slender, vanilla-bean C-shapes, finally splitting lengthwise along their seams. Now splayed open, they've revealed and released their tiny, black greatest hopes—next year's California poppies. For now, the seeds lie dormant, no bigger than those black dots speckling your morning bagel or lemon poppyseed muffin.

If, as the old Welsh saying goes, every apple seed is an orchard invisible, then every California poppy seed is a blazing orange spring meadow or mountain-slope super bloom in waiting.

Just down the way, along our morning walk on the road, where the gravel tracks take a small dip down and then jog up to the left, marking a culvert over a hillside drainage, the pipevine seed pods (whose teapot-shaped flowers lit this spot in January) have also dried and cracked open along their seams, now taking the form of honey-colored, open-ribbed, wooden lanterns waiting for a stray slant of sunlight to light them fully.

When this happens, it's easy to see how these persistent and durable structures could have served as models for just about any hanging lantern from any culture the world over—Japanese, Italianate, Greek, Islamic Ramadan-famous lanterns, minuteman lanterns of the American Revolution.

JUNE 10: NEW MOON

An article in *Modern Farmer* earlier this year featured the story of Alicia Serratos, a young woman who spent hours during the lockdown portion of 2020 "assembling kits containing organic vegetable, herb and flower seeds, envelopes and plant markers to help communities establish seed libraries."

These so-called seed libraries, generally based inside of and on the model of public libraries, were first conceived and realized in 2004 in Gardiner, New York, by Ken Greene (who goes by K), who was then working at the Gardiner Public Library. Greene had been part of the library's community outreach efforts to increase their books and programs dedicated to growing, farming, and gardening to serve its rural ag community.

In 2002–2003, the Gardiner library hosted two different local food challenges. The relative difficulty people had in being able to source a significant percentage of their food from nearby sources highlighted to Greene a series of related facts: that there needed to be a greater diversity of local food being grown; and for that, you needed a greater diversity of seed. Finally, this experience highlighted that most people in his community, Greene included, did not know where "seed actually came from before arriving at the food and grain or garden center where you bought it." This revelation about his own and his community's disassociation from seed initiated his subsequent career focus: seed library founder. He set out to learn about and steward a diversity of seed, and then went on to become the cofounder/owner of Hudson Valley Seed Company.

While learning about the work of Seed Savers Exchange, about the consolidation of seed in the corporate and commodity spheres, and the blocked access to some seed or aspects of seed based on plant patents or plant utility patents, Greene says, "I got to thinking about SSE's story, and I was kind of like, well, we could do that. I could learn how to save seeds, I could try to remove myself from this system that I think is toxic. And if we do this as a community and everybody brings their shared seeds to the library, then it works just like the books: we're sharing knowledge. And we're sharing stories, whether it's the genetic story (and I think of this as the nonfiction genre), or the whole range of human stories around these seeds. In human seed stories, you have every fiction genre you can think of: mythology, spirituality, romance, adventure, crime and mystery, coming of age, and family."

At first, the idea of the seed library within the public library was a hard sell. People did not understand it or get why it was important. Greene spent several years building the idea, developing materials, talking to garden and farm groups, to other libraries, mentoring others who wanted to get a seed library started in their own communities before it really felt like the idea took hold. But once it did, it became another avenue for raising seed awareness among people who might otherwise never have known or thought about it, and for fostering seed-saving skills and seed literacy.

Greene's slight variation on the age-old seed swap was ingenious: it made seeds grown and saved by real people within their community visible to people who had long been distanced from their own agrarian past. As Greene noted, "Two-year-olds coming to story time, their parents, their grandparents; young adults in need of a computer, a jobs board or even internet access on a hot or cold day, or career-shifting elders" all had an opportunity to encounter seeds and seed-growing gardeners. Just like that, a whole new perspective on the world opened to them.

As luck would have it, one of the Gardiner Library interns working with Greene had been involved in the Bay Area Seed Interchange Library (BASIL) Project, founded by and within the Ecology Center in Berkeley, California. BASIL was established in 1969 as a nonprofit focused on "improving the health and environmental impacts of urban residents," and their model was another direct inspiration for Greene's first formal "seed library" iteration.

For Greene, seeds have always represented generosity, mutual aid, and mutual care: "You grow one cucumber, and you have far more seeds than you could need for next season—or the next. The plant is inviting you to share them!" More than setting out to run a business that "makes money and has the latest varieties," for Greene, seed work "is about helping people have meaningful relationships with seeds, and fall in love with seeds, so that they care about where seeds come from, where they're grown, and what is the meaning of seeds in our lives. What does it mean to plant a seed? It's a very heart-centered place. Everything else needs to fall into place around that."

The story of Alicia Serratos makes clear that people are receptive to learning about seed in this moment. She pushed back against the COVID-19 pandemic by sending out more than 100 "Three Sisters Seed Boxes" to people young and old. The boxes were filled with seed donations from Seed Savers Exchange and with literature and a map of existing seed libraries in the United States supplied by the Community Seed Network (CSN), itself only recently established in 2018.

CSN is a free and open seed knowledge and resources network formed to support the national seed library community. The network concept was initiated by seed savers in Canada and the United States looking to protect seed-saving rights. That original concept evolved into a joint project of SSE and SeedChange, a Canadian open-source, local seed advocacy group.

The Three Sisters planting of corn, beans, and squash together is a centuries-old American Indian technique, and Native Seeds/ SEARCH describes that "for many Native American communities ... it represents their most important food crops [and ancestors]." When planted together, a Three Sisters garden concept is polyculture at work: each helping the others to "thrive and survive," the beans fixing the nitrogen in the soil, the corn providing support to the twining bean, and the squash vine with its big leaves shading the crowns and roots of (and holding moisture in the soil for) the beans and the corn. The intertwined efforts of Serratos, SSE, CSN, and the box recipients, and seed libraries generally, are polycultures as well.

Another key figure in the seed library movement in the United States is Rebecca Newburn. Newburn cofounded the Richmond Grows Seed Lending Library in Richmond, California, and it was she who initially worked to track, digitally congregate, and share resources for the seed library community as it grew across the country. The Richmond Grows website seedlibraries.net now lists more than 800 seed libraries sharing local seed in communities around the world. That is quite an enterprise: grassroots, staffed almost entirely by volunteers, built on the honor system, supported by donations. Although seed libraries primarily feature seed for edible crops (vegetables, fruits, herbs) and common seed-grown flowers, as of the early 2020s native plant seed libraries were sprouting up as well, including a flagship model in Maricopa County, Arizona, founded by Danielle Carlock.

Popularity reached such a level that in June 2014 the Pennsylvania Department of Agriculture notified a soon-to-open Mechanicsburg seed library that if it did not meet state-mandated seed-labeling requirements, it would be in violation of state seed law. This was a red-flag notice for the whole movement. The cost in labor and dollars of potentially having to meet such commercial requirements threw the viability and sustainability of seed libraries into question.

By mid-2014, a coalition mobilized to counter this challenge, with legal help from the Sustainable Economies Law Center (SELC), based in Oakland, California, and with funding support from the Clif Bar Family Foundation. Newburn of Richmond Grows was an early partner in the national Save Seed Sharing Campaign. For the campaign, the SELC developed the Seed Law Tool Shed, an online, public, "crowdsourced database of state seed laws and analysis," to help seed libraries and exchanges navigate and understand current laws.

In 2015, the first International Seed Library Forum in Tucson, Arizona, hosted by the Pima County Public Library, brought together over 100 seed advocates to discuss the state of the seed library movement and state seed laws, and to develop strategies for growing the national and international network of community-based seed sharing.

Unanimously, the group passed the Joint Resolution in Support of Seed Libraries, providing language and templates for legislation to protect seed sharing. Following on this work, in 2016, the American Association of Seed Control Officials voted to amend the Recommended Universal State Seed Law to exempt seed libraries from commercial regulations.

Chalk one up for the little guys.

The whole episode, however, is another example of what are essentially contrasting worldviews. On one side is belief in the inherent benefits and competitive controls of capitalism (albeit heavily weighted in favor of big business and big agriculture by subsidies and sheer resources), and on the other, a belief articulated by the SELC that "neither our communities nor our ecosystems [or their foundational seeds] are well served by an economic system that incentivizes perpetual growth, wealth concentration, and the exploitation of land and people."

Also noted by the SELC: "Communities everywhere are responding to these converging economic and ecological crises with a grassroots transformation of our economy that is rapidly re-localizing production, reducing resource consumption, and rebuilding the relationships that make our communities thrive.

As new solutions for resilience emerge, many are running into entrenched legal barriers: laws originally designed to protect people from the ills of industrialism are now preventing many communities from growing and selling their own food, investing in local businesses, creating sustainable housing options, and cooperatively owning land and businesses."

Writer Annie Dillard is well known for this sentiment: "How we spend our days, is how we spend our lives." This is true of our minutes and hours too. True of our pennies and dollars to our overall budgets—the smallest units of expression. Are we spending countless hours ensuring seeds' shared safety and access, or their restriction and corruption?

JUNE 12
Seed is of course where most of our food, or the food of our food, originates. And an amazing majority of that seed is completely dependent on pollinators pollinating. We are at perhaps peak insect season here now, with nighttime temperatures warm and still warming, and some moisture in plants and soils remaining from our last soaking rain of May 15. The crickets, the mosquitos, the bees, the flower flies, the bee flies are all singing, crooning, and buzzing to the vibration of the universe as we tend toward the summer solstice.

California has a high diversity of native bee species (directly related to the high diversity of native plant life). Of the nearly 4000 species of bees native to the United States, nearly 1600 species make their homes in California. In this summer moment, the intensity of purpose of many of the small native bees and flies is both audible and visible. At least four or five species of bumble bees; anise, yellow, and pipevine swallowtail butterflies; admiral and California sister butterflies; myriad moths, along with a healthy number of dragonflies; and—of course—nonnative honeybees all forage in the canyon daily.

Stories about pollinators fill the local, national, and global news—the pest-beleaguered honeybee, the declining seasonal numbers of monarch butterflies, the alarming declines in global insect pollinator populations over the last 10–30 years (or more).

As a society we are still not doing nearly enough to help offset or slow these declines in insect life. Examples of this fill our days: the telltale orange-red line of dead foliage along roadways and agricultural field edges this time of year illustrates the continued use of toxic herbicide in our region (and you can easily multiply that across all agricultural areas of the United States); the proportion of nonnative, non-wildlife-supporting, neonicotinoid-laced plants sold in the "garden centers" of our big box stores; the mown, blown, herbicide-sprayed, irrigated turf lawns that populate the "landscapes" of the 18 suburban-lot houses that fill the viewshed from my home office (and you can easily multiply that across all suburban areas of the United States). These "views" remind me just how far we have to go. I'm grateful at least for the six front yards in my office viewshed that have converted to gravel-mulched, dry-loving native plants.

Reading Gary Nabhan and Stephen Buchmann's *The Forgotten Pollinators*, I am more and more clear on how un-versed we are in where seed sits (or sets) in the magnificent order of operations that is the seed-bearing plant kingdom.

Forgotten Pollinators is clear that every step or link in this order of operations is "crucial," but in learning the distinct aspects and relationships of each link, you know and value both the individuals and the whole better. This clarity illuminates anew that without the hydrology of the rocks, no creek; without the healthy creek bed and riparia, no seedbed; without seedbed, no community of oaks, alders, willows, carex, *Darmera*, and seep monkeyflower. These plant communities are likewise in a circular relationship with the bugs and birds, without whom, no predators, without whom ... and so on.

It is a classic trophic cascade that in fact shapes all of our days, and that we often blur out. Even when we do see some of the links—oh look, a butterfly! Oh look, a hummingbird is at the monkeyflower!—how often do we see and then acknowledge the architecture of the entire ecosystem that is supporting that one lovely moment? It's sort of an odd change-up in some ways, as though we can see one note, or maybe even a chorus, or a chord, but we have lost the ability to grasp the complexity of the whole symphony.

To think about and understand our own place in these lines of life support is to recognize how reliant we are on every other life and life cycle: from the mycorrhizae in the soil, to the beneficial bacteria on the skin of pears that help our gut biomes digest them, to ancient relationships between maize/corn kernels and mutualistic endophytes (bacteria or fungus) on their seed coats that allow them to grow in nitrogen-depleted soils.

Nabhan and Buchmann take this line of logic further, making the connection that when a plant (or an insect) is designated as endangered, this acknowledgment also "implicitly acknowledge[s] that all the creatures—especially those specializing on this plant for nectar, pollen, larval or seed food—are also endangered."

Nabhan's interest in seed, in plants of the desert Southwest where he makes his home and where he helped found Native

Seed/SEARCH to conserve the declining biodiversity of native foods and seeds, is really about "conserving relationships." He traces this back to his study of the work of Rachel Carson and moving the idea of *Silent Spring* toward the apocalyptic idea of a "Fruitless Fall."

To him, trying to comprehend the extent of our intricate, interrelated roles—seed, elements, plants, pollinators, humans— is related to trying "to imagine the contours of one another's humanity."

JUNE 20: SUMMER SOLSTICE

JUNE 24: FIRST FULL MOON OF SUMMER
To celebrate the solstice and the first full moon of summer, John and I take a few days "off" from everyday life of his work in gardens and the constant to-do list of my life at the desk. We head to one of our favorite spots in the northeast corner of California—the Warner Mountains. The area is remote, and although we come most years to visit our plant friends and communities, we are almost always the only people camping and among very few enjoying the state-designated "areas of botanical interest."

The unique natural history of this area, situated on what is known as the Modoc Plateau, was described by geographer Thomas R. Vale in the 1970s. He noted the volcanic geology dating back 66 million or so years, including the uplift of the Warner Mountain Range, which runs parallel to the California-Nevada border for about 55 miles. Its highest elevation is just under 10,000 feet. The mountain range includes a very steep east-facing escarpment above a scenic valley, and a much more gently inclined western slope, broken up by spring and snow-melt streams. The Warners receive most of their annual 20–24 inches of moisture as rain and snow in winter and early spring. As with most mountain and alpine areas, the higher you go, the more rain or snow there is, and the more average precipitation, the greater the mass of plant life, until you hit tree line and move into alpine environments.

Here, sagebrush (*Artemisia cana, A. tridentatae,* and hybrids) and juniper cover of the lower and midelevation western slopes and higher merge into a coniferous forest of white fir and yellow pines (*Pinus ponderosa* and *P. jeffreyi*). Some lodgepole (*P. contorta*) and white bark (*P. albicaulis*) pines show up occasionally. The valley floor below and the alpine slopes above these more forested areas are fairly uniformly populated by sagebrush steppes and their associated low-growing flowering perennials, annuals, grasses, and ephemeral wildflowers and bulbs, the diversity of which is incredible—especially given the extremely dry, often windy, and in winter really cold, conditions.

Vale's description, inclusive of human-introduced and managed livestock grazing, set the scene for an analysis of obscured or unrecognized cultural human impact on this "wilderness" area, specifically the makeup of its forest species, as a result of suppressing the natural element of fire and introducing the "un-natural element" of grazing livestock as early as European settlement in the 1840s. Both happened in spite of the fact that the Forest Service designated this a wilderness area in 1931, and in 1964 it was incorporated into the National Wilderness System with the passage of the Wilderness Act. Vale's conclusion was that "in the Warner Mountains, land-use policies ... have resulted in alterations to the vegetation over the last century even within the ... 'wilderness.'" Fire suppression led to increased white fir populations and decreased establishment of yellow pines. Grazing by domestic livestock caused an invasion of trees into open brush and grasslands, which is natural succession, but one now shown to have been managed well by organically occurring wildfire cycles and seasons, and intentional Indigenous land management. The acceptance of these changes reflects the difficulty of recognizing the difference between natural phenomena and "cultural" alterations to an ecosystem.

Decades after these observations by Vale, John and I note small variations to the areas we're familiar with since our last time here, post-most-recent fire and continued grazing across the "wilderness area": the density of forest here, the intensity of burn scars there, the proliferation of invasives everywhere.

The way into the wilderness area shows extensive burn scars from the 2020 Fork Fire. We cross several of the streams noted by Vale as we drive up to some rustic camping sites, through aspen groves near a small lake and marshy area, and dotted by old but still used cattle corrals. The aspen groves rise up to meet the pine forest, and they are underplanted with sweeps of seasonal wildflowers that change significantly as you climb from the marshy areas to the drier slopes. We camp adjacent to a meadow with a wet and a dry side, both aspects part of the herbaceous understory to the midelevation sagebrush and other shrub ecosystems.

We come with several days' supplies for hiking, and well-worn and margin-noted lists of the known plants of the wilderness area. Several hikes extend south (and in elevation, up) from our campsite, allowing immersion in a whole handful of the ecosystems here—beginning in meadow, down to the marshy lake, up into midelevation forests, into wetlands, across remnant snowfields, and into alpine meadows below summit scree.

A favorite hike takes us steeply up through the dry, quiet ground and dappled light of tall conifers. Climbing and curving and crawling over fallen tree trunks, we eventually make a long, slow turn to the left and round a bend. The forest suddenly opens. Beneath an arching blue dome of sky, open and exposed rocky outcroppings stretch before us.

The windswept, reddish contours could be described as a moonscape except for the many small plant islands visible if you look closely. Widely spaced convenings of plants assemble in pockets between clusters of sagebrush. They huddle at the bases of gnarled curl-leaf mountain mahogany (*Cercocarpus ledifolius*), which are anywhere from 200 to 1500 years old and 20 feet high at their tallest, stunted and sculpted by seasons and years of weather. In fact, biodiversity swarms in little windblown eddies of time and space on the leeward side of anything with mass: sage, mountain mahogany, rocks, sticks, the dry mineral slopes themselves.

To look out across this extraordinary space on a clear day, vulnerable to the full force of the wind and sun yourself, with 100-mile views to the east (Nevada) and west (across Northern California), you can almost see the planet revolving: you are bearing witness to time and life and perhaps its meaning accumulated and accumulating. You can see weather moving, soil forming, seed forming and shedding along the forceful lines of the wind and watershed almost simultaneously; you can see herbaceous plants, geophytes, vines, shrubs, trees, and their related communities growing up, receding, evolving, adapting, adjusting, and coping all in the moment, in plain sight, all around you.

It is existential. It is breathtaking.

Fragrant, small-flowered, pink creeping phlox (*Phlox* sp.) intertwines with rigid tufts of prickly sandwort (*Eremogone aculeata*), and occasionally short stands of deeply orange paint-brush (*Castilleja* sp.). Low-growing dark purple allium (*Allium* sp.), whose two strappy drying leaves curve into a heart shape around the nearly ground-level flowering head. White morning glory (*Calystegia occidentalis*), blue-purple penstemon (*Penstemon* sp.), and several lupines (*Lupinus* sp.), and so many more smaller, grassier community members we have yet to learn or identify, all tuck and root together in these lively pockets of volcanic grit and soil.

In some ways, each individual plant is competing for protection from wind, sun, heat, and cold in their seasons, competing to catch what little moisture there is in this fast-draining, desiccating landscape. But in many ways they are joining forces to protect one another, to bio-accumulate what organic matter of foliage and twigs—and clearly seed—get caught in their matted stems and crowns; to aggregate what dew and rainfall they each gather and hold more efficiently together than separately.

The dusty trail, which is sometimes hard to differentiate from the bare expanse of first gently and then precipitously sloping soil and mineral on both sides, is intermittently bordered by two different milk vetch (*Astragalus* sp.), by dusty maidens (*Chaenactis douglasii*), by softly mounding colorful sulphur buckwheats (*Eriogonum* sp.), and by the fragrant minty foliage and pale to deep purple flowers of coyote mint (*Monardella* sp.). The plant combinations—of low and high, of blue and yellow swathes accented by whites and reds, of contrasting mounding and spiky forms—are so proportional, so balanced we are always left with the impression of perfect design.

In the open spaces of what looks like nothing but hard-packed grit, solitary outcrops of tiny individual navarretia (*Navarretia* sp.), the pincushion-like flower heads half the diameter of a penny, each flower one "pin," appear here and there, along with lone quarter-inch-high shocking bright purple monkeyflowers, and individual or small clusters of two or three bitterroots (*Lewisia rediviva*), whose large, soft pink, many-petaled, almost succulent flowers opening right at ground level seem completely unsuited to this environment, and yet here they are, popping up like buried treasure.

This volcanic basalt plateau lies between the vast desert of the Great Basin and the incredible, plant-rich California Floristic Province, and it includes some of the most threatened ecosystems in North America. Ecosystems struggling with the consequences of fire suppression, the correlated forest expansion, the overgrazing livestock herds playing out side by side with the threats of inundation and genetic swamping by invasive species, and the inching effects of climate change. The plants who have evolved here under these extremes seem as hardy as they come, but of course they are alarmingly fragile.

This place gives me a new understanding of the word "diaspore." In a 360-degree ring around any vignette of plants anchored together for survival, or single outcrop of one plant going it alone, there is a sweep line in the grit made by the foliage, flower, or seed head brushing the substrate in the constant wind. A wind shadow, something like a snow angel. When, finally, some part of a seed stalk or seedhead breaks off and travels from the mother plant, the whole structure released by the plant—be it one-tenth of an inch long or two feet across—constitutes the diaspore.

The astragalus bladder-like seed pods—fuzzy white or kidney-bean flecked red—do this: when ripe and ready, the individual bladders full of seed break off from the mother plant and blow about in the wind, banging and breaking against the grit and rocks, and with every blow seeding the next generation. The daggerpod (*Phoenicaulis cheiranthoides*) is named, like many plants, for the shape of the fruit—which dry to become astoundingly effective at wind dispersal. The daggerpod's stem, from which the flower and then fruit capsules project, rises from a tiny basal cluster of thin, almost needlelike, silvery green foliage. Each stem bears three or four of the seed capsules shaped like daggers (or airplane propellers). Each flowering stem stands perpendicular to the basal leaves below them; the many dagger-shaped seed pods on each stem are arranged both radially the length of the stem and perpendicular to the stem, thus parallel to the ground below. With even a small breath of wind, at least one if not more of these daggers will have its flat side creating resistance to that wind and eventually either the entire stem of daggers or the one resistant dagger will break at its point of connection . . . and fly away, sometimes lifting, sometimes shearing across the land. Likewise, the dried stalks and seed-filled umbels of the alliums break free at the soil level and, driven by wind, tumble across the landscape spreading seed. In all these cases, the structure that held, protected, and nurtured the seed(s) is an active part of its dispersal process.

Whereas, for instance, in the case of a dryland milkweed (*Asclepias* sp.), whose pods rarely release from the plant stalk, the "diaspore" primarily includes only the seed inside the pods and their silvery parachutes, individually called a coma, which allow for wind and/or water flotation.

You can see all of this and the need and purpose for it so clearly here—from the spikes covering the succulent rounds of native gooseberries, to the dry and light windblown allium and daggerpod seed heads; from the spiraled silvery plumes projecting from the mountain mahogany seed enabling it to auger down into hard dry grit, to the tubular cones of penstemon seed rattling out their charges—in this landscape of impressive, sharp extremes.

These seed-born and seed-bearing lives have convened and reconvened over the millennia to figure out ways to live—and work and reseed—together.

When we return home, we have new hope about the state of the world, new expectations, often related to resilience, adaptability, the long view, a capacity to think in terms of millennia versus the most recent political cycle. Sometimes it takes the brightly exposed plane of the unfamiliar and not-everyday to allow us (get us?) to really see the extraordinary in our seedy everyday lives.

JUNE 26
Do our hopeful expectations have the power to enact real change?

February 2021 saw the first Slow Seed Summit, hosted by Slow Food USA, and the tenth annual Seed Library Summit in April. Artist and heirloom seed activist Jeff Quattrone was a primary organizer of the first, and the keynote speaker at the second.

He was surprised to be asked to give the keynote for the Seed Library Summit, and when I asked why, he said, "It's just hard to believe. No matter how hard I work at it or how seriously I take it, that anything like this—the proliferation of seed libraries, of seed people—is really happening, it's just so beautiful. So unexpected."

Quattrone turned to community gardening following an auto-immune disease diagnosis and the Great Recession of 2007–2008. For him, this led to an increased interest in and curiosity about foodways and from there to an interest in seed.

Slow Food USA works to counter the increasing industrial-ization and globalization of our food and agricultural systems. Quattrone learned about Slow Food's Ark of Taste, a catalog and campaign to save local, place-based foods at risk of being lost to history from disuse in modern food systems: breads requiring an at-risk grain, heritage animal breeds, individual plants and their seeds.

Quattrone comes from a historically agricultural area of New Jersey, notable for its tomato breeding and canning industries, so he was dismayed to learn that one side effect of industrial-ization and globalization working hand in hand for "efficiency and scale" was the impoverishment of the genetic diversity of our foods, and how heirloom and culturally significant foods can easily (and have) become "functionally extinct." After reading an article about how seed libraries maintain seed stocks, he set out to create a seed library network in his home region of South Jersey, beginning in 2013.

In the subsequent years, Quattrone helped to launch more than 10 seed libraries, consulted on others in the United States and abroad, and consulted with other anti-GMO, seed saving, and protection groups. As a graphic artist, he's created a line of "power to the people" seed propaganda images—for instance, an image in which the yellow petals of a sunflower become raised arms ending in a fist representing defiance, strength, resilience, resistance. This image also summons the ancient, cultural importance of sunflowers as food and regional signifiers to Indigenous peoples across North, Central, and South America.

Part and parcel of the Seed Savers Exchange history, of the seed library movement, and of the idea behind Slow Seed is a desire to maintain the connections of individuals, cultures, and places with their traditional foods born of seed. Because, as is increasingly clear, especially in the face of devastating losses, these intact or re-woven connections are inextricably tied to cultural survival.

The celebrating and documenting of these stories and connections across cultures was not new to 2020 and the pandemic and social-justice upheaval of the year, but can be traced back hundreds and thousands of years at food gatherings, seasonal festivities, and communal rituals of both joy and mourning.

Our human connection to seed comes to us directly through the foods with which we identify. This is as true for Jeff Quattrone as anyone else.

Quattrone's community garden is just two miles from where seedsman W. Atlee Burpee had his Sunnybrook Farm experimental station. "To have the opportunity to grow and revive the 'Sunnybrook Earliana', a functionally extinct tomato"—which Quattrone pronounces like a good South Jersey kid, *tomayta*— "just a few miles from where the originators grew it and made their own selections," is everything Quattrone loves: history, food, place, art, and seed "coming together" in a garden plot. While doing research at the Smithsonian Gardens library, where a good portion of the Burpee papers are held, Quattrone was able to read the actual seed journals of Burpee's trialing the 'Sparks Earliana', from which they would later make the selection for their 'Sunnybrook Earliana'.

For Quattrone, the Jersey tomato is a perfect illustration of how seed is at the intersection of local food, local culture, and (as importantly) local economy: "There was a lot of food system innovation around the tomato in Jersey at the turn of the nineteenth century, around breeding for taste and disease resistance. They did not need to select for shipping or storing, because the breeding, growing, processing, and canning were all right here." For him, this model exemplifies locally based, circular economies that could be part of a re-envisioned seed and food shed in the future. When Quattrone started his Library Seed Bank project and research, his "stretch goal" was to rediscover one "lost Jersey tomato." As of 2021, he was at "three, with two more" expected to be announced shortly.

But perhaps his greatest stretch goal is this: re-imagining a less environmentally and culturally costly food system starting from seed.

JUNE 27

For K Greene, founder of that first public library–based seed library in 2004 and then cofounder of the Hudson Valley Seed Company (HVSC) in 2009, this intersecting connection between seed, food, art, and culture is expressed in visual art of a slightly different but still poignantly connective variety.

As a holdover from his love of the unique power of public libraries, Greene and partner Doug Muller established Hudson

Valley Seed Company's mission to not only uplift seed, but to uplift the human stories and re-viewed, reclaimed histories held in seeds as well. This is a growing aspect of the independent seed stewardship world—seeds of the African diaspora, of the Asian diaspora, and ancestral seeds of cultural relationship to Indigenous people and cultures of North America—being reconnected to their people on their long road to reestablishing community sovereignty. To remedy in part hundreds of years of displacement, erasure, diminishment, and attempted genocide. This history and process is often described as "rematriation" because women are so often the seed keepers in land-based and agrarian communities.

In 2009, HVSC wanted to build into their business model multiple aspects of the work that were of equal importance to them, "not just the biological stewarding of these little life beings, but all of the symbolic and metaphoric and mythologic narrative that comes along with them." For Greene this was all part of the "seed literacy that was so lacking. Most of the people who came into the library had no consciousness of seeds, let alone where they come from, at all, even if they were people that regularly went to a farmers' market. And stories are the perfect hook to engage people and their curiosity, to bring them to wanting to learn about seed."

Their first year in business, HVSC had 14 varieties of seed. Greene's idea to meaningfully incorporate storytelling into the young seed company was to commission original art for each variety of seed, and he chose a different artist for each packet. He began each commission by telling the artist the story of the seed as he knew it. And then he would "let them do what artists do. They are cultural seed savers—looking at all these different pieces of what helps us understand who we are, what we want, what our hopes for the future might be, and they take all those pieces and translate them into something visual." Something that, Greene described, "tells the story in a way that is beyond words— it's emotive, it's open to interpretation, it allows and invites the viewer to integrate themselves into the feeling of that story." The resulting art is one way HVSC preserves and shares the stories of seed, embodying the belief that saving and sharing seeds is about "cultural creation" and re-creation.

By way of example, Greene shared with me the story of HVSC's 'Cornell Bush Delicata Squash', its art packet, and the synergy between the story, the seed, and the artist.

The seed was developed by Molly Jahn and George Moriarty in the organic breeding program at Cornell University, New York State's land-grant institution. In Greene's experience, "most university-based breeding programs seem to focus on developing new offerings that can be released widely as a hybrid, from which seeds can't be saved and grow true to type, or with a plant variety protection, or some other control mechanism in place so that the financial investment in the development can be returned and increased by the university that developed it and by whatever seed company picks it up."

The development of 'Cornell Bush Delicata' at this public organic breeding program "meant that Molly Jahn created an open-pollinated variety, that could be saved by farmers from season to season, but also 'saved' as an open access resource for the betterment of farmer and gardeners and agriculture going forward. The 'Delicata' is like a dumpling squash. It's small, it's tender, you can eat the skin. The Cornell variety, developed as a bush form from a vining form, made it especially good for small-space growers." But after the newly developed seed was released into the trade, somewhere along the way it got crossed, and whatever the accidental cross was, it affected, "not in a good way," both the texture and taste of squash grown from the subsequent seed, which was still available under the original name.

Noticing this loss of the original variety's traits, Greene "worked with Cornell, who had archived seed from the original introduction, to grow out and replenish the original seed stock line until HVSC had enough to start sharing."

Each year Greene knows which forthcoming varieties he would like to commission art for, and he looks through his files of artists who have applied to be part of the program to find the best fit. He "feels like the match.com of seed and artists." When he looks through the portfolios each year, he will get a feeling of "Yes! This artist needs to meet this plant. I am sure they will hit it off."

When he was looking for the right artist to create the artpack for 'Cornell Bush Delicata,' Greene came across the work of Sarah Paulucci, "which very much focused on hands, and the act of creating something." When he'd interviewed Molly Jahn about the development process, she'd shared how "she had collected the squash pollen using a paint brush to hand transfer to the different varieties she was using for the potential cross the traits she was looking for." For Greene, the human hand as the vessel through which many seeds have passed over time plays such a crucial role in the lives of these seeds. He knew this was a fit.

Sarah came up with the idea of "a hand with a paintbrush carrying both pollen and vibrant yellow paint." The visual narrative is multi-layered: creating new plant varieties can be an art form and process, just like the art of gardening, and painting, and culture building.

HVSC now commissions art for about 12 new seed varieties each year. Each piece of art is used as the basis for their respective seeds' packets. The art-based seed packs are known as "artpacks." As of 2022, HVSC had more than 200 original pieces of art in the collection. The HVSC artpacks and their artists beautifully represent and reflect the biodiversity inside the packets: "What we're passing on is not only the seed or its biology, but the story and the invitation to grow and become part of the seed's story—witnessing all of that coevolution of humans with that seed that has come before you planting it in your garden. As you're watching that unfold and caring for it, you are now part of that seed's story."

Which is both beautiful and complex, bringing up sometimes difficult questions, the way good stories do. Greene routinely asks of himself and the HVSC community, "What does it mean to be part of the story? What does it mean and how do you care for a story that has come into your hands and into your soil that might be part of a different culture or a different part of the world, or ancestors who are not your ancestors? These are important and ongoing questions and conversations."

The art from these legions of artists of all backgrounds, aesthetic styles, artistic modes, and materials, provides a "doorway into" the conversation sparked by these questions and allows that "conversation to continue to evolve over the years."

Holding this seeming unity of opposites is an art in itself, not unlike the sometimes-unexpected capacity of any seed: "How do we steward these seed lives respectfully? How do we hold onto and share their histories and narratives respectfully and authentically? How do we do this and maintain a viable business based on the need to sustainably support the people and seed within it and the mission of it? This is the work of really seeing what our current food, economic, environmental, and social structures are" and experimenting with healthier ways to re-envision them and manifest the answers to these questions. Starting from seed. And the circular, cyclical nature of the seeds.

Close to the end of our conversation, Quattrone says to me, "There is a concept we talk about in the seed gardening world called backyard biodiversity. Seeds have a way of adapting to where they are growing to a certain extent. If you are growing and saving the best seed year after year, you are self-selecting the best seed you can grow for yourself." Your own landrace, as it were. Quattrone encourages everyone who can and wants to, to save their own seed. If not, "get involved with your local seed library, volunteer time. If policy is your thing, then get involved with policy work in your region. Match your passion and skills to the seed work that needs doing." As he sees it "every seed that gets saved [in backyards, in seed libraries and local exchanges] takes a little bit of power away from corporate control," its narrowing and diminishing of this great diversity and seed heritage, and distributes it back to the people, the places, and the seeds. "It's a very quiet and subtle madness," he admits, "but good for that. One seed at a time."

SEED SAVING

JULY

Seed Conservation

NEW MOON, JULY 10
FULL MOON, JULY 22

JULY 3

The cattails (*Typha latifolia*) are tall and arching, the colony of green strappy leaves flagging the edge of the swimming channel in the creek. On these hot, hot days (113 yesterday) we linger with the birds—the chat, the phoebe, the robins, along with bumble bees and swallowtail butterflies near or in the cooling water—shaded by the alder, willow, and expansive oaks at the far edges.

This young stand of cattail—new this year and joined by many willow saplings—holds down a sandy curve of the creek bed formed by the current's ongoing deposits and withdrawals of materials as it makes its way. The cattail colony has sent up just one stout pillar of a seed head. Daily we can see it lengthen, finally growing out of its protective sheath, and as time passes, the maturing seed turn to a deeper and deeper brown.

At their feet, in the rocky pools just at the water's edge, the bright yellow spring-blooming monkeyflower (*Erythranthe guttata*) is all but done blooming, one or two trailing yellow flowers marking the last of them. The spent stems are now woody staffs leaning out over the current, ornamented with inflated papery seed pods, translucent and golden with the low late-afternoon light refracting within and through their globe lantern forms.

The creek-side watercress too is nearly past blooming, its seeds beginning to disperse; the twin purple pods hovering above the large-leaf *Darmera* have a little further to go.

A remarkable number of seed pods remind me of lanterns, so many "lights unto our path."

JULY 7

We spend the day cutting back flowers on the invasive broom we were not able to pull in February. At least cutting these back gives us the sense that we are helping stay the tide of that unwanted, unchecked seed.

The Himalayan blackberry is steadily reclaiming sections of the creek-side ecosystem—a tangle of roots and shoots and thorns. The birds love it as cover, all of us partake of the berries, but there is always a dread that these berries (or any invasive) are outcompeting, strangling, choking, dominating (the way colonizers unchecked will do) the soil life, the water, the air, the other plants whose lives are needed, are adapted here.

JULY 10: NEW MOON

In place, or in situ, conservation of seed and plant genetics includes the natural so-called seed bank held in the soil and the plants that produce those seeds and add to the bank year after year. Plants and seeds sown and grown purposefully by humans are another form of in situ conservation.

The newly planted native gardens John designs and installs, John's wildland interface native and cultivated canyon gardens—these are individual examples of some variety of in situ conservation. Even my tiny town garden, with its mix of sentimental English and European garden plants balanced by climate-loving native California plants, is some very small, scattershot version of in situ conservation of the plants and seeds (and conditions) being cultivated. Your garden, and its plants, is too.

Many botanic and public gardens are more strategic and formal versions and sites of very purposeful in situ conservation. The Atlanta Botanical Garden's (ABG) Conservation and Research department, for example, features a Conservation Seed Bank focused on the collection and preservation of germplasm of targeted native imperiled plant species from the southeastern United States, the Caribbean, and Ecuador. The ABG focuses on supporting, protecting, and researching in situ conservation in all of these regions first, with backup provided by their seed/gene bank, which holds seeds and pollen for imperiled species restoration efforts and for in situ and ex situ research of threatened populations.

Similarly, in Phoenix, the Desert Botanical Garden (DBG) and its historic living collection, established on what was primarily Sonoran Desert scrub, has been dedicated to conservation and research since its founding in the late 1930s. Director Kenneth Schutz told me that by 2023 the garden's goal is to have the living collection include 85 percent of the world's known cacti and agave species. The DBG began collecting and maintaining seeds of rare, threatened, and endangered plant species in the early 1980s as part of the national network of botanical gardens that founded the Center for Plant Conservation, and the DBG is the only one specializing in Sonoran Desert plants. The garden and the seed bank work hand in hand. In 2021, the DBG opened their brand-new Ahearn Desert Conservation Laboratory to house work the garden is doing to photograph, test, store, and germinate desert seeds.

Take *Pediocactus knowltonii*, a tiny cactus that grows only on a 25-acre patch in New Mexico. The new conservation lab has helped to document and protect this cactus. "Compared to a saguaro fruit, which can produce more than 1000 seeds, *P. knowltonii* can only produce between four and 20 seeds in a single fruit," a significant challenge for the species. The DBG collects and stores *P. knowltonii* seeds to germinate for reintroduction to the wild, in appropriate places and conditions. Further, with the lab's capacity, the DBG also serves as the Southwest regional orchid seed bank for the North American Orchid Conservation Center; and they partner with the Chiricahua Desert Museum and the Phoenix Zoo to test seeds "eaten by rodents later digested by snakes," to determine whether snakes, important species for desert regions, are significant or efficient seed dispersers.

That's a new one on my list of seed dispersers.

The USDA oversees another mode of in situ conservation. Although its Fort Collins facility primarily holds seed, plant physiologist Dr. Stephanie Greene explained that "while seeds are generally the best way to store plants, in terms of a living propagule, sometimes we need other means as well." For some crop plants, seed is not the best way to save genetics.

Beyond plants that have recalcitrant seeds, which do not store well if at all, crops that are primarily clonally propagated likewise can't be stored as seed. "Apples are a perfect example," she went on, citing that many of the apples we love are grown by cuttings that are then grafted onto a reliable root stock. "You can pick a 'Granny Smith' apple, but if you grow out the seed you will not get a 'Granny Smith' apple tree. Saving the actual tree in an in situ collection in order to take cuttings is the appropriate method."

The USDA maintains an active in situ collection of apple trees in Geneva, New York. "In total, 6883 diverse apple varieties are maintained there between the field plantings, their stored seed, and stored cuttings." This includes 1565 seed lots of wild *Malus* species including approximately 950 seed lots of *Malus sieversii*, the main progenitor species of the cultivated apple (*M. ×domestica*) from central Asia. Most of the varieties used as parents for breeding new varieties of apples in the United States come from what is known as the "North American gene pool," which dates back to seedling orchards planted when European settlers first arrived [in what is now Geneva] between the seventeenth and nineteenth centuries. It is often referred to as the "Johnny Appleseed gene pool." Many enduring varieties—including Red Delicious, Golden Delicious, Jonathan, and McIntosh—were discovered as chance seedlings from this pool.

The USDA gene bank curators at Geneva take cuttings during the dormant season and send them off to Greene in Fort Collins. She takes the two-to-three-foot-long sections and cuts them into two-to-three-inch sections, each host to a dormant bud. These sections are then prepared so they can withstand submersion in liquid nitrogen at -196°C.

Seedswoman and gardener Shanyn Siegel pointed out, however, that the USDA's Geneva collection of apple trees, seed, and germplasm is actually a sort of hybrid ex situ/in situ conservation program, given that apples are not native and have not coevolved over the millennia there in Geneva, although some have been growing and adapting there for the last couple of hundred years.

The USDA works in partnership with other kinds of in situ collections of naturally occurring wild plant populations and their wild progenitors (parents) or congeners (like siblings or cousins). Each partnership is tailored to the needs of the plants. These partnerships gesture back to the USDA's Dr. Christina

Walters's goals and hopes around supporting on-the-ground, not just in-the-bank, seed and biodiversity conservation.

For example, the USDA also partners with the Forest Service and tribal and private landowners working on preserving the wild species of cranberry growing naturally across the northern mid-Atlantic United States and in the Pacific Northwest, where cranberry diversity is high. One key species is the large-fruited *Vaccinium macrocarpon* 'Aiton', which is the wild source of the cultivated cranberry. It "occurs in bogs [sites highly vulnerable to alteration or destruction] in eastern Canada and the northeastern and north-central United States, and south to the Appalachian Mountains of eastern Tennessee and North Carolina." The second key species is the smaller-fruited *Vaccinium oxycoccos*, "a secondary genetic relative of the cultivated cranberry. It occurs throughout Alaska and all across Canada, south through New England down to the Mid-Atlantic States, west to the Great Lakes states, and in the northwestern states as far south as the Oregon Cascade Mountains."

Both cranberry species bear the familiar fleshy red fruit form, a berry. But different from many other "berries" that bear their seed on their outsides, or within individual fleshy orbs clustered together, cranberries contain four small, open cavities that hold many small seeds.

These two species of cranberry are culturally significant food and medicine plants for Indigenous cultures across the regions where cranberries are native. This "complementary conservation" approach of including both ex situ and in situ conservation practices also includes collaboration and consultation with tribal groups across these same regions, to help ensure holistic success.

"The conservation of the existing genetic diversity, both ex situ in USDA-ARS gene banks and in situ on USDA Forest Service (USDA-FS) lands, will ensure that these resources will be readily available to cranberry breeders whenever the need for them arises. Preservation of wild populations will also ensure that they can continue to be used directly as sources of food."

While the needs of commercial breeders are listed before the use of the plant as local food, at least the plan acknowledges both as valuable.

The program description goes on to note that "in situ conservation allows plant populations to continue to evolve and adapt to changing environmental conditions in nature." Preserving entire populations, rather than limited samples sent to a gene bank, "makes conservation more effective. In situ and ex situ strategies act as backups to each other and maximize the potential for cost-effective long-term conservation of alleles, genotypes, and populations."

Maintaining a diversity of stakeholders and decisionmakers with different perspectives and potentially different values, including government employees, tribal members, and more general residents of these cranberry-growing regions, is integral to the complementary approach of this specific seed-banking project.

Cranberries are interesting studies in climate change because they are cold-loving plants with chill-hour requirements that, if not met, lead to yield and quality decline, and increased disease pressure. The nation's major cranberry-production regions are also important research centers for the genus: Massachusetts, New Jersey, Oregon, Washington, and Wisconsin. With "New Jersey and Massachusetts having experienced some of the most rapid warming," ARS scientists are clear that the more they understand cranberries' response to climate, the better they will be able to protect them and harness natural adaptations in future cultivation.

The variations on what's possible with in situ conservation are insightful as to the range of work being done and the range of findings. So many things stand to be learned by studying the plants in their natural places, being conserved intact with their wider communities of conditions, flora, fauna, and people.

JULY 13

Today, eerily close to the point of origin of the 2018 Camp Fire, and also sparked by Pacific Gas and Electric Co. equipment, the Dixie Fire broke out in the Feather River Canyon, not 15 miles northeast of us. Because of the wind conditions, this fire moves away from us, not toward us. My head—and the collective heads and hearts of our region—spins with the possibilities, the past trauma, the most feared future outcomes.

With heat and drought and north winds, this fire grows quickly, sweeping through acres and acres of rough, wild land—sloping, mountainous, forested, riverine. Small canyons, small towns, small farms.

A report published recently out of the northeastern United States, *Conserving Plant Diversity in New England*, provides a scientific framework and detailed mapping tool for "conservation action and land protection at the species, habitat, and parcel scales that will effectively save plant diversity—and thus overall biodiversity—in New England as the climate changes."

One hope of the report is that by identifying places of greatest biodiversity, there will be a clearer understanding of which habitat types and locations still need to be protected or better protected. The report overlays which of these diversity-rich places might already be conserved or "protected" from human development, and which are conserved for "nature." These are two different designations, as, for instance, a lot of land could be protected "from conversion to development" but not protected from the potentially biodiversity-damaging effects of logging, mining, or the aforementioned cultural impacts of grazing.

The sheer magnitude of fragmentation and damage to ecosystems already done, and the challenges inherent in the triage thinking of "trying to at least conserve 30% of our planetary, national, and regional biodiversity" as humanity's stretch goal by 2030 is staggering. There is hope that the New England report, its mapping tool, and its collaborative model for collating data from a wide number of agencies and regional community sources could be a template for similar reports in other regions of the country and world.

Aside from policy implications, what is striking in this report is the authors' identifying and defining particularly climate-resilient and biodiverse landscapes.

To put the report's complex analysis—based on a host of overlays and data sets—really simply, climate resilience was found to be strongest in landscapes that are already accustomed to a wide range of climate variability. Mark Anderson is one of the report's authors and director of conservation science for the eastern region of the Nature Conservancy, a partner with the New England organization Native Plant Trust. As he explained the report's metrics, biodiverse "resilient landscapes" are defined by a range of topography, geology, hydrology, humidity, and exposure. He notes that microclimates seem to be key: native plants have adapted to highly specific conditions over time, and they have a lot of geographic and topographic variability into which a plant can lean and grow as conditions continue to change. Succinctly, these kinds of areas offer their plants the most options for adapting in the face of new conditions.

The area currently burning in the Dixie Fire is just such a place.

The report by Anderson and his coauthors extrapolates from the patterns of conservation, fragmentation, land management, and biodiversity to show that conserved land separated from other conserved land—and thus a conserved "island"—is significantly more vulnerable to damage and loss from climate change (heat, flood, drought). It also notes specifically that this kind of fragmentation "disrupts seed dispersal and [plant and animal] migration routes."

One of the author's really powerful observations is that "resilience exists across a spectrum, and habitats can be made more resilient." How? Anderson describes that habitats can be made more resilient by decreasing fragmentation and increasing concentration and links between conserved land, by decreasing disturbed and exposed edges, and increasing buffers for all habitats.

All this makes my mind swing back to the observations and findings these past 30-plus years regarding the interdependent relationship between the security of our world's food crops and the health of the planet's overall biodiversity, especially as expressed by the current health of the planet's wild crop relatives.

This is clear in Gary Nabhan's work, the work of Native Seeds/ SEARCH beginning in the 1980s, and has been corroborated again and again in the work of seed keepers and researchers.

Summarized, all of this combined research indicates strikingly similar findings: climatic diversity plus habitat diversity plus human cultural diversity equals more, and more resilient (to climate, to disease, to degradation by pests/invasives) biodiversity.

Nabhan notes, "Genetic erosion has certainly wasted a considerable wealth that once existed on the American continents," but he goes on to lay out why he does not think it will ultimately claim all seed, or all crop biodiversity. "The economic and psychological forces that aggravate crop genetic erosion and disrupt traditional agriculture simply do not penetrate all places and all cultures equally. After hundreds of years of economic or military domination by colonial powers, there remain agrarian peoples who continue to grow many of the same seed stocks their forebears did centuries ago." And there are others the world over who choose to plant their family's heirloom seeds rather than someone else's hybrids. In this, he sees great hope.

In the 1980s, Nabhan described findings around the International Maize and Wheat Improvement Center at El Batán in the state of Mexico, which had been releasing hybrid corn cultivars on a worldwide basis. However, it was found that immediately surrounding the center, "over half of all the corn planted remains open-pollinated seed saved from local harvest ... despite half a century of pervasive advertising and public education encouraging corn growers to obtain improved, hybrid seed from off-farm sources."

Further, Nabhan noted, echoing exactly what the newest New England plant diversity report found, that "the more marginal the land is in arability, the greater the probability that native crops will retain their advantages over introductions." Nabhan concluded, citing the work of late anthropologist Edward Spicer (1906–1983), that one of the predictive characteristics in many of these "resilient" agrarian communities was that if enough members of a community "expressed an affinity for shared" cultural signifiers (seed, crops, foods, religion, religious, or spiritual ritual) and values through time, across the generations, their agriculture *and* culture stood a better chance of remaining vibrant and viable. "Once inoculated," Nabhan wrote, "with the values held within their community, children acquired a certain resistance to the trappings of the dominant culture. Perhaps," he reflected, "these values act as 'cultural antibodies' which react to outside influences in such a way as to overcome their negative effects."

Ethnographer Eugene Anderson referred to this "as an ecology of the heart" and extrapolated from that: "Without an intense, warm, caring, emotional regard for the natural world, we will literally be incapable of preserving it." Areas and people who have persisted in their traditional farming "do not simply conserve indigenous seed stocks because of the economic justifications; the seeds themselves become symbols, reflections of the people's own spiritual and aesthetic identity and of the land that has shaped them."

In essence, Nabhan, in his own work and his review of the work of others studying agrarian ecology in "patch communities" around the globe, documented the same correlations found in Anderson and colleagues' report: climatic + habitat diversity + climate inconsistency + cultural diversity/tenacity equals more, and more resilient, biodiversity. For food, for wild crop progenitors, for wildlife, and for, and because of, resilient, adaptive humans.

There is a striking, and poignant, call and response between Nabhan's observation that disruptions to traditional agricultural systems can't affect everyone everywhere simultaneously and this thought from 2021's *Conserving Plant Diversity in New England*: "Plants experience climate at the micro scale (inches to yards), and thus sites that include variations in topography and hydrology create a mix of microclimates that have the potential to buffer the impact of climate change. ... Resilience exists across a spectrum, and habitats can be made more resilient."

It is (and has always been) the most challenging to colonize the most ignored lands, people, economies that support and allow the conditions for the greatest biodiversity.

These heterogeneous lands, growing practices, and cultures seem to embody some of the most important lessons we can learn from seeds: the harder the situation, the tougher the survivors; the more diverse you and your solutions and adaptations, and the more you share these forward, the better your chances; the more of you, the better your chances. (In my mind, I read these as: generosity and abundance, and redundancy, redundancy, redundancy).

For the greatest security in our seed and food crops, we need to protect seed and seed-producing plants of wild relatives and their associated ecosystems; one of the best ways is to support and sustain the cultural integrity of people around the globe who maintain a cultural relationship with seeds, plants, and ecosystems.

Therefore, our global seed and food security is inextricably linked to native plant and seed protection and by extension inextricably linked to respecting and supporting (or at the very least not dismissing or destroying in blind capitalism) land-based cultures and land care globally.

All of this would be infinitely more possible if we—Western capitalistic cultures—actually shifted a significant number of our values to those of land-based cultures. How do we accomplish that? How do we do this more quickly? Will any progress be quickly enough? How many generations will it require to build such adaptation into our own cultural seeds?

The Feather River Canyon and its adjacent landscapes to the north and east, the landscapes in the path of the Dixie Fire, could be described in all of the ways these studies hold up as best-case land and human-scale scenarios for biodiversity—a mosaic of diverse habitats, of geologies, hydrologies, topographies, of small towns and farms, rich American Indian cultural homelands, as well as European, Hispanic, and Chinese diaspora through European colonization, and subsequent immigrations of so many more, Basque to Hmong.

JULY 14

As the California experience has demonstrated and traditional practices incorporating prescribed fire have perennially proven, there is real benefit in the clearing, recycling, and regeneration that comes with mid-to-low-intensity, regular-interval fire. Overabundant fuel is diminished; ash, char, and even smoke feed the soil and the plant life; the most aggressive competitors get a setback while the less dominant get a chance at life. In these fires, soil and animals (from decomposing microorganisms and insects on up the chain) can also experience renewal.

Studies indicate that certain habitat types formed of plants that have evolved to rely on fire for good seed dispersal and germination (among them some pines and conifers as noted earlier) benefit not only from the presence of fire, but are better main-tained by "frequent interval low-intensity fires."

According to Forest Service tables, in the California oak wood-land, ponderosa pine forest, or mixed evergreen forest habitats, "frequent interval low-intensity fires" in a healthy cycle means they happen naturally every 5–15 years. Further, in regions where fire plays a historic seasonal role, the seeds of many native plants that don't require fire still germinate better when they are intermittently exposed to a cycle of smoke via smoky air or smoky water.

After nearly 150 years of active human fire suppression and the prohibiting of cultural prescribed burning in California, cata-strophic high-intensity fires have been happening much more fre-quently than every five years. And many areas that haven't burned lately are absolutely choked with dangerous deadwood fuel loads—much of the area of the Dixie Fire had not been allowed to burn in well over 50 years. Firefighters, emergency responders, and even ecologists must weigh these questions as they consider how to handle such fires: Does the area need the clearing that fire provides? Will a high-intensity fire and the incredible pres-sure of massive firefighting—hundreds of miles of bulldozer lines cut for fire breaks, aerial deployment of fire retardant, the car-bon footprints of helicopters, fire trucks, and bulldozers—be too much for the landscape? What else—rare or unknown plants, wild progenitors, overall biodiversity, seeds, and adaptive strategies—might be on the loss list from this most recent human-caused and human-caused-climate-change-exacerbated fire?

JULY 15

This canyon John calls home holds a remarkable amount of edible and herbal native plants—from acorns, to miner's lettuce, to starchy spring bulbs and redbud's young pea pods, to summer blackberries (native and nonnative), fall manzanita berries, and grapes.

Last year John identified a native yampah (*Perideridia* sp. maybe Bolander's, maybe Kellogg's) in a small, seasonally damp draw up the hill from his house.

Yampah is a magnet for pollinators, and when the foliage is disturbed it emits a pungent, soapy cilantro-like scent. It is one of the many native plants with a long American Indian culinary history—the seeds, the leaves, the tuberous roots. Independent and traditional (not GMO) breeder William Whitson, based on the central coast of Washington State, sees potential in yampah because of its valued history and because the only trait it's missing in order to be a good domestication candidate is a larger size. He sees yampah as a good "wild crop progenitor" or ancestor to future local crops.

Wild crop relatives and their presence and health in the landscape, especially in that seam between wild and cultivated, is of abiding interest for many economists and ecologists, including Colin Khoury, international food crop ecologist perhaps best known for his work on food diversity from the dietary perspective. One thing made obvious by his collaborative research into the spaces of greatest diversity of wild crop relatives, and the landscapes and people associated with them around the world— from rice, to beans, to maize, to soy, to agave, to cranberries—is that these specific kinds and locations of biodiversity (places with high wild crop progenitor diversity) are incredibly valuable to the future. They are also incredibly vulnerable to erosion, conversion, and outright loss. In part this value and this vulnerability is due to many such important places and peoples being the epicenters for the speciation of the plants that are now global staples—as rice is to Asia, corn and squashes are to Central, South, and North America, wheat is to the Fertile Crescent of the Middle East, potatoes are to Peru, and so on.

As Nabhan, Khoury, and others articulate, the best hope for the seeds of these communities and landscapes lies in a diversity of responses to conserving and caring for them. This includes meaningful and traditional relationships in situ, ex situ, and everywhere and every way we can come up with.

Khoury is the senior director of science and conservation at the San Diego Botanic Garden. He was born in Southern California, and on his road to becoming a leading international crop genetic conservation scientist, he experienced the full gamut of how our world grows, banks, and cares for seed. He grew up at the nexus of historic avocado and citrus orchards, eating pineapple guavas, alongside areas of then-still-intact distinct coastal sagebrush chaparral of Southern California, a gorgeous, rugged, heat-, drought-, and fire-adapted native ecosystem much of which has been lost to development, and what's left remains under serious threat from more development as well as climate change.

Khoury has remained particularly interested in the intersection of urban, rural, and wild spaces and ecological and regenerative—often seed-based—agriculture as a potential way to improve sustainability in our world. He traces the best models for these ideas to his childhood landscapes.

Before completing college, Khoury went to work on diversified farms in the southwest and, early on, he was taken with the colorful and textural diversity of beans while working on a cereal grain farm. At this same period of his life, two books came out that profoundly influenced his thinking: Nabhan's *Enduring Seeds* and Cary Fowler's *Shattering: Food, Politics, and the Loss of Genetic Diversity*, in which Fowler postulated that "it was through control of the shattering of wild seeds that humans first domesticated plants. Now [over] control of those very plants threatens to shatter the world's food supply, as loss of genetic diversity sets the stage for widespread hunger."

Khoury went on to become the "Bean Curator" at Native Seeds/SEARCH, where he safeguarded and cared for a collection of 350 to 400 varieties of native and adapted beans. The heritage of these beans originated largely from American Indian cultures of the southwestern United States and northwestern Mexico.

For Khoury, small-scale, community, and regionally based farming is and will always be "one of the most beautiful and most just ways to make a difference and care for land, seed, and people fully." However, from his work at Native Seeds/SEARCH and as a farmer, he saw wider connections that he wanted to make, beyond the direct impact of community-based farming. While in graduate school, Khoury went to work for the Crop Trust (formally named the Global Crop Diversity Trust) then in Rome, where a lot of the United Nations and international food agencies were based. As of 2013, the Crop Trust has been based in Bonn, Germany.

The Crop Trust, per Khoury, "is trying to secure enough funding, enough social/cultural support, and enough science to help the network of regional, national, and international collection seed banks into the future. One of the mind-blowing aspects to this work is that it's a forever job. These seed banks never expire in their importance and will forever have needs. Seed banks in Colombia, in Nigeria, in Ethiopia, the Russian Federation, and on. That is a big task to conceptualize, in tandem with the long-term backup center—the Svalbard seed vault."

For him, the preparation for and then the actual opening of Svalbard between 2007 and 2009 remains one of the "most powerful examples of goodwill among nations and institutions" he has ever witnessed. "It needed a country like Norway, which has worked for so long at international collaboration, with some degree of neutrality, to make it happen." On the other hand, he added with no small amount of audible grief, "it was also painful and shocking as well. There was a lot of pushback and misinformation about the seed vault promulgated online, especially by nonprofit seed organizations" he had formerly felt aligned with. It was a clarifying experience seeing that who he had considered the "good guys" and the "bad guys" was not so clear cut. That those he had thought of as the "small, good guys could also lie or fib for an end that fit their worldview." One of the most disturbing rumors about Svalbard was that to populate the bank, seeds were being taken away from communities by large corporations like Monsanto or Syngenta, who would then control and use the seeds for patenting.

There are very serious issues, he acknowledged, as someone who has spent his career trying to support seed in its place and secure long-term backup support for it in local and international seed banks. And, he admitted, "within these issues are deep fears that are real and have threads of truth. In these times, there are—and should be—real concerns about intention." The consolidations and mergers of large, industrialized agribusiness corporations, with the financial bottom line as their motivating principle, need checks and oversight. If we—lay people and gardeners—do not remain informed, then we will be easily swayed by fear and sound bites.

"It is a hard job to be a functioning human, to go to work, to want to garden and be engaged with the world for pleasure and beauty, for taste and health, and still remain well informed on business and politics. It is a hard ask," Khoury offered. "Further, finding people and organizations that are trustworthy" is time-consuming and involved. The trick, to his mind, is how you track these issues without closeting yourself in an echo chamber, without giving up your critical-thinking capacity and your willingness to question media sources, governments, businesses, or yourself. He also reminds us that "even the big corporations like Syngenta or the Gates Foundation contributing to the Crop Trust *can* contribute funding to an endeavor without any underhanded motives or hope around controlling that endeavor's basis—the seed. These groups may want positive PR and they may be virtue signaling as well as investing in what we hope they value, but their funding is needed."

The whole experience blurred Khoury's formerly binary thinking as a young man of 20 years old: "Big companies can do positive things, small NGOs can do harmful things—and certainly the reverse is true as well."

Khoury has realized that "agriculture and diversity within agriculture have direct relationships to human health, to environmental sustainability," and—a pivotal third part—"to equity and justice." The last two, in his experience, are inexorably inter-twined with climate change.

I had a conversation with poet and environmentalist Camille Dungy in which she remarked on what a great job we as Western "developed" countries have done at separating ourselves from nature in the name of survival and comfort the last 150-plus years, but that we've done this at the cost of no longer understanding our own human interdependence with and integral reliance on nature. She is not alone in this observation. Khoury's pathway reminds me how effectively we have broken our human needs down into component parts and siloed them into their designated lanes: how we live on the planet and environment here, how we feed there, how we work together for social justice here, nature and climate change there.

As complex as it is to see the web that strings these parts together, we must. It is Khoury's "big picture." We subdivide in order to see what we're dealing with, but at the cost of losing the sum for the parts.

It's all related. We're all related. We sometimes say this, but how can we really see and seed this understanding in a way that durably roots a cultural worldview built on this?

This is all so relevant to how we care for the world around us—from seeds to other people. It is why we can't just change law, we can't just change seed patenting bureaucracy or funding models—we must change our cultural expectations and intentions.

When we're trying to get our head around the big pictures of the big questions, it is harder and less convenient to work from the sum rather than the interrelated parts, but if we don't, aren't the picture, the ques-tions, and the answers predestined to be woefully attenuated, off the mark, and incomplete?

JULY 16

A belief in the socio-agro-ecological model of small-scale, multi-cropping, diversified farmers prompts the question: Who represents an urban/suburban/post-wild version of this model and these kinds of growers in the "developed" global West?

❖

Plants- and seedswoman Heather McCargo is one. As noted earlier, McCargo is the founder of Wild Seed Project, which focuses on returning native plants to the Maine landscape. McCargo is interested in the relationship between seed-grown native plants and re-weaving healthy ecosystems wherever they may be. Her goal is to "return native plants to the spaces right outside all of our doors" starting with her own.

McCargo grew up with a wild-foraging kind of mother who introduced her to Euell Gibbons's *Stalking the Wild Asparagus*, in Western Pennsylvania "on deep soil of the last glacial-age at the beginning of the Great Eastern Hardwood Forest," an ancient North American old-growth forest extending from the Gulf of Mexico up to Canada. Per McCargo, "Its incredible diversity had changed little in centuries until it began to be cleared for agriculture and logged and burned as fuel for settlement in the eighteenth and nineteenth centuries. Once home to rich bio-diversity—more than 110 species of primarily hardwood trees, including oak, chestnut, maple, beech, and hickory, and more than 40 species of mammals—by the 2000s, Eastern Deciduous Forest in North America had been labeled a site of global biodiversity concern. Less than 0.1 percent of this original forest now remains intact."

Attending Hampshire College, McCargo was introduced by a wildlife biologist professor and mentor to the interplay between the wild and the domesticated—and the benefits and consequences of these interfaces in our plant world.

This is often a preoccupation among people catalyzed by a deep interest in seed.

McCargo interned with John Torrey, director of the Harvard Arboretum at the time. Her interest and knowledge about seeds first "germinated" while working with Torrey studying the nitrogen-fixing capacity of alders. During research, McCargo helped propagate alders and other plants in the Harvard collections from seed. And, for some of the plants in the arboretum's collection, there was "no information on how to germinate the seed: Did you have to file the seed coat? Did you have to pour 80° water over the seed?" McCargo learned as she went, and Torrey shared what experience he had. For any germination test, Torrey and McCargo always put some percentage of seeds outside in the elements, rather than protected in a lab or greenhouse. And, McCargo reported, "these often seemed to do particularly well." Every germination test taught her something and was miraculous in its own way.

McCargo went on to work and learn at native plant gardens from California to New England.

It was during a year of living in Barcelona with her own high-school-aged children that McCargo noticed and became concerned with "just how homogenous the ornamental horticulture of the world is from one city to the next. It didn't used to be that way." She wondered "how, if most of the world's population lives in cities, do native plants specific to their places withstand [survive]? And, how do urban dwellers connect with their native environments in order to support and maintain them?"

For her, the magic of growing plants from seed has never dimmed, and she feels that when you're growing any plant from seed, "you're more of a partner or a midwife" than anything else, which is a very different relational understanding than many have with plants—of owner-object or even parent-child. And from the concerns she observed in Barcelona, she conceived the idea for Wild Seed Project, which she launched in Maine in 2014.

Wild Seed Project's mission is to inspire people to take action in increasing the presence of native plants grown from wild seed. The vision being "that people create and repopulate landscapes to be abundant with native plants which then safeguard wild-life habitat, support biodiversity, and mitigate the effects of cli-mate change."

And not inconsequently, native plants imbue a sense of place, helping Barcelona to look like Barcelona, and Portland, Maine, to reflect the landscapes and cultures of Portland, Maine.

While cultural and place-based identity were part of what inspired McCargo, there was also a very real and, she felt, over-looked aspect to the work: "The real value of growing from seed is sexual reproduction, which creates new combinations of genet-ics. When you take a cutting, you are cloning that plant. We need to be growing plants from seed in order to keep genetic diversity out there as we replant and restore habitat. But in our concern about biodiversity, we are not talking about cloning and its con-sequences nearly enough." The math of genetics and biodiversity supports her point.

There is an urgent call in our world—for homeowners, rent-ers, apartment dwellers, commercial landscapers and designers alike—to plant more native plants. Invertebrate-conservation nonprofit the Xerces Society, individual state-based native plant societies, wildlife conservationists, scientists like Doug Tallamy, founder of Homegrown National Park, activists like Edwina von Gal, founder of Perfect Earth Project and Two Thirds for the Birds, and legions of others have asked home gardeners to dedicate any-where from one-third to two-thirds of our individual home land-scapes to the native plants of our broader regions (with any luck removing irrigated/overfed turf grass and other non-ecologically functional or natural-resource-costly plantings in the process). This will also re-weave our urban, suburban, and exurban areas into the diminishing tapestry of remaining native vegetation cor-ridors for wildlife. Not to mention helping with carbon seques-tration, air and water quality, and climate resilience (minimizing heat islands, managing stormwater, etc.). In an ideal world, home gardens would become the connective pathway the New England plant diversity report called for between more and more isolated protected landscapes, thereby bolstering their capacities.

McCargo thinks this is a must. But what she recognized simul-taneously to these calls for planting more natives is that much of the new native plant supply is coming "at scale." And in her line of work with plants, she knows that means "cuttings, divisions, and at even greater scale, by tissue culture," all of which is cloning. "If all we do is clone, we undermine the greatest amount of diversity possible across a species. With the increase in native plant gar-dening, we have to be aware that if we are cloning plants rather than growing them from seed, we risk depressing the genetics of our native plant landscapes." The problem entangled in having a great many clones of a relatively few "mother plant" individuals is the reduction in vigor, in fertility, and in overall fitness within that species as a result of closely related plants reproducing. This not only damages biodiversity, but stops plants from evolving, adapting, and passing learned knowledge and traits down to the next generation via their seed.

McCargo took heed, like John Dickie at the Millennium Seed Bank and his explanation of seed bank standards, of "the imperative of collecting seeds representing as broad an assemblage as possible of any species' phylogenetic range of expression and diversity."

This should be a formative and transformative aha moment for gardeners, seed students, and environmental gardening advocates.

The benefits of increased genetic diversity and avoiding inbreeding depression that result from growing from seed, however, come with offsets as well: as the demand for native plants rises in tandem with the rise in rare, locally rare, or endangered species, the less anyone wants to encourage the wholesale collecting of seed. "Our seed is too precious to risk people over collecting, collecting at the wrong time, collecting and then not being ready to plant or propagate in a timely way thereby wasting the seed," McCargo explained. As well, many plantspeople and nursery people note that the efficiency and scale at which desirable plants can be cloned through tissue culture for home landscape, house plants, or the floriculture trade takes immense pressure off wild plant collection and depletion.

McCargo still carries the *Newcomb's Wildflower Guide* she got in her college days in the 1980s, and she is depressed by how many plants considered to be abundant then are now rare or locally rare. This decrease in populations of enough plants in our native landscapes means that not only does their vulnerability to overharvesting and inbreeding depression increase, but the risk of outbreeding depression also rises.

Quick and simplistic review here (who remembers their Punnett squares from biology class?): Just like humans, each individual plant has its own genetic code. When plants reproduce sexually, each individual in the next generation receives a set of genetic information from each parent, and the ways these codes combine will determine a great deal about the offspring: from morphology (how the child plant looks) to phenology (when it reaches each of its seasonal maturation points: sets flower buds, flowers, has ripe pollen, sets and disperses seed, senesces, etc.). In all of the bits of information that make up any plant's genetic code, there will be *dominant* and *recessive* trait information. If one parent plant has passed their dominant gene for flower color, and the other parent has passed their recessive gene for flower color, the offspring will express the dominant color. If both parents pass the dominant flower color gene, then the child will not only be the dominant color but can then only pass that dominant flower color gene to its offspring. But if both parents are the dominant color, but also carry the recessive color as part of their color gene coding, and by chance they both pass the recessive color gene information to their offspring, that offspring will be the recessive color—and can only pass the recessive gene on.

Sometimes two parent plants are so closely related that they pass identical recessive genetic information on any given gene to their offspring. If that happens in more than one generation in a row, inbreeding depression can occur, resulting in weaker and potentially less fertile and vigorous plant stock.

When breeders work to create stable hybrids, referred to as F1 (or first filial generation) hybrid crosses, they are often (always?) crossing two plant lines with known recessive similarities in order to get a certain trait to express in the first generation—like a recessive flower color form. In the first generation of this cross, there will be what's known as hybrid vigor—good growth, good flowering, good fitness, but not seed that comes true to that specific trait the hybrid was expressing. For that, the breeder needs to cross the same two parent lines again—and offer out another F1 generation of plants. An F2 generation, which you get when you cross the F1s with their parents or with each other, or with their children, would begin to express inbreeding depression because the recessive genetics would have no opportunity to be masked by or mixed up with other genetics that have been bred out of the line. Which, if expanded exponentially, could endanger the health and survival of the species as a whole.

JULY 18

Seedswoman Shanyn Siegel is one of those plantspeople who has frequently "moved camps" in agriculture and horticulture, always looking for one single scientific discipline or agronomic field that would have "the most" impact on improving the sustainability and health of our world. She worked in sustainable agriculture and then sustainable horticulture, specializing in organic vegetable gardening and organic seed production. With deep interest in the "hard sciences," she took a degree in soil science from the University of Massachusetts Amherst and went on to work in plant pathology. The study of pathology, and therefore resilience and resistance, "inevitably led to a closer study of genetics, and that led to an even deeper interest in seed—and their amazing genetic diversity."

Siegel honed her seed conservation skills as collection curator and head of preservation for Seed Savers Exchange (SSE) from early 2008 to late 2012 and through 2014 as part of the team working on *The Seed Garden*, a comprehensive guide to "the art and science" of seed saving published in 2015 as a joint project of SSE and the Organic Seed Alliance. While at SSE, Siegel brought the seed bank up to international standards: sorting, categorizing, and combining duplicate species, varieties, and cultivars; and improving record keeping, labeling, storing, and germination testing for the longevity and purity of the collection.

Working with SSE's large ex situ conservation bank, however, eventually left Siegel feeling removed from the "on-the-ground conservation of ecosystems, and their ongoing adaptability in the landscape." In part her interest in being a bigger part of field conservation came up because at SSE, she was working with edible cultivars, bred by humans for centuries—plants already selected (and therefore narrowed down genetically) for their traits and genetic expression. She realized she wanted to work more with wild genetic resource conservation, "where you're not dealing with prepackaged sets of genes [cultivars], but the wild assortment of all genes out in the universe."

She turned her focus to maintaining the diversity within both natural ecosystems and food crops, "making sure we are conserving all of these resources, because it is that genetic diversity that enables us and plants themselves to adapt into the future." This took her to the Mid-Atlantic Regional Seed Bank, the seed bank of the Greenbelt Native Plant Center (GNPC), a facility of the New York City Department of Parks and Recreation that comprises a 13-acre greenhouse, a nursery, and seed bank complex on Staten Island.

The GNPC grows native plants for New York City projects using only local ecotypes (a population of a species that is adapted to local conditions and survives as a distinct group). Their seed is sourced from native plant populations in the NYC metropolitan regions, and healthy populations are sought out as close to home as possible, within the 25 counties that cover the 100-mile radius of NYC, 14 counties in New Jersey, and one county in Connecticut.

Realizing the risk of outbreeding depression in the restoration of lands or the creation of new native plant habitat gardens was a big epiphany for Siegel. Understanding the ways in "which non-locally native seed affects wild plant genetics and the wild seed bank and any plants or seeds' long-term adaptability is of real concern."

Back in the west, the California Plant Rescue is a "collaborative of not-for-profit botanical institutions working under the auspices of the Center for Plant Conservation to conserve the wild species of California and the California Floristic Province, primarily through field work and long-term seed bank collections." The goal of the member organizations including California Botanic Garden, California Native Plant Society, and the Theodore Payne Foundation, and partners, from the California Department of Fish and Wildlife down to local agencies and governments, is to conserve as seed or living collection the entire California flora in conservation collections, with an emphasis on seed collections, but more importantly to have secured all of the more than 1000 listed rare plants by 2025. In part these collections "provide the raw materials for the enhancement, restoration and reintroduction of wild plant populations, while also providing an insurance policy against extinction." Simultaneously, the work improves the scientific knowledge around these plants' biology and ecology via field observations, germination testing, and propagation, increasing the success of "comprehensive strategies for plant conservation and recovery."

When Siegel states emphatically that "we need on-the-ground conservation, seed banking, and seed-grown ecosystem restoration ... we need it all," she equally and adamantly notes her belief that "all" includes "people enjoying their home landscapes—the joy of gardening and horticulture and loving plants the way they are." In her mind, "this is key."

Both Siegel and McCargo highlighted the importance of the process and the patience required but also the deep enjoyment of gardening with seed. McCargo emphasized "facing our own fears and the future by investing in and planting with patience and care seeds that we will never see mature in our lifetime." The work of these women, and organizations such as Wild Seed Project, the Mid-Atlantic Regional Seed Bank, Greenbelt Native Plant Center, California Plant Rescue, and the Center for Plant Conservation, seem to me to model the joy, faith, and great expectations of gardening wherever we are.

As noted, Tim Johnson, now the director of the Botanic Garden of Smith College, was Siegel's colleague at SSE. He pointed out a connection between these aspects of joy, faith, and great expectations as they relate to the uptick in seed orders at the beginning of the pandemic: "Even though we know it is more expensive to grow our own food in small home gardens, there is a recurring reverse correlation between the economy and an interest in gardens and seeds. The economy tanks and people turn to gardens and to seeds. The economy 'improves' and there's a downturn in garden and seed sales."

How do we transcend this? How do we use this 2020-and-onward moment of social, environmental, and economic interest in seeds to deepen these seed-born interests beyond the reach of economic fluctuations? Because as Johnson's economy and gardening correlation implies, it's not actually about money—it's about something else. It's much more about being human, what it is to be alive, and a strong desire to survive well.

JULY 23: FULL MOON
It is the full Holly Moon according to the Celtic full moon tree calendar, but if you ask the plant community of our canyon, it's the full smoke moon, full young-buckeye-conker moon, full narrowleaf-milkweed-bloom moon …

Yesterday another fire sparked, not far from the Dixie Fire, and the two have merged, becoming the single largest fire of the year so far. The smoke rolls in and out with the wind, but someone (plant or human) is always in its path for better or worse. Poor air quality is being registered as far away as Denver. The sun is a red orb by day, and even if the Delta variant of COVID-19 were not a concern, the smoke would force us to keep our masks on.

The fire has grown to 167,430 acres with 18 percent containment. Governor Gavin Newsom declared a state of emergency for Plumas, Butte (our county), Lassen, and Alpine Counties. We have John's important documents at my house in town, his important items—family photos, etc.—ready to go in the car at a moment's notice. Even in town, I have these same things ready in case we are asked to evacuate, as we were in 2018.

I know this is no different for natural or cultural disaster refugees the world over. It is the state of the world and the mindset from which our decisions about the future of the world—including how we view and care for seed—must be, *are* being made.

JULY 28

Maybe the problem with large-scale consolidated seed is twofold—or threefold? At first glance it is about greed; at second glance perhaps it is both greed and bullying. Dominating aspects of our human natures? The same traits that drove the Crusades and the imperial age in search of "a New World." But maybe these are coupled with not only our most overbearing selves, but our most scared selves, cautious and anxious about our own survival?

The impulse that leads us to hoard food, the impulse that leads us to hover over our children and hold them back—from driving or fledging or individuating from us in any way because we are afraid of losing them, because we are afraid for their survival without us, and our own survival hinged to theirs?

I hear all of this in the undertones of mass seed production: a desire to own, to control—but also to protect. In varying degrees and measure it is a fascinating calculus and cocktail of anxiety combined with aggression combined with arrogance combined—again—with our deepest seated/ seeded existential insecurity.

Seeds are both like and not like our children, and in most respects we are like and not like their children. In so many ways, over and over again, we are born of and beholden to them, learning from them even as we germinate and grow them out and on.

There are many leaders and teachers and mentors in the world doing this work at various layers, levels, lenses, but can enough of us learn from these leaders and the seeds themselves the traits of patience, listening, persistence, faith, and adaptability?

Seed Memory

NEW MOON, AUGUST 9
FULL MOON, AUGUST 22

AUGUST 2

John has cleared out one of the raised beds in the fenced vegetable garden for fall crops: our first succession planting of favorite winter spinach and carrots, both of which always seem so out of place in this apex of summer's heat—112 degrees Fahrenheit and dry, breezy today, smoke from the Dixie Fire rolling in and out. The idea of cool winter days, of the rainy season, of fresh, cold carrots and crisp spinach winter crops seems very far away. Almost unimaginable.

Spinach trials in the home garden this season include Palco (*Spinacia oleracea* 'Palco F1') from Territorial Seed up in Oregon; Red Malabar spinach (*Basella rubra*) from Johnny's Selected Seeds in Maine, 'Flamingo F1 true spinach', also from Johnny's, and finally, from Redwood Seeds, just an hour or so northeast of us in Northern California, a packet of 'Winter Bloomsdale'. Redwood describes it as "our favorite for early-spring overwintered spinach production. Heavy, Savoy-type, thick leaves, with great flavor. Winter hardy in well-drained soils yielding the first field spinach of the year." John likes the way these heavier leaved spinaches cook up with eggs in the morning, in pasta dishes, in soups.

For carrots (*Daucus carota* var. *sativus*), we go with organic 'Scarlet Nantes' from the Living Seed Company over in Point Reyes Station on the California coast; heirloom 'Kuroda', a carrot from Botanical Interests seed supplier out of the Denver area; organic 'Rotild' snacking carrot, from Renee's Garden, now based in central California; and, finally, we try a variety recommended by John's daughter: 'Scarlet Keeper'—a workhorse carrot!—from High Desert Seed and Gardens in Montrose, Colorado.

In an illustration of how short the distance can be between our most common produce choices and their wild progenitors, one relative of our common eating carrot is Queen Anne's lace, (*Daucus carota*), an invasive species in much of the United States, including this canyon.

John and I are not—and in our independent paths to our now shared path, have never been—bent on eating only our own produce or bent on any notions of "self-sufficiency." We are bent on maintaining the joy, effort, process (sanity), and passion of engaging with soil and the tiniest forays into our own survival—entwined with the pleasure of seasonal produce and seasonal shifts in our landscapes. Seasonal understandings and love of food, flowers, and forage.

Our own edible gardening efforts add salt (as it were, via sweat equity), amplify the real work of the farmers, the land, climatic processes, and appreciation of the beloved plants. For us, these are the real sufficiencies.

AUGUST 3
We try to plant our carrot seed while the moon is waning, toward the new moon on the ninth, purportedly the best time to plant root crops (whose energy grows down); but, we also know that historically the seeds and greens of carrots were of medicinal and culinary interest and so tell ourselves it seems OK to sow the seed in the waxing moon (drawing the energy up) too.

Many cultures still honor traditions by singing songs of praise and gratitude, welcome and wonder, to their ancestral seeds. These are the seeds most associated with their foodways, medicinal knowledge, rituals, and long-term coevolutionary survival.

Rowen White of Sierra Seeds in Northern California—whose blog is actually entitled *SeedSongs*—regularly speaks of the importance of offering song and prayers for seeds as sacred members of one's family and community. Chris Bolden-Newsome, a fourth-generation Black farmer, speaks of his father offering blessings over their seed. In *The Unlikely Peace at Cuchumaquic: The Parallel Lives of People as Plants: Keeping the Seeds Alive*, Puebloan spiritual leader and author Martin Prechtel notes that by offering blessings or prayers to seeds, we are recognizing the "holy in nature." Vivien Sansour of the Palestine Heirloom Seed Library shared with me a Palestinian blessing traditionally offered over newly sown seed: "May we eat and be able to feed others. It's up to God and it depends on our service—our service to the plant, our service to the soil." She says, "The seed, the seed, the seed—what is it but a continuation of ourselves? Aren't we all seeds?"

I try to think of seed songs or prayers that have come down through my own mashed-up European descent—and very few come to mind, one or two nursery rhymes at most. Given that I am a gardener with at least five known gardening generations before me on both sides of my family, why are these few rhymes/songs the only ones I know or can conjure up in my own garden life? Does this affect how we Europeans as a whole have treated the earth? I think it might.

AUGUST 5

Rowen White, to my mind, is the unofficial poet laureate of Seed, with a capital existential S.

Over the past several decades, cultural seed keepers have been striving to not only recover the diversity of their specific peoples' seeds and foods, but also associated ceremonies and rituals. These seed keepers and teachers are striving to imprint the importance of integrity, not as a form of cultural separatism, but to strengthen the global collective memory about the importance of diversity and the gifts (and seeds) fundamental to that. There has been enough of perpetuating pervasive homogeneity. Indigenous seed people are among the most vocal and visible of this caliber of seed teachers, and leading voices include White, Prechtel, Sansour, and many others who mentored them and whom they have mentored.

White was born within Akwesasne, a Kanien'kéha (Mohawk) community along the Saint Lawrence River, which is bisected by what is now the border between upstate New York and Canada. Her parents worked on "legal issues defending Indigenous sovereignty, such as land and water rights, including for the Native American Rights Fund." While at Hampshire College as an undergraduate student assigned to care for an heirloom tomato seed collection being planted out at the college farm, White discovered for herself the capacity of seeds to transmit cultural stories and histories, and to see in that their potential to enliven cultural understanding and identity. Of this epiphany, she wrote, "I think equal to my joy and enthusiasm in learning and opening this new doorway of understanding was this palpable sense of grief and longing. Understanding that as a Mohawk woman, as someone who understands who I am and where I come from, that we are and continue to be agricultural people, and yet I had no idea of the foods that fed my ancestors, and no sense of intimacy with or responsibility to them." She determined to draw on the energy of both that joy and grief "to set out on a path to discover the foods of my ancestors and really begin to renew what I eventually found out were the original agreements that we had with these plants to take care of them. It is through these relationships with plants and seeds that I'm finding my way home to a deeper understanding of being human."

After she and her young family relocated to Northern California in the early 2000s, White started a seed business born of her new community, a region that is home to a vibrant local food and farmer network. But she soon realized that what people really wanted and needed as well as seeds were the tools and skills to "follow that passion all the way back to the seed, to knowing who is taking care of the seed and stewarding it." As a result, White moved the direction of Sierra Seeds, of her land-based seed bank kiva, and of her own leadership work firmly toward education around seed literacy and seed-related cultural preservation— what she describes as "rehydration."

White has developed Seed Seva, an ongoing and seasonally based eight-month mentorship curriculum to educate and steward new seed keepers and seed growers. Throughout it, White shares her own seed knowledge, history, and relationships— from the basis of both Western academic science and her own ancestral, and lived, Indigenous cosmologic, spiritual, and cultural experience and scholarship. She includes lessons on seed care and cultivation from a wide variety of seed leaders: plantspeople and breeders such as Dr. Alan Kapuler, cofounder with his wife, Linda, of Peace Seeds; and Frank Morton, cofounder with his wife, Karen, of Wild Garden Seed, both in Oregon and both dedicated to open-source seed and seed breeding. Seed Seva also honors culture keepers and gardeners such as Mary Arquette and Winona LaDuke.

Through the eight months of "educational modules," White leads each cohort of students to engage with themselves and with each other around questions of their own seed ancestry and seed-impacted experiences. She encourages students to foster a loving, responsible, and reciprocal relationship to seed. She writes, "By bridging both practical hands-on skills with Indigenous knowledge and reverence, we are cultivating a way of seed stewardship that is based upon service to life and seeds. Finding ourselves again by rekindling a relationship with our food that is mutually beneficial, and truly honors the seeds for all that they continue to share with us. Writing ourselves back into the story of the sacred dance between humans and plants that is dynamic, evolutionary and resilient. Seeds are sacred."

White draws particularly on her deeply personal perspective, "beyond the biological and scientific aspects of seeds." In her experience, when we "engage the heart and engage the layers of that spiritual and emotional and cultural connection, it rehydrates cellular memory, like a dormant seed. We are all bound in a reciprocal relationship with plants and seeds, and that reconnection builds true sustainability into the system." She sees hope in "a great resurgence of Indigenous tribes building healthy and resilient food systems as a cornerstone to cultural and ecological renewal programs, as well as a means to reclaim Indigenous economies and true economic and political sovereignty."

She serves on the board of the Native American Food Sovereignty Alliance and has been instrumental in forming the Indigenous Seed Keepers Network (ISKN), a formal intertribal group that works to secure funding, share skills, and prioritize. They seek to find or create "culturally appropriate solutions to restoring seed stewardship of traditional foods," and are working toward creating a seed bank/library and training for Indigenous mentors.

White is a powerful, poetic, and fierce advocate for seed rematriation—reintroducing seeds into their communities and places of origin. Rematriation, she says, "is an intentional shift of word choice from repatriation of things to their tribal origins, because seeds are traditionally the responsibility of women, and it speaks as well of seeds returning to the Mother Earth." The ISKN works with organizations housing historic collections of Indigenous seed to find where "seed important to tribal communities might exist outside of their mother communities" and to return them home. These include Seed Savers Exchange, Chicago's Field Museum of Natural History, the University of Michigan, the Science Museum of Minnesota, the Yale Peabody Museum, and many other institutions.

Although ancient and ancestral seed ceremonies have not always passed through generations intact for a wide variety of reasons, the destruction wrought by colonialism across the globe high among them, White points out that Indigenous cultures still refer to seeds as relatives, part of a worldview where all living things share kinship. Indigenous coalitions are developing "new ceremonies and songs to welcome [the seeds] back home into the rich soil of our everyday lives." This in turn is working to heal the ongoing "intergenerational trauma and rage" and disenfranchisement of Indigenous peoples, deeply affected by colonization and acculturation.

"In cultivating trusting relationships with people who have historically been our adversaries," she says, such as institutions that took and have held heritage seeds, "when we lay down those differences and look to the seeds and this work with the seeds, we find a means of reconciliation and reparation."

White also sees a deeper revolution brewing, as more people examine food, economic, and justice systems that do not serve the majority of people: "Staring down industrialized food systems and GMOs will take us all reclaiming our responsibilities for our relationships with seeds, plants, food. That reclaiming can be healing—it can be glorious and healing and beautiful and flavorful."

AUGUST 6

Elizabeth Hoover is another seed-forward woman who has spent her academic career (currently an anthropologist and associate professor in the Department of Environmental Science, Policy, and Management at University of California, Berkeley) immersed in cultural seed and food preservation and documentation. This has often translated into seed and seed knowledge rematriation, often in concert with Rowen White.

In their work, both women are working to deconstruct and reimagine the boundaries, constraints, and capacities of the often-exclusionary social and cultural constructs like "academia," "success," and "accomplishment."

The daughter of avid gardening parents, Hoover says that she's "been with the seeds and the plants in the dirt since I could move around. Both my parents did a lot of gardening, and my dad was very serious about it." While doing the research for her dissertation, Hoover interned at Akwesasne, the Kanien'kéha Nation's homeland, where she worked with cultural seed keepers Mary and Dave Arquette and the Akwesasne Task Force on the Environment (ATFE). Finding and returning seeds original to the people of Akwesasne, as well as other Indigenous tribes, became integral to Hoover's ongoing academic research. Hoover spent the summer of 2014 traveling North America to document Indigenous seed, food, plants, and gardens for a book project titled *From "Garden Warriors" to "Good Seeds": Indigenizing the Local Food Movement*, with an eye to providing interconnection and therefore increased support among the many growing endeavors.

Hoover credits the title of her project to the Indigenous cultural seed and garden work of Dream of Wild Health, led by Diane Wilson in Minnesota when Hoover served as a volunteer. "Good Seeds" comes from the English translation of a Mohawk organization at Akwesasne: Kanenhi:io Ionkwaienthon:hakie, or "We Are Planting Good Seeds." This title, Hoover points out "refers not just to the organic and Haudenosaunee [according to the ATFE, the Mohawk Nation is one of the original five nations of the Haudenosaunee or Iroquois Confederacy] heritage seeds that they are planting in the community garden, but also the knowledge and motivation they hope to instill in fellow community members."

More recently, Hoover's work has focused on getting recognition for groups restoring horticultural knowledge to their fellow community members and encouraging more people to garden and eat healthy food, and in so doing come to know their culturally important seeds, which can even mean that "conversations at night over cups of tea after long days of pulling weeds or breeding corn center around how to fund these garden projects, how to get more community members interested, how to involve more youth."

Hoover also embraces helping heritage varieties persist by growing her own "plump scarlet runner beans, climbing dark-red cranberry beans, blackish-purple Haudenosaunee sweet corn, towering Seneca stripe sunflowers," relishing how "seeds are now passed among friends and relatives rather than purchased from a conglomerate."

Another active contributor to the Indigenous seed movement is Pat Gwin, senior director for the Cherokee Nation's Environmental Resources group. He was educated in biology, botany, wildlife sciences, and chemistry, and has written about the history and early years of the Cherokee Nation Seed Bank (CNSB), which was catalyzed in 2005 and 2006 by the optimism surrounding the imminent opening of the Svalbard Global Seed Vault. The CNSB serves members of the Cherokee Nation and is based in Oklahoma, where the Cherokee were forcibly relocated by the US government in the 1830s from their traditional homelands in parts of what are now North Carolina, Tennessee, Georgia, and Alabama.

Gwin emphasizes the statistics that "some 100,000 American Indians were forcibly removed from what is now the eastern United States to what was called Indian Territory, including members of the Cherokee, Choctaw, Chickasaw, Creek, and Seminole tribes." Gwin compares and contrasts the seed growing, tending, selecting, and saving done by his ancestors in 1491 with his and his team's work today trying to establish and relocate any of the descendants of the seeds of their ancestors with which to populate their own cultural seed bank—even if it must be in a very different climate. To date, the CNSB collection includes history-rich seeds such as 'Cherokee Tan Pumpkin', 'Cherokee White Eagle Corn', 'Trail of Tears Beans', several gourd selections, Indian corn beads, and native plants including 'Rattlesnake Master' (*Eryngium yuccifolium*), 'Wild Senna' (*Senna hebecarpa*), and 'Possum Grape' (*Vitis cinerea*).

The CNSB sourced their first collection of heritage Cherokee seed from Carl Leon "White Eagle" Barnes in the Oklahoma panhandle, from Kevin Welch and Sarah McClellan-Welch of the Eastern Band of Cherokee, and from the Science Museum of Minnesota Native American exhibition. In their first 10 years, the CNSB expanded to maintaining, growing, storing, and sharing "approximately 5000 packages of seed each year with Cherokees and educational institutions that cater to Cherokees." They grew to include the husbandry of wild plants and the native plant garden "that supplies the Seed Bank and in which they maintain more than one hundred varieties of plants." Each year, Gwin notes, Cherokee "elders request that other plants be added to the site. Simply displaying culturally important plants is then no longer enough; culturally appropriate propagation is required to allow for annual harvesting and use to perpetuate [ritual] and traditions."

Gwin reminds us of an old Cherokee saying: "No self-respecting Cherokee would ever be without a corn patch," and says "it was the plants that kept them alive and, in fact, what made them Cherokee. One could not exist without the other."

If we as humans see ourselves in our seed, perhaps our seed can help us see and save the best of who and what we are.

AUGUST 7

I have a slurry of black cherry tomato pulp and seeds in a glass jelly jar in the pantry. I rinse living bacterial and fermenting fungal goop off them daily, helping to prepare their seed coat so I can then dry and save them for sowing next spring. They are our favorite cherry tomato but have been hard to find the last few years and so we are hoping to grow our own seedlings next season.

❖

Earlier this year I attended a virtual event hosted by *Emergence Magazine* about the cultural healing capacity of food. The event featured speakers Rowen White; Lisa Lee Herrick, a second-generation Hmong writer; and Kalyanee Mam, a Cambodian American writer.

The three discussed the cultural power of food and "the memories encoded within seed," and this phrase drew me in. I am white, of English-Scot-Irish descent. My maternal grandfather came to the United States in the 1920s as a polo player and horse trainer—in many ways to get away from, to "succeed" beyond a life of often impoverished land-based subsistence. He told us a strongly imagistic story of being one of five children growing up very poor in Melton Mowbray, England. My grandfather and his brothers would "borrow" their mother's only heeled shoes to sneak into the neighboring fields and steal potatoes to stave off hunger. My paternal family immigrated from Scotland, Northern Ireland, and England a century or so earlier and worked in belt factories and railroads on the East Coast for generations. There is little to no consistent occupation or preoccupation in my bloodlines of recent memory aside from the sheer work of trying to make a living in an increasingly industrialized world, where every societal positive-reinforcement cue—dollars, enough food to eat, social status—led many people away from the land.

Interestingly, among my ancestors was a "successful" florist in New York City who lived at the turn of the twentieth century, but it was the building he bought for the business, not the floristry, that, at least on paper, sustained his children. Both my grandfathers were lovers of flowers as well as vegetables, and they grew and tended both—my English grandfather, the polo player and horse trainer, grew tea roses, camellias, magnolias, and the front of his house in South Carolina was draped each spring in the fragrant purple clusters of wisteria flowers. In late spring and summer as the pods of the wisteria ripened and dried, there would come a day when they would blast open—the torque of the drying and constricting putting pressure on the seams of the softly downy pod and then *Bam!* The whole front porch was alive with seeds pelleting and ricocheting across the floor, walls, onto the hot summer South Carolina gravel drive.

My paternal grandfather, living outside of Boston, Massachusetts, his entire life other than four years serving in the navy during World War II, lovingly tended a series of spring flowering fruit trees and an adored asparagus bed. He grew old-fashioned gladiolus, nasturtiums, zinnias, and scabiosa in summer as cut flowers, which were displayed inside the house all summer. The small, brain-like seeds of the nasturtiums were the first seeds I saved and grew myself. The leading edge of their dark green lily pad leaves peeking out of the soil remains an incredible revelation to me. Their edible and tropical, spurred orange, red, and yellow flowers equally so. Was a few generations of people immigrating and living in urban areas all it took to lose our cultural ties to seed, to so easily shift to cultivating only what we find aesthetically pleasing, even though the urge to cultivate *something* clearly endures? How did we lose so quickly any allegiance to the seed that sustained our family in earlier times?

These questions make what White, Herrick, and Mam talk about—even deeper memory—all the more fascinating. Each of their cultures has retained memories of growers and tenders in a longer, expansive seed line—not unbroken (horrifically), but strong and more visible (audible) daily as a result of these seed and culture keepers' cultivation. They have seed stories about nourishing foods, and these stories now feed them spiritually and creatively through the act of telling them, even if history has reduced them to somewhat faint traces, as far as they can see, find, and feel, in their lineage.

How do you root out, reroot, in order to hear stories that have been unspoken, to hear songs that have been unsung for so very long? We need pathways that allow for empathy, insight, understanding, song, and celebration. Merely understanding the physical science of seed doesn't make the act of growing truly satisfying—we need the epigenetics as well as the genetics. Many voices and hands from many cultures are modeling and offering just these kinds of pathways to us all.

AUGUST 8

The days are hot—118 degrees Fahrenheit in the forecast this coming week. Nighttime lows are in the midsixties, which makes the days more bearable. We manage the canyon house with very little if any air conditioning by opening windows at night and closing them in the morning before the temperatures begin to rise. The oaks around the house provide daytime shade—but by late afternoon the warmth is oppressive. The creek makes this easier to handle, and we often walk down with a beer in the late afternoons to wade, swim, paddle, cool off—it is a luxury we are grateful for beyond measure.

Along the creek's edges, the now-many cattail seed heads are cinnamon colored, downy with their millions of tiny seeds packed together, torchlike. They form their flowering stalk with the pollen-producing portion situated at the top of the stalk, and the seed-producing portion just below it. In some species of *Typha*, these two portions are contiguous; in others they are separated by a few millimeters. It is clear in seed as in all manner of life that we each need some full spectrum of expression. As the seeds ripen, the breezes and the rustling of their lower leaves will send a few of the tiny, tiny seeds—just visible bits of fluff floating on air currents—down the creek.

On the oaks, acorns are forming, not as many this year as last—the result of now extended drought. But they are there. Slowly fattening up in the way that these trees (and their kin across the Northern Hemisphere) have formed their fruits for millions of years.

Aldo Leopold once sagely wrote, "Preserving every cog and every wheel is one of the best calculations of intelligent design."

And might we add, saving every seed?

AUGUST 9: NEW MOON

We have been hearing a screech-owl in the early evenings recently and this morning saw a large and serenely white-faced barn owl sitting—still and undisturbed by us—in the twisty branching of a blue oak across from where John's driveway meets the dirt road. We were surprised and pleased. It always feels auspicious to see other lives not part of your everyday—a veil lifted, a reminding hint at all that we do not know, do not see, and yet is just right there, beyond our most obvious radius of attention and awareness.

Some of our favorite seedeater companions on the road, the acorn woodpeckers, are noisy and beginning to liven up the canyon. Here year-round, these matriarchal communities are most vocal, social, and active as summer begins to wane with the acorns coming on, and in spring with nesting.

The universal concept of "mothering"—mother plants, matriarchy, matriation, matrilineal—is a recurring theme in the seed world, for obvious and human-narrative reasons. Women have been traditional seed keepers; seed-bearing plants display sometimes female-associated characteristics—producing offspring being among them; and then there is the sheer love of, respect for, concern over our own "mother" earth and her maternal and generous abundance on which we as a species have depended and continue to depend. But if the plant world teaches us anything, it is that much of life is way beyond any binary definition of female/male—and that it's profoundly reliant on a savory cocktail of diversity.

The seedways of Indigenous North American cultures are not alone in experiencing a renaissance of leadership voices in caring and cultural seed work. Descendants of land-based cultures around the world are likewise finding and reclaiming their seed and their voices in defense of a worldview and a future imbued with respect for the natural world, for the processes of life, for ancestral knowledge, and for the symbolic and literal power of seed as we collectively face the uncertain future.

Owen Smith Taylor and Chris Bolden-Newsome are the cofounders of Truelove Seeds, "a spiritually rooted cultural-preservation and rematriation-focused seed company" on half an acre outside of Philadelphia, Pennsylvania. "Lifting up the idea and hope of collective cultural evolution." Taylor and Bolden-Newsome believe that through their own "ancestral work" with seed—each of them individually researching what human ancestral seeds (and roots) they could—they found each other, and in this way their "ancestors arranged" their 2012 marriage.

They are firm in acknowledging that doing this kind of work is entirely different for a person of European descent (Taylor) than it is for people of Indigenous ancestry, of African (Bolden-Newsome), or Asian or any other "nonwhite European" ancestry. As Rowen White, whom Taylor and Bolden-Newsome consider among their mentors, shared, this kind of cultural seed work not only uncovers lost seeds and seed stories, but history of "trauma, devastation, erasure, loss, and elimination."

For Taylor, it is both "heartbreaking and hopeful that people are so hungry, literally and spiritually, for information on this level." He's found that "people are excited to learn. To meet a new plant is still magical access, one that is important to humans throughout time." Plants that make us "us" and make home "home" are of particular interest to him. He really wants to understand how any plant that represents "home" for someone works, and how he can help that plant and its seeds make it to the next generation. "We've had 10,000 years on this planet saving and working with seeds. To be here now in the United States, where the majority of humans have a difficult time recognizing where seed actually is on a plant, is phenomenal." It is not like this for the entire world, he pointed out; much of the world is absolutely still living within and reliant on local land-based food and seed supply. This is one of the reasons Taylor likes working with the enormous diversity of immigrant populations in the Philadelphia area, "who come with such different, and rich, cultural plant and seed literacy and knowledge to share."

For Taylor and Bolden-Newsome, their focus not only on seed of their own ancestries but on the history held within that seed are of equal importance, another recurring theme in cultural seed work. This dual purpose is manifested in their seed-growing, seed-keeping, and teaching work. To reintroduce this knowledge and these skills to others, they invite in seasonal apprentices and volunteers. "To help steward the culture keeping of the work" is just as vital to Truelove as the seed keeping itself. "Because you can help teach someone how to save the seed, but you cannot tell their story unless that story is yours. Otherwise, it must be told by them. And this is true for each of us."

Prior to cofounding Truelove with Bolden-Newsome, Taylor's preliminary seed education included four years apprenticing and working with William Woys Weaver, an internationally known food ethnographer and author focused on culinary history and heritage seeds. He is the founder of the Roughwood Center for Heritage Seedways, a nonprofit devoted to heritage foods from heritage seeds. In 1932, his grandfather, H. Ralph Weaver, established "the oldest private seed collection in the Eastern United States [which by some estimates] houses the largest collection of Native American seeds in the country." Since Weaver discovered and took up caring for the collection in the 1970s, it has expanded to "over 5000 varieties of heirloom food plants seed."

Simultaneous to Taylor's work with the Roughwood collection, he and Bolden-Newsome were invited in the early 2010s to be part of a "seed keepers collective" and to attend the annual Great Lakes Indigenous Farming Conference in northern Minnesota. This was where they "really began to learn the histories and ideas of seed stories, seed rituals, and seed songs." They were sent home with a mandate from the conference elders "to start their own seed networks." When he looked at the Weaver collection again, Taylor was struck by how few of the seeds actually connected to either his or Weaver's personal family stories.

When Taylor and Bolden-Newsome launched Truelove Seeds in 2017, Taylor asked himself, "How do I start a seed company selling seeds of meaning to me, not just other people's seeds? And how do I help other people tell their own stories and learn to tell my own story in my own words through this work?" Their answer: offering open-pollinated seeds grown by more than 50 small-scale urban and rural farmers committed to community food sovereignty, cultural preservation, and sustainable agriculture. Taylor asks everyone who works at Truelove Seeds farm, as well as all 50 of the farms from which they source seed, to identify at least one seed that tells their ancestral story in some way. Through interactions both purposeful and serendipitous, Taylor has found and been given meaningful seeds speaking to both his Irish and Italian ancestry. He does this to support each person on the team in their own ancestral work, "and because it immediately infuses their engagement with the seeds with so much depth and meaning ... it makes it personal." He hopes this will not only last for their lifetime but will be something they pass on to the next generation. In addition to Rowen White, Taylor counts Ira Wallace of Southern Exposure Seed Collective in Virginia, and Leah Penniman of Soul Fire Farm in upstate New York as his mentors on this life path, and as "Mama Ira Wallace reminds us, our seeds are among our greatest family heirlooms."

"If we are ever going to address seed (and cultural) blindness and apathy," Bolden-Newsome believes it needs to be through this kind of powerful and "attached work, not detached curiosity but deeply rooted personal value."

Bolden-Newsome, originally from the Mississippi Delta, is the oldest son of farmers and justice workers Demalda Bolden-Newsome and Rufus Newsome Sr., as well as being "a fourth-generation free farmer since emancipation in 1865." Following natural agriculture practices, Bolden-Newsome focuses on "cultivating healthy soil for life-giving crops while learning and teaching Pan-African practices in farming and foodways."

He is also cofounder and codirector with Tyler Holmberg of the Sankofa Community Farm at Bartram's Garden in Philadelphia, on the grounds of the historic house and garden of renowned 1770s colonial European North American botanists and plant and seed collectors John Bartram and his son, William Bartram. For Bolden-Newsome, working with community, students, and plants at Sankofa is "focused on the seed stories of southern African Americans in the north. Encouraging all people to find out how we got here." The seed keepers gathering at the Indigenous Farming Conference in Minnesota really illustrated for Bolden-Newsome how the "seed becomes metaphor, and text and story, and therefore sacred. A vessel for culture." He described how meaningful it has been to seek out people who can flesh out the stories in the seeds and imbue them with meaning: "How they use the leaves, how they use the seed, how they cook the fruit ... it's on par with sacrament."

The Sankofa Community Farm at Bartram's Garden is a beautiful and intentional overlay and re-envisioning of one time period's practices and paradigms with new ones, often working to compost the travesties of the past. "To develop an African focus for [Bartram's] farm's core purpose," where it had long held an acquisitive and colonial focus, Bolden-Newsome and Holmberg engaged in many conversations with the "community gardeners, student interns, and local leaders." The concept of Sankofa is derived from King Adinkera of the Akan people of West Africa. Sankofa is expressed in the Akan language as *se wo were fi na wosan kofa a yenkyi*. Literally translated, it means, "It is not taboo to go back and fetch what you forgot." As Bolden-Newsome elaborates, in this context, it symbolically includes what people were forced to leave behind.

Taylor and Bolden-Newsome consciously carry seeds with them—in their pockets, in their wallets, as an invitation to their ancestors to "walk with them" as they teach and live. When they were looking for a new house and farm after losing the lease on their original land, they carried fava beans in their pockets, in an embodied prayer asking for Saint Joseph to help them in their search—Taylor has Italian ancestry and Bolden-Newsome is Catholic. "Once you put this kind of quest out into the universe, you get so many different answers," Taylor observed.

Bolden-Newsome was holding two different peas in his mouth as we spoke, "preparing them to sow and having them keep him company." Bolden-Newsome also almost always keeps a black-eyed pea in his pocket or wallet, which he explained "is a custom in Mississippi for Black people as a protective and grounding force, because this pea is a symbol of prosperity in southern African culture, and they are said to be the eye of God."

AUGUST 29

I am home after three weeks on the road for both work and family. Family time included driving my eldest daughter across the country to begin her own adult life, move into an apartment, and start a new job.

This morning, I sat in this daughter's bedroom and realized that she will likely never come home for good again.

It is my first real experience with empty-nester syndrome, and I found myself sobbing. Sobbing like my 33-year-old self after the death of my mother. Weeping inconsolably.

To be clear, I would not have it any other way; I am happy, my life is full and satisfying. And, after all, this was the goal all along: for them to grow, to mature, to disperse. To keep an emotional bond, but not need to be physically close or in my shadow. Do plants and other animals feel this?

Maxine Kumin's poem "The Envelope," which I read at my mother's memorial on a warm early-summer day beside the South Carolina tidal marsh she loved, comes to mind. In the poem, we—me, my mother and

grandmothers, my aunts, my two sisters, my two daughters—are all
nested vessels tucked inside one another.

I am not (by far) the first, won't by far be the last, to know: We are all seed
inside seed inside seed. We are all doing what we can to fly, to prepare,
to root and leaf out, to flower, and to successfully set some manner
of seed ourselves for a future we cannot know and can only intend to
seed well.

AUGUST 30

John tells me it is the first clearish morning in weeks. The heat and
dryness of the season, and smoke from the ongoing Dixie Fire have all
escalated. The air quality index, or AQI, an acronym I was not familiar
with until 2018 when the Camp Fire burned through our region and left us
breathing smoke for months, is as low as it's been in that same time.

The Dixie Fire, which is now the single largest fire in the state's history,
has burned 756,768 acres, is at 48 percent containment, and has had up
to 5982 total personnel dedicated to it. On August 18, the Dixie, "burning
on the Plumas National Forest, Lassen National Forest, Lassen Volcanic National Park, and in five counties: Butte, Lassen, Plumas, Shasta,
and Tehama," became the first recorded fire to crest the massive Sierra
Nevada. The eastern flank of the fire is now described as "secure" but
the western flank (toward us) is still burning and being managed. "The
drought, combined with dry, hot weather and strong winds, has resulted
in very active fire behavior," according to local meteorologists.

Taking advantage of the clearish feeling, we walk up the road to check
in on things I have not seen in weeks because of travel and heat and
smoke. The morning is unusually quiet—blessedly free from the daily din
of helicopters overhead ferrying water back and forth from reservoirs
to fire's edge. We stop on the road and chat with a neighbor who asks
if we've been to the Oroville dam recently. We have not. He describes
a militarized zone surrounding the beleaguered dam and its severely
depleted contents. He describes multiple stations of highway patrolmen
all monitoring the feeds from live cameras positioned in, and around all
sides, of the dam structure, the overflow, the spillway. He describes vast
stretches of multi-strand razor wire worth hundreds of thousands of dollars blocking access to a dam that used to be a destination viewpoint.

We contemplate whether this newly ensconced military zone is to protect the aging infrastructure of the dam, or to protect its very, very precious water holdings.

Walking up the road, we note the slow decline of some of our biggest oaks. We are not sure what specifically ails them. Perhaps it is the combination of this year's monumental drought on top of smoky dusty heat conditions on top of the hard hit these trees took three years ago during the Camp Fire. Perhaps their immune systems were down enough that these latest insults of prolonged heat and deep drought have finally tipped them?

Senescence is a beautiful and necessary phase in life's cycle, but we still feel the sadness of losing so many at once—not knowing if it is their time or if they have, as we guess, been pushed here prematurely. We're grateful to the lives the declining trees have shared; we are grateful for those that are not in apparent decline; grateful for those that remain shading and feeding and hosting entire communities of birds and bugs and microorganisms within this watershed.

We count small numbers—this is no mast year—of fresh green acorns brightening the canopies of the vibrant oaks; every now and then you hear or see a young nut being knocked to the dirt below by squirrels or acorn woodpeckers. We walk our mile up the road to the roadside spring to see how it is faring, if it is flowing, and if so, the extent of its overflow, which will often creep into the dirt of the road itself sometimes 10 feet across the surface, sometimes 50 yards down the road. It is a handy annual barometer for water.

When we make it to the spring, the road is dry, the roadside is dry, which feels a little worrisome, and yet not unseasonal. Dryness notwithstanding, the toyon on the slope above this point in the road has set healthy, heavy clusters of fruit, the buckeye as well is speckled with buckeyes, and there's a wide colony of understory narrowleaf milkweed in full bloom, the lowest blooms having been pollinated and already set seed. The drying follicles stand brightly beneath the open blooms, waiting to open themselves and release their contents of silky plumed seed.

What any one life can and will adapt to is often surprising.

SEPTEMBER

Seeds of Culture

NEW MOON, SEPTEMBER 6
FULL MOON, SEPTEMBER 20

SEPTEMBER 2

On a day that rises with little smoke, I wake early and am greeted by the beautiful sight of a pure white, fragrant *Datura wrightii* in full bloom in my front courtyard town garden. A remarkable sight to see its white, open face on its stately tubular neck lifted to the morning—for now. Having just opened late last night, the flower will fold back into itself with the direct sun of midday. Each flower's fertile window is less than one day long.

The same plant was a phenomenon in 2019. Its arrowhead-shaped leaves increased in perfect fractal relationship, dividing and subdividing just like the limbs and branches of a tree, like the tributaries and branches of a river. It rose to almost three and a half feet tall and took over at least a four by four corner of the courtyard. By late August, the plant was at its peak bloom and each morning we'd count the number of buds that looked ready to open that evening—for one night only. Datura blooms have famously been subjects for artists throughout time, including ancient pictographic cave artists in Kern County, California, between 130 and 400 years ago, and Georgia O'Keeffe, who was painting *Datura stramonium* in the 1960s in New Mexico. The trumpet-shaped blooms reach maybe 10 inches in length, 6 to 7 inches across at the open end of the trumpet. It forms in a perfectly pleated roll, and as each bloom opens, the petal unfurls in a spiral. Near the full moon in September 2019, we had 40-plus blooms open in one evening. From late August to late September that year, John and I would stay in town and at dusk take our evening drinks to sit with the datura as her blooms audibly—a soft plosive: pft!—opened from bud to bloom. We would witness hawk moths, carpenter bees, and honeybees arrive for the nectar.

Each prickly seed pod resulting a few weeks later from these pollinated blooms is topped by a recurved and scalloped calyx, and the pods ultimately crack open from the bottom, like an upside-down sea urchin, dropping dozens of flat black seeds onto the courtyard ground. So many of the seeds that we packaged them up and gifted them forward that year.

Today, John and I leave by midmorning for the seven-hour, 400-mile drive to Southern California to visit the Theodore Payne Foundation and for a speaking engagement. The I-5 corridor running down the middle of the length of the state is an overview lesson in US history, in colonization and development—and impact. The highway is in rough disrepair, abandoned orchards—dead or dying—along either side in many stretches of the long agrarian Central Valley. As we drive, I notice over and over again along the parched roadsides and field edges masses of gently mounding, silvery gray datura plants and colonies. Sometimes known as sacred thornapple (a name descriptive of the plant's prickle-studded orbed fruit), datura (which is toxic to humans and animals in large doses) has psychoactive properties and is associated with Indigenous rituals and medicinal practices where it is native.

These same stretches of the highway are also punctuated by billboards declaring "Food Grows Where Water Flows," which date back to the 2014 drought and farm crisis. Little summer moisture ever existed here naturally, but the soils and climate developed over eons of winter water make good growing conditions—if you can pipe in the water when it is not naturally there, and when most nonnative crop plants are grown.

Overland transport from river basins, ditches, diversions, and reservoirs serves the region's vast farming needs. According to the California Department of Agriculture, in 2022, the state supplied over one-third of fresh vegetables and two-thirds of the fresh fruits and nuts for the United States. This infrastructure also supports the needs (and wants—like irrigated turf lawns) of California's human population, which has grown to 39.4 million. This human pressure has exacted a toll on the river flows, other surface and groundwater reserves, and aquifers across this reliably summer-dry landscape.

When we arrive in LA, we meet up with my two copresenters, one of whom is Kat High, an adviser of Indigenous ancestry to the Satwiwa Native American Indian Culture Center, the Autry Museum of the American West, and the Antelope Valley Indian Museum. When I mention to her how much datura we saw on the drive down, she looked at me intently and asked, "Do you know why?" Beyond the fact that these plants like full sun, good drainage, and dry, disturbed conditions without too much competition, I said I did not know.

"Because they are telling us we need more ceremony, Jennifer. We need more ceremony and attention paid, everywhere. By all of us."

❖

SEPTEMBER 3

An artistic rendition of *Datura wrightii* (artwork by California native plant artist Lesley Goren) is also featured on some of the branded T-shirts at the Theodore Payne Foundation for Wild Flowers and Native Plants (TPF), which aims to educate people about the role native plants play in the local ecology, their place in our gardens, and how everyone can take part in making our built environments "more life sustaining," starting with Southern California. Located on 22 acres of canyon land in the northeast corner of the San Fernando Valley, TPF has a long-standing full-service native plant nursery, much lauded native seed and bulb conservation program, bookstore, native plant art gallery with revolving exhibitions, and well-marked demonstration gardens prized by regional gardeners.

Seed Program Manager Genevieve Arnold, who came to TPF in 2010 after a decade working in the seed program at what is now California Botanic Garden, gives us a tour around the gardens, nursery, and seed rooms. The seed collection was started in 1903 by founder and plantsman Theodore Payne, and it is maintained and has been expanded with scrupulous care. The TPF Seed and Bulb Program tends and grows over 200 species of native wildflowers, grasses, ground covers, shrubs, trees, vines, and bulbs and includes plants grown from ethically wild-collected local seeds, on TPF grounds or permission-granted private lands, and from which all subsequent seed stock for TPF will be collected.

Arnold reiterates what Heather McCargo reinforced earlier—that the seed from these seed-grown plants will result in genetically diverse, well-adapted native plants that help support local habitat. "All original wild seeds from which plants are grown are collected under permit. A portion of these wild-sourced seeds are stored in the Long Live LA Conservation Seed Bank ... which helps bridge fragmented habitats of the LA Basin while preserving, protecting and supporting precious wild stands."

TPF's Seed and Bulb Program further aims to build genetic diversity in the urban environment by providing native seed and bulbs to home gardeners, researchers, school gardens, education programs, and community groups. They collaborate with regional seed conservation and restoration projects, including Seed LA, the Los Angeles Regional Native Seed Network. They document all provenance information for each kind of collected seed: where collection was made, fruiting and seeding habits of the species, associated photographs, seed viability and germination data, and anything else of importance.

In 2020, the nearly 125-year-old nonprofit hired their newest director, Evan Meyer, who also came from California Botanic. Meyer helped develop a new master plan with landscape designers Terremoto to include an updated seed and bulb house at the top of the property. One of TPF's newest projects is the Native Plant Landscaper Certificate Program, a course offered in both English and Spanish focused on improving professional landscape managers' capacity to care effectively for native plant landscapes. It includes lessons on "how to identify native and California-friendly plants," including their seed and seed stages.

❖

If we as a world are ever going to move the needle on the standards of home and commercial landscapes toward a seed-grown, food-and-habitat-supporting, climate-resilient standard, it will not be by home gardeners alone or public gardens or ecological restoration work alone, it must be with all of these stakeholders involved—and it must include a well-equipped, paid, supported, and trained professional sector as well. TPF, and all of its partners including California Botanic, Seed LA, and even design firm Terremoto, is helping to set a model to grow this corps.

SEPTEMBER 6: NEW MOON
We are leaving soon for a 10-day road trip through the Southwest. We will visit family and we will visit the Native Seeds/SEARCH Conservation Center outside of Tucson.

Preparing to be gone, we pick blackberries along the creek and nectarines in the orchard, and John makes us a new moon nectarine and blackberry pie. We plant our next succession of spinach seed. We harvest the last of the 'Shirogoma' white sesame seeds, which we sourced from Kitazawa Seed this past spring.

The seed work of the Asian diaspora in heritage preservation and reclamation cannot be emphasized enough. Seeds and plants, ornamental and culinary, even garden tools and methods derived from Asian cultures and history are fully integrated into this twenty-first-century US gardened world, although the cultural point of origin for these seeds, plants, tools, knowledge, and ways is often obscured or simply not known or shared. These cultural interrelations trace back at the very least to the gold rush, to the building of railways across the US west, and to the expansion of commercial agriculture in the early and mid-1800s. The re-membering of these cultural seed ways has been underway in some respects for more than 100 years, with the work of seed people like the owners of Kitazawa Seed company in San Francisco, but in other respects is finding new ground in the last decade, with the youngest generations of plantspeople taking leadership roles.

Kitazawa Seed was founded in 1917 in San Jose, California, by Gijiu Kitazawa. Forced by US policy during World War II to suspend his business and relocate to an internment prison camp from 1942 to 1945. Kitazawa returned to California and restarted the business in the postwar era. Originally serving Japanese American farmers and growers, the company evolved to grow, source, and offer seeds from a wider variety of Asian cultures. In January 2022, Maya Shiroyama and Jim Ryugo, Kitazawa Seed's owners and stewards since 2000, transferred ownership to True Leaf Market Seed Company, a wholesale non-GMO, non-GE seed supplier and owner of several seed brands founded elsewhere, based in Salt Lake City, Utah.

A next-generation person focused on cultural seeds of the Asian diaspora is Kellee Matsushita-Tseng, a floral and edible food farmer and seed keeper. She is a *yonsei* (fourth generation) Japanese-Chinese American, born and raised in Los Angeles. Matsushita-Tseng's background is in anti-death penalty work, education, youth empowerment, and community organizing. Interested in building a movement toward seed sovereignty as a means of cultivating community health and working for collective liberation, Matsushita-Tseng has served on the board of directors at the National Young Farmers Coalition, has organized with the Asian American Farmers Alliance, and grows with and for Second Generation Seeds.

In conversation with Matsushita-Tseng, she and I quickly entered into the heartbreaking question of how to preserve biodiversity with integrity and the care and modulation of story and human acknowledgment that should travel with it and invite others to do the same—to honor the past and the process and the posterity at once. In Matsushita-Tseng's experience, she says "seed are sort of a container, a vessel, and they're a channel through which we can connect to our past, our future, our selves, so while they are living, breathing ancestors, they are also this site of really potent exploration."

Matsushita-Tseng says the values and intentions she carries "have been deeply put into me by the [plant and activist comrades] who were willing to create the things they needed to survive and thrive, because those survival tools didn't exist before that." These values, survival tools, and humans were and are literal and figurative seeds.

Matsushita-Tseng and Second Generation Seeds, as with most seed and cultural preservationists, work from within the palpable dilemma of a sense of urgency over biodiversity and cultural preservation and a sense of cultural caution, thoroughness, and necessary process requiring time, vigilance over sources, stories, details of the seed conserved along with the seed itself.

The Second Generation Seeds collective is a group of Asian American growers devoted to the preservation and improvement of heirloom Asian herbs and vegetables by offering organically grown, open-pollinated varieties. They are committed to continuing traditional foodways and to inviting "our community to reclaim the narrative around Asian crops." One of the group's goals is to incentivize small-scale seed production by creating meaningful economies for Asian American farmers and food advocates.

Like most cultural seed keepers, Second Generation believes that "seeds are storytellers, protectors of our traditions. In choosing to grow them and save them each season, they remind us of our collective memories, and we commit ourselves to keeping those memories alive for generations to come."

Second Generation Seeds has worked as a group with Seed Savers Exchange to plumb and tag the depths of the so-called "Asian Seed Bank section of the SSE collection." In that process, Matsushita-Tseng and others have found that "so much information was not preserved along with the seed—from the name of the people from whom it was collected, to any name or date on the seed. It is challenging to go through [the collection] after the fact and try to reconstruct any framework." Matsushita-Tseng emphasized the "trust and intention needed in tending to networks of people" as well as networks of plants, places, and seed to avoid this happening again.

Second Generation Seeds offers a handful of heritage varieties, including 'Joseon Shorty', a Korean cucumber; 'Cha Jogi', a "wilder form of red perilla [a green], native to the mountains of Korea, Japan, and China. Considered a fundamental plant in Traditional Chinese Medicine"; 'Lady Choi' peppers; and 'Black Chestnut' soybeans (which are strikingly beautiful in their black-and-white almost fingerprint pattern). In coming seasons, the collective is aiming to "continue to grow and evolve." They continue to add new varieties to their online shop. The Seed Stewards, an online network that facilitates space- and task-sharing in-person events, when possible, in 2023 will be "focused on highlighting the growing and learning of the farmers who are part of the first cohort for our seed fellowship program, launched this year. We will continue to have broader community events as well, mostly focused on live cook-a-longs and in person tastings or variety showcases." In addition, "community partners facilitate storytelling sessions to help us collectively remember the place crops have had in our histories, while chefs and food energize the conversation by creating culinary iterations steeped in tradition."

However, per Matsushita-Tseng, some of the importance of the work lies in not just "preserving static varieties of heirloom seeds, but understanding the throughlines that make them beloved and identifiable to our communities, and then negotiating what that looks like in our current cultural, climactic, and regional contexts."

The diversity of seed people—as well as the seeds themselves—are quite literally the spice of life. Think how many seeds produce the spices we use daily and come from cultural richness over time and space: from allspice and anise, cayenne, cardamom, and cumin, to mustard, pepper, sesame, and vanilla. Grown, smoked, dried, ground, the list is long, tantalizing and steeped in cultural and culinary wealth.

SEPTEMBER 7

Today is Rosh Hashanah—one of the two "New Year" points in the Jewish seasonal year—the other being in spring at Pesach, or Passover.

Rosh Hashanah, which takes place on the first two days of the Jewish month of the autumnal equinox, in 2021, also marks the beginning of Shmita, the Sabbath or Sabbatical year, which, according to Jewish tradition, calls for Jews "to work the land for six years and let it rest in the seventh. Shmita is also known as a "year of release . . . in which debts are to be forgiven, agricultural lands to lie fallow, private land holdings to become open to the commons, and food storage and perennial harvests to be freely redistributed and accessible to all."

The first reference to Shmita in the Bible is in the Book of Exodus. Hazon, one of the largest Jewish environmental organizations in the United States, glosses Shmita in this way: "Understandably, Shmita challenges all who learn about it to think about what our obligations are to land and people in general . . . In recent years, a growing movement of thinkers and activists has pointed to Shmita as a means of addressing the global environmental problems and economic instability of the 21st century and of challenging contemporary expectations of continual economic growth, development, and individual gains."

The questions we struggle with are as perennial as the plants and seeds we love and who sustain us.

SEPTEMBER 9

I'm reading a recent analysis on seed from Food & Power, which reports that "dominant seed corporations have built their market power over producers in several ways," including by "designing seeds to terminate—or, to fail to germinate—after one harvest, forcing farmers to purchase new seeds from them each season," and designing their seed and pesticides to work together, pushing "farmers into a 'pesticide treadmill.'"

Food & Power is a food systems and equity watchdog website that "provides original reporting, resources, and research on monopoly power and economic concentration in the food system." Its mission is to investigate "how corporate power has shaped the food industry, and how monopolization is impacting farmers, consumers, entrepreneurs, and distributors."

The recent report added that corporations like the 2018-merged Bayer-Monsanto "simply bought many of its smaller seed and genetics rivals to further its control over genetic traits," sometimes muscling their vast financial resources to sue "small, independent farmers who attempted to save Monsanto seeds from season to season, or who unknowingly cultivated Monsanto seeds after they or their genetics blew over from a neighboring farm, for patent infringement."

Ominously, the report concludes: "Concentration in the seed sector is deeply tied to concentration in the agrochemical sector. The same four multinational corporations (Bayer-Monsanto, Syngenta, BASF, and DowDuPont) control 75% of plant breeding research, 60% of the commercial seed market, and 76% of global agrochemical sales. Accumulating power across both chemical and seed sales help these companies sell more of all of their products. Because these corporations are so dominant, farmers have few options when seeking alternatives to corporate agro-industrial giants." Farmers using Bayer-Monsanto products are now also tracked by the industry's pervasive use of "big data," which "critics worry will be used by the corporations to control pricing and supply." This puts our farmers, our land, our water, and our environment, cultural histories, and legacies at greater and greater risk.

One woman pushing back heavily against this type of consolidation is Vandana Shiva. She is a long-standing cultural seed keeper whose work dates back four decades. She has been a direct and indirect mentor to many of the cultural seed keepers who have come after her. Shiva has been working on environmental justice since the 1980s in India, and she has become one of the most lauded international faces and voices championing diversified, local, land-based agroecology as the foundation for food and economic systems. After a 1984 industrial disaster at a synthetic fertilizer plant in Bhopal, India, killed more than 15,000 people, injured hundreds of thousands more, and left devastating environmental pollution for what would prove to be decades, Shiva was catalyzed into political and environmental action. She was "forced into sitting up and asking why agriculture was so like war."

Questioning the global agricultural predicament after the Green Revolution led to her books *The Violence of the Green Revolution* and *Monocultures of the Mind*, and to her founding of Navdanya, a seed bank, farm, and nongovernmental organization promoting biodiversity conservation, organic farming, the rights of farmers, and the process of seed saving.

Navdanya translates to "nine seeds." It also means "new gift." Navdanya brings to farmers "the new gift of life in the face of extinction of species and the elimination of small farmers' free exchange of seed."

As Shiva came to believe, "blindness to diversity and self-organization in nature and society was clearly a basic problem in the mechanistic, Cartesian-industrial paradigm," in which humankind is perceived as separate from the material and natural world, which is subsequently perceived as a machine outside of humanity or life. As she tracked the research, she learned that "monocultures produce less and use more inputs, that's destroying the environment and impoverishing people."

Shiva was instrumental in a coalition in the 1990s that fought to overturn patents granted to the USDA and a manufacturing company on the neem tree (*Azadirachta indica*), its oils and seeds, and their natural insecticidal properties. Neem is a legendary medicinal tree of India and has been documented, she says, as an "integral part of the Indian way of life for centuries. The history of the neem tree is inextricably linked to the history of the Indian civilization." Neem has been used since ancient times for disease protection, as repellent against pests in stored flours and grains, and as an insect repellent on crops. It is a significant ingredient in Ayurvedic medicine, a medicinal tradition originating in India thousands of years ago, and still depended on there and around the world for health care. Despite this widespread cultural use, it took Shiva's coalition almost a decade to overturn the patenting of neem and its naturally derived active ingredients. The group was finally successful in May of 2000.

Between the mid-1990s and 2021, more than 200,000 Indian farmers died by suicide, and this is largely attributed to intense indebtedness. Shiva estimates this is directly "caused by the high cost of unreliable seeds sold by corporations." She traced the fact that suicide rates are highest in regions dominated by and dependent on commercial seed, the strongest correlation being in regions "where genetically engineered BT cotton has been sold," and where farmers were leasing their land from larger landholders. There were few to no suicides in places where farmers still had access to and used their own and other heritage seeds.

Shiva concludes with raw honesty: "These are seeds of suicide and seeds of slavery. My inspiration for saving seeds came from Mahatma Gandhi's spinning wheel, through which he fought the British Empire nonviolently." Shiva extrapolates as well from Gandhi's 1930s "satyagraha," a protest march and act of civil disobedience against British taxation of and monopoly of salt. In 2006, Shiva and Navdanya undertook a seed satyagraha, traveling across India distributing (dispersing?) heritage crop seed to farmers and making a public "commitment to refuse to cooperate with patent laws and seed laws that prevent farmers from saving and exchanging seed. Seed freedom is our birthright, and without seed freedom there is no food freedom."

Shiva was determined not to allow the age-old act of saving seed to become criminalized or controlled by authorities, within or beyond India. Navdanya has created more than 20 community seed banks through which seeds are saved and freely exchanged among more than 300,000 members. Collectively they have reintroduced and reinvigorated culturally selected and environmentally adapted seed stock, requiring very few inputs to survive, for "4000 indigenous rice varieties, 2200 varieties of millets such as barnyard millet and finger millet, pseudo cereals, pulses, oilseeds and vegetables, 205 varieties of traditional wheat, and 151 species of trees including orchard fruit."

In 2021, an award-winning documentary about the life and work of Vandana Shiva, *The Seeds of Vandana Shiva*, was produced by Becket Films. In 2022, the film was shown as part of COP27 (the United Nations Climate Change Conference) in Egypt and will be available for individual download and streaming as of 2023. A subtitle to the film reads: "When You Control Seed, You Control Life on Earth."

SEPTEMBER 11
We got on the road early yesterday to make the drive to Tucson, stopping halfway last night near Palm Springs, a revered oasis of the Indigenous Cahuilla peoples, but since the early 1900s a snowbird and tourist destination, and now a sprawling electric-lit metropolis in the desert. We left early again today to make the most of the cool temperatures as we head into the Sonoran Desert—we drive down through the Coachella Valley, along the Salton Sea, across the southern portion of the Algodones Dunes Wilderness area, along the United States-Mexico border and then, hugging the border, down into Tucson.

The Coachella Valley has become a vast human-engineered experiment in agricultural enterprise and mechanization. It runs essentially northwest-southeast and is described as "an arid rift valley in the Colorado Desert." Situated just southeast of the southern end of the Los Angeles Basin, it is the western edge of the miraculous arid expanse that is the Great Basin. The Coachella Valley is bounded on the northeast by the San Bernardino and Little San Bernardino Mountains, and on the southwest by the San Jacinto and Santa Rosa Mountains, and it includes the northern portion of the Salton Trough, also called the Cahuilla Basin, the ancestral home region of the Cahuilla.

According to Cahuilla history, they comprise nine distinct groups who were the first known human inhabitants of the valley, and who have lived there for over 3000 years. In the 1700s the population was nearly 15,000 people. With the 1863 smallpox epidemic brought on by European settlement, "80% of the Cahuilla were killed." Per the most up-to-date records on the Cahuilla website, there are currently around 3000 registered members in the tribe.

Formed in part by movement of the San Andreas Fault, the Salton Trough includes the Salton Sea in its middle, and the Imperial Valley south of the sea within the United States, as well as the Mexicali Valley and Colorado River Delta south of that in Mexico. The valley is the northernmost extension of the Sonoran Desert to the southeast, and as such, is extremely arid. And yet, over 100,000 acres of the valley is irrigated by way of the behemoth Coachella Canal, a concrete aqueduct constructed over a decade from 1938 to 1948 that literally redirects the Colorado River. Providing drinking water to Los Angeles and San Diego, the canal also makes agriculture here possible. And yet, with climate change, aging infrastructure maintenance, and increasing awareness of the complex and multilayered environmental impacts of this human-created irrigation and intense, large-scale agriculture, the canal is also recognized as being increasingly expensive and perhaps untenable.

In the 2020s, the Coachella Valley Water District (CVWD) reported that the valley's crops are valued at about $600 million. Also according to the CVWD, a founding member of the Salton Sea Authority, "the district has been a part of efforts to restore the Salton Sea for decades."

The Salton Sea was first created naturally between 1905 and 1907, in a once-a-century event of Colorado River floodwater filling the Salton Sink, a large, natural topographic depression. The area's elevation is the second lowest in the United States, surpassed only by Death Valley, and forecasts were that the desert's intense heat would evaporate the sea in 8 to 14 years. But the 34-mile-long, 9–10 mile wide "sea" was designated as an irrigation drainage repository in 1928, and agricultural drainage (runoff) of more than a million acre-feet a year, plus all of the fertilizers and pesticides in that runoff, have continued to fill the Salton Sea ever since. Over time, the large inland body of water became an attractive destination (before large quantities of fertilizer and pesticides)—for vacation, for water play, for fishing, and for birding—and was among the most visited tourist attractions in California. And, as the CVWD points out, "as the largest body of water entirely within the state, it became a crucial stop for migratory birds seeking food along the Pacific flyway."

The conundrum as distilled by the CVWD is that "because the Salton Sea is fed by farm drainage and has no outlet, as water evaporates it leaves the salt [and other long accumulated poisonous agricultural residue like selenium] behind. As a result, the sea is now saltier than typical ocean water." After more than 100 years of agricultural accumulation, the seabed has become toxic to all life around it: birds, fish, mammals, soil, produce, and humans.

In April 2021, the California Water Board issued warnings for people and their dogs to avoid water contact in the Salton Sea after harmful algal blooms were detected and a dog died following a swim in the sea. The Colorado River Basin Water Quality Control Board has been conducting monthly monitoring of cyanotoxins in the Salton Sea, which "can affect the skin, liver and nervous system of people and other mammals." Water has been diverted from the Salton Sea to growing desert communities since at least 2003, and this diversion, combined with the desert's naturally high evapotranspiration rates, has caused the sea to shrink, exposing its toxic seabed laden with pesticides, salt, and industrial and other pollution.

Every time the wind blows here, which it does often and fiercely in the natural desert environment of the Salton Trough, the legacy of more than a century of water diversion and artificially supported, often large-scale, mono-crop agriculture fed a constant diet of chemicals, becomes airborne dust breathed in by everyone downwind.

We drive by acre after acre of date orchards, which seem climatically if not culturally appropriate, but also mile after mile of other crops: table grapes, lemons, limes, oranges and grapefruit, onions and leeks, peppers, alfalfa, artichokes, avocados, beans, beets, cabbage, carrots, corn, cotton, cucumbers, dandelions for salad greens, eggplant, figs, barley, oats, rye, wheat, rice, hops, lettuce, mangoes, nectarines and peaches, persimmons, plums and prunes, pomegranate, potatoes, radishes, spinach, strawberries, sugarcane, tomatoes, a variety of herbs and spices, and other vegetable crops.

Finally, as we drive, I read that the valley is a large producer of "domesticated grasses, flowers, and trees ... widely grown for warm weather climates and sold for use in golf courses and landscapes."

All this, growing in a region that the US Geological Survey estimates naturally receives an average of only six inches of precipitation a year.

By 10 a.m. it is 104 degrees Fahrenheit. Driving through this valley, in a second year of extended not just normal seasonal drought, in the driest time of year—late summer—is like driving through a living encyclopedia entry on European colonization of this continent. This is what results from failed policies of "Westward Expansion," industrialization, the horrifyingly too-close-to-successful attempted genocide and erasure of Indigenous peoples and land ethics, and the indecent water and land use that are our modern-day existential sinkholes.

Whether intentional, or created with "good intentions," so much of the viewshed is dying or scarred and littered by overuse, abuse, arrogance, and abandonment/avoidance afforded by disassociation and dissembling.

Driving in an air-conditioned, gas-powered car, it is easy to look away—and hard *not* to look away.

From the Coachella Valley, traveling along the Colorado River as it makes its way through the desert, we enter the expansive, almost mystical and surreal contours of the Algodones Dunes, an ancient sand dune field that straddles not only the border between California and Arizona but also (as made clear by a snaking black wall) the human-political border between Mexico and the United States. On the US side, as you cross into Arizona, you also enter the Yuma Indian Nation, a sovereign nation in its own right.

There are signs warning drivers not to stop, not to get out of the car, not to pick up hitchhikers. The language of the signs and their placement make it clear that these warnings are in part to protect passersthrough from potentially "illegal" immigrants coming across the border from Mexico, and in part to protect the laws and lands of the Yuma, especially with the ongoing COVID-19 transmission and the disproportionate impact of the virus on American Indian populations.

Human-engineering intrusions into these unirrigated portions of our journey include not only border walls and roadside immigration checkpoints, but wind farms on the crests and windy slopes of nearby ridges, and acres of solar arrays covering open desert on such a scale it's hard to grasp. These are interspersed with enormous feed lots for thousands of cattle.

With river cleaving to desert, humans cleaving to land and climate, all that can and does divide and separate us is in full view. It is visually arresting and symbolic of the uneasy, often awkward balances and imbalances between humans and nature, Indigenous cultures and colonizing forces, foreign and domestic policy.

But seeds recognize few of these human boundaries. Mountains, yes. Rivers, yes. Sand dunes, yes. Militarized border wall, no. State-line signs welcoming and then bidding you good-bye, no.

Desert scrub landscapes dot the drive between stretches of human development. Spindly, spiny, towering, vase-shaped clusters of ocotillo cactus are vibrant green—leafed out after a recent rainfall. *Fouquieria splendens* is characterized by a panicle of many red flowers at the tip of slender, spined stems. These rare blooms in the desert provide nectar and pollen to migratory hummingbirds and resident carpenter bee colonies. Carpenter bees often nest in ocotillo's woody stems. Pollinated flowers are followed by plump green to reddish fruit capsules, which dry and split lengthwise to release between 9 and 20 papery-white winged seeds per fruit.

Teddy-bear cholla cactus naturally underplant the ocotillo; they are so heavily spined that they look fuzzy and wear a halo of yellowish glowing prickles when backlit. *Cylindropuntia bigelovii* tend to spread vegetatively and by detached stem pieces rooting, and far less frequently by seed, many of which are apparently not fertile.

Sagebrush (*Artemisia* sp.), whose herbal astringent fragrance characterizes the petrichor, post-rain scent, of this place; creosote bush (*Larrea tridentata*), the white hairs of its capsule fruits glowing in the desert's angled light; agave, sometimes known as century plants; yucca, and many, many low-growing, wind-and-sand-stunted sparse grasses fill out the landscape.

When we rise just slightly in elevation, thick-trunked and stoutly branched saguaro cactus, some more than 20 feet tall with 6-foot arms, appear in the landscape. *Carnegiea gigantea* bloom at the top of their stems and arms, and once pollinated, form fleshy, egg-shaped red fruits that dry and dehisce to reveal pink flesh filled with many shiny, black, also egg-shaped seeds up to one-third-inch long.

The Tohono O'odham culture, whose land we are now traveling across, are said to "divide the year into 13 lunar 'months,' starting with Hashañi Mashad, or saguaro [harvest] month. The saguaro-fruit-wine-imbibing ceremony to bring the summer monsoon doubles as the O'odham New Year's celebration. Their annual cycle or year begins with harvest and preparation for the monsoon season in late summer."

Individual ocotillo plants can live between 60 and 150 years; saguaros live 150 to 175 years with some living well beyond 200, according to desert biologists. Creosote bushes, like aspen, spread vegetatively (clonally) as well as by seed—the oldest clonal-ring creosote colonies in the Sonoran Desert are over 5000 years old, and a ring colony in the Mojave is thought to be more than 11,000 years old.

The day's accumulation of starkly contrasted images, spaces, communities, and concepts coalesce into what seems like a never-ending reel of depressing impressions. These poisoned fields of big ag? These plastic-covered-hydroponic-greenhouse/warehouses with bumble bees indentured for pollination services? Acres of solar arrays killing desert habitats? Gallons of carbon-creating fossil fuels to get here? This soil overtilled to grow plants that don't belong here with water not naturally occurring here to feed these miserable meats that "feed" us?

The challenges, diversions, false questions, and protective mechanisms that often make life harder, not easier, are legion, but so too are the expressions of parts of solutions. As with anything, the binary viewpoint is likely not helpful. We must learn to look at a spectrum, and how we each activate our own expression along the spectrum of the multitude of ways to seed better solutions.

We feel the discomfort of being complicit participants in our society as it currently functions—even if we're just "passing through."

SEPTEMBER 13
We arrive in Tucson in the midst of a weeklong celebration of Sonoran food held by all the local restaurants, each one developing a menu of dishes, drinks, and desserts that include seasonal, local, and native produce of the Sonoran Desert.

We spend today at Native Seeds/SEARCH headquarters and tour their seed bank, offices, conservation center, and gardens.

The low reddish-earth-colored adobe building is fronted by a large water-harvesting tank, and a front entry wall tiled with a mosaic depicting the diversity of wild fruits and flowers of the area: native amaranth grain, pea pods, colorful dry beans, different-sized sunflowers, blanketflowers, native dwarf blue flax, and low, blue, creeping phacelia flowers are all there. Donors to the organization are also recognized here: names etched into gourd-shaped tiles, surrounded by artistically rendered gourd flowers and foliage. The bottom of the tile mosaic is bordered by a river of colorful corn kernels.

Behind, the conservation seed garden grows out the season's selected stock. Small fruit trees stand out, and lofty native and sacred *Nicotiana rustica*, known as "papante tobacco" is grown under isolation tents.

In the seed storage, cleaning, and processing rooms inside the center, we meet the staff and volunteers, the educators, the local and regional farmer coordinators. We meet native green "pima" cotton bolls and seeds, rare Hopi lima beans, a naturalized okra from Texas. We meet the hooked seed pod of what we call devil's claw or unicorn plant in Northern California but is basket claw here—after the use of the mature seed pod fibers in basketry and the use of its jet-black seeds as a dye source.

Native Seeds/SEARCH's original accession of basket claw, *Proboscidea parviflora*, dates back to a collection from Santa Rosa Village, Tohono O'odham Nation, Pima County, Arizona, in 1978. Basket claw has tubular pink or yellow flowers that when pollinated produce long (6–10 inches?) fleshy and fuzzy green capsules that curve at the tip to form the signature claw. As this capsule matures and dries, the green fleshy outer flesh dries out and sloughs off, and the woody interior splits lengthwise to form a two-sided claw, which "grabs" onto the hooves or ankles of passing mammals, who then disperse the seeds inside as they try to shake the pokey capsule off.

The accession notes indicate: "Devil's claw is believed by the Tohono O'odham to have been brought into existence at the same time as humans. In their creation story, I'itoi, the Great Spirit, gave each tribe a basket on the third day. So that each group would be able to tell its baskets apart, I'itoi gave to the people *'ihuk* [devil's claw], and showed them how to weave its fibers into designs in the baskets." Evidence of the plant has been found in caves in the Southwest dating from AD 300; basketry using devil's claw splints date to AD 600 in Arizona's Gila River watershed. Growing wild throughout the Americas, devil's claw is believed to have first been cultivated in the "Southwest by the Hohokam a thousand years ago." The Tohono O'odham and Pima still grow this plant for the fruit pods, which are used for food as well as basketry by many groups including the Apache, Yaqui, Cahuilla, Yavapai, Hopi, Shoshone, and Tarahumara.

One thing that stands out as unique in the work of Native Seeds/SEARCH is the integration of both food crop seed and wild plant seed. A rich overlap that exists in the world, exists abundantly in areas with high wild crop relative biodiversity, but it does not always exist in our human-derived systems that try to patly divide cultivation from wildness.

The walls of the NS/S offices and group spaces are covered in posters and maps: some tracing the source of each seed in the collection, the locations of growers across the US Southwest and Mexico, others illustrating native bee species and the pollinator cycle. A large black poster depicts scanning electron microscope images of nine colorful seeds in an amazing—a *wild*—diversity of forms with the title "Phantoms of the Desert: Seeds of Tuma-moc Annuals."

Tumamoc Hill, just west of the city of Tucson, is a national historic landmark and an "860-acre ecological preserve and site of the University of Arizona's Desert Laboratory since 1903." The hill's name is taken from the Tohono O'odham place-name Che-mamagi Du'ag—Horned Lizard Mountain—indicating the pro-found cultural importance of this site. It includes a 2500-year-old settlement, and the entire preserve is notable as a cultural land-scape "reflecting four millennia of significance to the communi-ties that have known the hill."

Annual plants of course live out their entire life cycle—from seed germination to seed dispersal and mother plant death—in one year or season. Germination for annual plant seeds is gener-ally dependent on both heat and moisture; in a desert environ-ment this means that some annuals can remain dormant for years between seasons in which conditions allow—in which heat and moisture occur in enough abundance at the same time—for germination and fresh seed set. About half of the immense diversity of the more than 2000 plant species in the Sonoran Desert are annuals. Researchers at the Tumamoc Desert Lab, led by Larry Venable, study the germination strategies and needs of these seeds to learn more about desert adaptations.

The academic lab has been on this site for 120 years, humans have been living here for more than 2500 years, and yet we still have not discovered all the ways that the plants of this place have adapted to live here, rest here, wait here, and then—like a miracle—one spring or monsoon season gather just enough rain, at just the right moment, to resurrect. When they do, they transform the entire viewshed from what appears to be barren into miles of wildflowers—miles of green, yellow, white, blue, purple, red in all shapes, sizes, and forms hovered over by the lively sounds and cycles of bees, flies, moths, butterflies, bats—as far as the ear can hear and the eye can see.

SEPTEMBER 20
Today is the full harvest moon, it is the first day of the seven-day Jewish harvest festival, Sukkot. It is also the first day of Chuseok, the three-day Korean harvest festival.

We spend the week after our NS/S visit with parents, children, and grandchildren before beginning our multiday trek west and home. We have a lot to think about in the way of seed protection, preservation, and the growing urgency around all of these things. A lot to think about in regard to adaptation, loss and degradation, but also of transformation.

Seeds provide constant lessons in adaptation and transformation.

It is at the intersection of the urgency of immediate protection and preservation of cultural seed that Vivien Sansour, founder in 2014 of the Palestine Heirloom Seed Library, has found herself. Born and raised until her early teens in Palestine, she and her family immigrated to the United States in the 1970s.

A lot of Sansour's connection to seeds and plants is "born of joy, but there is equal if not greater measure of pain to be found there." The latter comes from her own experience returning to Palestine as an adult and endeavoring to locate and share forward seeds of environmental, agricultural, and culinary meaning to her region and its people. With every seed and seed history she finds, it seems she also uncovers a great loss or a tragic, criminal injustice to a person or a place or a community of people and seed.

But, she adds with clarity, "the plants carrying the history, the joy, and the pain in need of understanding and acknowledging and processing" help Sansour to make sense of life. "We know from seeds that there is no such thing as always joy or always woundedness and pain. We know instead there is always cyclical change and that inevitably something will transform and move us to the next stage in the cycle."

"Seeds," says Sansour, "help un-school us in the arrogance of knowing anything for sure, of consistency, of stability at all times. They help make us comfortable with impermanence, which is of course deeply reminiscent of many religious teachings. To really gain the benefit of gardening and seeds and what they teach us is to allow that surrender, to be humbled by the process of putting these living things in the ground and hoping it will grow into food or beauty or medicine but never really knowing what will happen."

As she has done her work in Palestine, finding seeds, finding stories, building community, she has found herself being slowly and steadily re-woven into her own culture, her own cultural identity, one seed offered out from an "old chocolate tin storage box kept under a bed at a time, one grandmother hug at a time."

Since 2014, Sansour has recovered many interesting seeds, including khyar abyad, a fragrant white cucumber; baladi bandora, a tomato that tolerates drought; 'Jadu'I', once a widely grown watermelon renowned for its size and flavor; and 'Battir' eggplant. Palestine was a center of diversity for wheat varieties until the early 1900s. "Now, from hundreds of varieties, Palestine grows only three at scale," she says. Sansour has helped to revive one heritage wheat known as 'Abu Samra', which translates to the "Handsome Dark One," a wheat with dark black "whiskers" on the fruit and a rich, nutty flavor. "Women talk about it like a love who is long gone."

Sansour's goal is not to be a "diligent farmer" but rather a tireless seed disperser. "The true seed library grows in the farmers' fields," she explains. "I want to see as many farmers as possible using the seeds," all chosen over time by the Palestinian people specifically for their drought-tolerant, climate-appropriate, storage, and flavor traits.

She came to see how her forebears *had* worked diligently to bring the world these "seeds that did not require violence towards the earth in order to grow food, violence towards the earth in the form of irrigation and diversion of water, or manipulation of soil. These seeds were adapted to thrive off the moisture of the rainy season, off the moisture held in healthy soil after the rainy season, and off the moisture of dew."

These seeds and this history demonstrated to Sansour that no matter what mainstream agricultural or cultural histories included, her ancestors and Palestine "had made and continued to steward offerings of great contribution to the world of agriculture: okra, tomatoes, watermelon, cucumbers, wheat, wheat, wheat, wheat, and barley. Collectively these are known as Ba'al seeds [the name of the Canaanite deity of fertility]."

Sansour recognizes that the world is a wounded place, but she found in seeds "a possibility to keep expanding little oases. When future generations come to start something of their own in the world, they will find these seeds to start from. I did not start from scratch because there were all of the grandmothers and grandfathers who did this work before me. In this way, we understand each other not because we share a language, but because we share an understanding of seeds and plants and how we want to see and understand the world. Because we share a vision of how we see the world, how we want to see the world." Sansour finishes, "These are trying times, but they are also opportune times calling us to ask ourselves how mediocre or how brave do we want to be? We have a choice." She hopes we will come out braver.

She is a germinating force who prays fervently: "May we eat and may we feed others. It's up to god and our service to the seeds, plants, and service to the soil."

SEPTEMBER 22
After watching a still nearly full moon sink behind a gently craggy rock ridge last night as we went to sleep in our roadside campsite making our westward way home, we woke this morning on the autumnal equinox, in an open, painted desert of a valley somewhere in Utah. From our sleeping bags and then our camp chairs with coffee, in a gravel wash beside

the small dirt road we are traveling, we watch the bright morning moon set over the striped cliffs to the west and the brighter, glowing sun rise over a scrub-clothed ridge to the east.

Our 360-degree uninterrupted view takes in both at once. An expansive celestial balance.

We spend the day making our way slowly through this valley. We do not see another vehicle for 12 hours, allowing us to stop and walk and photograph and witness at a very human pace, a moment's whim, the flash of a grass head, rock outcrop, or flower.

Only a few trees are apparent—wind-sculpted juniper and pinyon pine, a few rugged and likewise wind-clipped Emory oak, and later in the day, aspen and cottonwood as we rise out of the valley and enter forests that clearly receive far more annual precipitation. Shrubby rabbit brush and sage, in what seems like barren rocky soil, on closer inspection include an amazing diversity of wildflowers and grasses in bloom and seed: short, scrappy but bright white and wide-blossomed evening primrose; stunted and muted pale pink dwarf milkweeds; small single gaillardias; bright yellow *Stanleya* plumes; pink sand verbenas; trailing purple-red four-o'clocks; white sage; black sage; and so many we do not know any names for but are so happy to be in the presence of.

This is a dry, rocky landscape that dwarfs us, our car, our ability to walk a few hours or miles in one direction and reach nothing in the distance. It wears its geologic age in visible, colorful, windswept layers, resolute in the face of wind, weather, night, day, lunar and solar years, centuries, millennia—time.

SEPTEMBER 23

The last few hours of our drive home, we are in the still-smoldering-in-some-places burn scar of the southwestern flank of the Dixie Fire, much of which is in Plumas National Forest. The northeastern and some central areas of the fire's now 963,276 acres are still active, but this section is what firefighters term "mopped up."

From the mountain town of Quincy, California (elevation 3650 feet), we drive through the often steeply sloped serpentine and granitic Feather River Canyon, previously dense with mature montane hardwood and mixed conifer forest and chaparral—thick with a tapestry of seasonally colorful black and live oaks, cottonwood, alder, ponderosa pine, Douglas fir, manzanita, Pacific madrone, wild grape, clematis, ceanothus, toyon, coffeeberry. Up the little tributaries from the Feather River itself, we have routinely come to visit stands of late spring and summer *Lewisia*, stream and lady slipper orchids, a symphony of lilies.

We, along with a multitude of birds, butterflies, bees and other insects, mammals, amphibians, and reptiles, seasonally visit wet meadows of official botanical interest, the home ground for endemic California pitcher plants, rein orchids, *Aconitum*, corn lilies, and so much more.

We, along with a multitude of birds, butterflies, bees and other insects, mammals, amphibians, and reptiles, seasonally count on the bloom in dry meadows of *Agastache*, aster, *Monardella*, and lovage where earlier this summer John sighted and photographed the now rare western bumble bee, *Bombus occidentalis*—the only sighting in Northern California in many years.

The western bumble bee is under study by the Xerces Society for having declined sharply since the late 1990s. There have been significant range losses in these regions, particularly from lower elevation sites in California, western Oregon, and western Washington. Bumble bees face a number of threats: pests and diseases, habitat destruction or alteration, pesticides, invasive species, natural pest or predator population cycles, and climate change. Commercial bumble bee rearing may also be among the threats to the western bumble bee. In North America, two bumble bee species have been commercially reared for pollination of greenhouse tomatoes and other crops: *B. occidentalis* and *B. impatiens*. Between 1992 and 1994, queens of *B. occidentalis* and *B. impatiens* were shipped to European rearing facilities, where colonies were produced then shipped back to the United States for commercial pollination. Bumble bee expert Robbin Thorp (1933–2019) hypothesized that these bumble bee colonies acquired a disease ("probably a virulent strain of the microsporidian *Nosema bombi*") from a European bee in the same rearing facility, the buff-tailed bumble bee (*Bombus terrestris*). The North American bumble bees would have had no prior resistance to this pathogen.

Dr. Thorp further hypothesized that the disease then spread to "wild populations of *B. occidentalis* and *B. franklini* in the West (from exposure to infected populations of commercially reared *B. occidentalis*), and *B. affinis* and *B. terricola* in the East (from exposure to commercially reared *B. impatiens*)." In the late 1990s, biologists began to notice that *B. affinis*, *B. occidentalis*, *B. terricola*, and *B. franklini* were severely declining. Where these bees were once very common, they are now nearly impossible to find.

I think of my small number of saved cherry tomato seeds, waiting for next spring in the cool dark of a cupboard back at home. I think of the year-round supply and availability of hothouse tomatoes shipped from around the world so we human consumers will never be without.

Do we know, when we choose a cluster of red tomatoes in winter and spring, that we are simultaneously choosing to pressure, disease, and disrupt the bumble bees of our world? And the ecosystems reliant on them?

As we drive the burn scar, we fall very, very quiet. The landscape is very, very quiet. We point, mostly—never taking our eyes off the scenes around us. Whole stretches—from the river's edge to the ridgetops high above—are burned to the ground, just white and black ash covering everything. In other areas, charred skeletal silhouettes of standing dead trees remain. Elsewhere, trees and shrubs are a lifeless dry brown, with likewise brown, curled, still dense foliage intact. Other pockets of trees, shrubs, and grassy slopes are green and seem wholly untouched, until we slow a bit more and looking closer still see the burn and desiccation on the under-sides and outer edges of these pockets—where the heat got too close, we see an ashy coating on the leaf colors.

At least 300 bird species made this forest home along with bear, deer, fox, coyote, mountain lion, bobcat, multiple species of bats, and untold numbers of snakes, frogs, toads, newts. Who knows how many specific and beautiful fungi live here in relationship to their trees and shrubs. We will not know until next summer if the western bumble bee has persisted here; we will not know for at least a year which soil communities have been destroyed rather than refreshed; for up to four years or longer we will not know which trees have died, which will stump-sprout, which have been systemically weakened in such a way as to shorten their lives.

It will be the dotted-about living pockets, the stretches of burned—but not mineralized or decimated or sterilized—soil in the midst of the scar, from above, from upstream and upwind of this negligent-human-started fire burn that will serve as seed banks for potential restoration.

SEPTEMBER 25
Back home, we are getting resettled into everyday life. I have a day at the desk and John takes and sends me a photo of a healthy pile of fresh (today's) bear scat under the 25-year-old 'Mutsu' apple tree. "A smallish bear, I think," he writes, based on the size of the pile and the relatively few broken branches in the old tree's canopy.

The pile of poop contains almost all seed: wild grape, toyon, coffeeberry, and a whole lot of this season's manzanita.

SEPTEMBER 29

I ask again: What are seeds if not a microcosm perfectly situated inside of a lived life? And what are our lives if not most appropriately contextualized within our lived experience on this planet?

I am no longer seed bearing, I have blessedly aged out of this capacity naturally, but my daughters are of childbearing age, and they now carry a shared and new genetic narrative forward.

If we as a species so completely dominate, disrupt, dismember the world around us that we end the natural and healthy seed-bearing cycles for all other creatures and life forms, what then?

Many gardeners and seed keepers echo a thought in their persistence and age-old relationships and responsibilities, that how we measure anything in the garden is over revolutions of the sun and moon, over layered multiples of seasons, as Gary Nabhan expressed it, this calculus over a "lifetime that equals partnership; a partnership not formed with a signature, not un-formed with a signature, [rather] built and/or deconstructed over the same periods and measures of time."

When is "courage conjured," Nabhan wonders, perhaps in being present with mortality? Mortality, and its alter ego (or nemesis?) immortality, are bound together in seed, and in this union, seed holds the powerful memories and contracts of place, of plants, and of our human nurture and nourishment.

As Martin Prechtel admonished and pleaded, "Let us get small, unarmed, brave, and beautiful" as we tend to and ensure "the glorious continuing" that is a seed.

We should live our lives as seeds.

SEED FUTURES

Going to Seed

NEW MOON, OCTOBER 6
FULL MOON, OCTOBER 20

OCTOBER 4
It has been one year since I started this renewed and intensive engagement with the state of seed in the world. I also can't help but mark time
by reflecting that I am a little over a month away from outliving my
own mother.

In California, the so-called water year ends September 30 and
begins again on the first of October. The first California Drought
Report of the month shares what we intuitively know: California
and the West are in severe drought, with impacts accelerated by
climate change. The weekly report shares some new statistics:
"The water year that ended Sept. 30 was the second driest on
record. Storage in some key reservoirs will reach historic lows
this fall. Fifty of California's 58 counties are under a drought
emergency proclamation. Californians are asked to reduce their
water use by 15 percent over 2020 levels to protect water reserves
and help maintain critical flows for fish and wildlife wherever
possible." In the final month of this last water year, 168 wells were
reported dry, with the state providing water to areas of water

"outage" in at least six counties. Fish and wildlife are expected to be significantly impacted, as are economies associated with fish and wildlife.

Some days the world seems viewable—understandable—only through the lens of urgency, crisis, loss, degradation, separation, and competition over accelerated use of limited natural resources.

In Diane Wilson's novel *The Seed Keeper*, seeds are the first characters, with voices of their own, that readers meet. The seeds' words focus on the importance of interrelatedness. The whole book in many ways is an exploration of what Wilson refers to early on, through the voice of an elder American Indian woman, as a societal "drought of memory." We're urged to reclaim "the natural laws that bind us all," despite the painful truth, also articulated and illustrated through the stories of the characters in the book (primarily the American Indian), that "forgetting is easy, it's the remembering [of loss, trauma, violence, violations] that wears you down."

OCTOBER 6

Plants- and seedsman Jeff Quattrone says that in his work tracking down heritage tomato seed and stories in New Jersey he was still struck, some 15 years into it, by "just how deep gardening goes—how deep our relationship to seed goes. It is an expression of who we are as people."

I recall Tim Johnson, from the Botanic Garden of Smith College and Seed Savers Exchange, saying, "Even now in the era of big ag—where most of our food comes from very large industry—gardening is still a very powerful folk and oral tradition. You can read every book you want on how to grow a tomato, and you still have not *grown* a tomato." In a world where every question can be answered by an algorithm, for Johnson, gardening is refreshingly the one area where he still gets his information person-to-person, by calling his gardener community to ask "Where did you source these seeds? When did you sow them? Harvest? What are the caveats, the intricacies?"

I recall Johnson's observation of an "inverse relationship between the health of the economy and gardening and seed sales." As previously noted, when the economy sinks, seed sales go up. Many of the seed growers and suppliers that came to life in the 1880s, 1930s, 1970s, 1990s, or in the Great Recession of 2008 seem to have been born of a desire for imagined self-sufficiency, for less reliance on paper currency, industrialized food systems, government oversight, and seed supply well beyond their own reach or regions. The origin dates of seed banks, seed growers, seed companies seem to bear this out: D. Landreth in Pennsylvania (1784); Comstock, Ferre and Co. (founded in 1853, purchased by Jere Gettle of Baker Creek Heirloom Seeds in 2010); W. Atlee Burpee (1876); Ferry-Morse (1856); Johnny's; Territorial (1973); Fedco (1978); even the native seed sellers Plants of the Southwest (1976), Larner Seeds (1978), and Native Seeds/SEARCH (1983).

Johnson went on to consider that beyond economic need, there's something else at work in this relationship. "It's the psyche of having food close at hand"—this wanting to survive noted earlier and desire to be in control of it, but also of connecting back to the people in your lineage that engaged directly with their (and so your) own survival. And, to the most modern point, "it's having the screen and headset off and losing the constant sense of anxiety, which growing food, flowers, herbs, even weeds in the garden allows us." It is an existential comfort to believe we can get back to the most essential and elemental aspects of survival if and when we need to.

One of the lines of inquiry in Diane Wilson's *The Seed Keeper* circles around these questions of genetic integrity, modification and genetic engineering in our food crops, and the specter of contamination the GMO and GE seem to let loose in our environments. Another line of Wilson's inquiry covers concerns over consolidation of seed genetics and control over them in multinational seed and petrochemical corporations growing and distributing at the largest scale.

Quattrone and Johnson are both worried about these conditions in real life, in different measure. When he was first doing the research and study to begin his first seed library in New Jersey in 2012, Quattrone was surprised by the extent of seed consolidation and genetic modification. The more he looked at the combination of the two trends in the context of the history of seed selection, sharing, and breeding, the more he was convinced "that modifying genes was nothing more than profiteering. Before GMOs, before accelerated consolidation and globalization in the 1990s, seed breeding was about creating better plants—for yield, for disease resistance, for flavor, for climate adaptation, and for the public to grow and use them and breed from them. In the age of GMOs, breeding is about profit and excluding anyone else from 'profiting' let alone benefiting from this breeding."

For him and his sensibilities in which "universal access is at the core of equality, the previous age of public access" made more sense to him, and the new age of corporate profits and patents not only makes no sense but actively disturbs him, because it "becomes about controlling food in our world" and controlling our world through that. "All corporations have a duty to their investors to be profitable, but this profit comes at the expense of access, and at the expense of life. In order to build a profitable bottom line, they have to build a structure of exclusion. Some profit comes as a result of producing more or producing a better idea or product, but this profit seems different—it is based on being the best at destroying access," which precludes both healthy competition and healthy cooperation.

Johnson is concerned about consolidation, but not necessarily anti-patents, because he appreciates a patent's ability to protect a useful innovation. However, he adds as an important caveat, he sees this protection as useful *only if* well administered and well monitored in the global genetic modification arena. But this caveat is seriously unwieldy and includes hard-to-ensure provisions in our current government and mainstream cultural models.

Johnson makes note that seed patenting is in fact quite young (the original protection was trademark protection—the next utility patent was the 20-year-cultivar protection), the ability to patent seed as technology is really new, and as Colin Khoury (previously of the international German-based Crop Trust, helping administer Svalbard's seed vault) adds, most European countries do not have such corporation- and profit-driven biases built into their governing ideals: "In Europe, there are far more social-good controls built into agro-environmental and seed laws."

Johnson sees patents as one tool in the broader kit of capturing and containing a market. "It gets harder to make the case that patents are used to encourage innovation when powerful companies are also doing things to crush competition. To literally crush them." He cites the history of sugar beet growers in the mid-2000s, when there was a push by "organic sugar beet growers to market their sugar beets as organic and non-GMO. They were growing organically because they believed in it environmentally and socially, and because they believed that someday the market would afford premium prices for their beets." But, in the middle of an industry in which a large percentage of growers plant GMO and pesticide-resistant beets, the GMO-dominated sugar beet consortium pushed the organic growers' marketing hopes down, because the GMO growers knew what this would mean for the market price of their nonorganic sugar. Declines. Johnson continues this observation: "When you combine patents with effectively antitrust tactics, you are no longer incentivizing innovation."

The prevalence of large GMO growers moving into global centers of diversity for a genus or species and growing those genetics also disturbs both Johnson and Khoury. By way of illustrating this specific global-centers-for-diversity worry, Johnson offers the example of GMO corn: the pesticide-resistant corn grown in Mexico, the global center for teosinte corn. "To have that epicenter for the biologic diversity of corn facing both external threats from loss of habitat and farmland, as well as internal pressures like genetic swamping from big GMO growers, especially when combined with overly aggressive patent laws," Johnson points out, "it becomes a sort of biological warfare," which becomes just a new iteration of modern cultural warfare.

While at SSE, Johnson served on the National Genetics Resource Advisory Committee, which advises the USDA, when they were reviewing recommendations for organic farmers in the event of conflicts around organic and conventional farmers. "The published opinion of the USDA was that organic is a 'value-added' product and part of the cost of that 'value add' is that organic farmers have to work harder to protect that value add from genetic contamination." To Johnson, this seemed "like yet another blow. That is not cooperative. Cooperation is thinking about the needs and fears and interest and concerns of your neighbor, your community. We as a country have continually favored the interests of larger agricultural corporations under the guise of it being in the best interest of us all. The result of that has been a reduction in the diversity of our food crops, a reduction in numbers of farmers, and the reduction in the diversity of those farmers with regularity."

It is not in the long-term interest of any, but it is certainly on record as being in the short-term financial interest of the few.

This became a very visible and real obstacle to Johnson in his SSE days. With corn, "you need two miles of isolation to protect crops from genetic drift," from other varieties, from GMO varieties. In Decorah, in the middle of Iowa, surrounded by commercial corn, there was one location on SSE's Heritage Farm that allowed for a 1.5 mile isolation grow out. The preservation team did an experiment with white-kerneled, white-fleshed corn, "because the seed coat is see-through, so if you get contamination from a yellow corn, you can see it, whereas in otherwise colored seed [which is most seed] you won't see that expression of the yellow pollen parent so immediately." Contamination happened, and then SSE "had to grow out their corn covering individual tassels and hand pollinating to avoid any contamination because you can't tell 10,000 acres of neighbors around you to stop contaminating your crops."

In the face of such overwhelming obstacles and "genetic swamping," you capitulate and try your best to adapt.

When you consider the work of Indigenous seed keepers and seed keepers of the African and Asian diasporas tenderly and determinedly building up the seed and story banks that were violently taken from them and lost for generations, losing one line of recovered sacred heritage seed to genetic contamination or an overreaching patent is the equivalent of attempted genocide and erasure all over again.

"Most of the consolidation is happening at the big commodity level," Johnson stresses. In our conversation you could feel in the tone of our voices, the cadence of our breathing, that we were at our very cores holding onto the fragile and tenacious hope of the diversity and the interconnecting, supportive seedshed of the seed business world composed of interested and engaged seed companies with stated environmental, economic, *and* social justice aspects to their missions. There are those that have persisted, and those that have joined the work recently: Fedco Seed, Peace Seedlings (a second-generation shoot of Peace Seeds), Wild Garden Seed, Territorial Seed, Siskiyou Seeds, Southern Exposure Seed Exchange, Baker Creek Heirloom Seeds, High Mowing Organic Seeds, Sow True Seed, Truelove Seeds, Adaptive Seeds, Living Seed, Second Generation Seeds, Experimental Farm Network Seeds, Uprising Seed, and among the newest additions, "Ujamaa Seeds, a project of the Ujamaa Cooperative Farming Alliance, a BIPOC-led collective which recognizes the need for increased diversity in the $15 billion seed industry in particular," and many more.

"These tend to not be the companies," Johnson pointed out, "that buy seed and repackage it, but that are growing it themselves," or in community, as community. Along with food or environmental justice, as well as social justice writ large, "adding their breeding collection and take on the seed is really refreshing."

These endeavors also recall the predictive elements of resilience noted by cultural anthropologist Edward Spicer that if enough members of a community "express an affinity for shared" cultural signifiers (seed, crops, foods, religious or spiritual ritual) and values through time, across the generations, their agriculture and culture stand a better chance of remaining vibrant and viable.

The germination, leafing out, and the possible damping off before real establishment of small seed companies is a temporal and spatial sine curve if ever there was one, and there is real vulnerability, Johnson indicates, in the fact that at this small-scale seed growing and selling level, "so much of the seed we buy looks like it is widely available, but in many cases the seed is coming to all these sellers from just one grower, and so if that grower or those few distributors decide to stop growing or stop distributing, that seed is critically endangered."

OCTOBER 15

If this year has made visible anything to me it is that, as Jeff Quattrone commented, "the larger the size of the mainstream river, the more room there is for an undercurrent." Cooperative, collaborative, generative, and enduring restorations in all of these arenas are being propagated by many adaptive and resilient seed and seed people. Seed and seed people have been and are modeling perennial restoration every generation, every season, interconnecting intergenerationally and interculturally from every corner of the world. Strengthening the fabric of our world as they go.

Recently, A Growing Culture, an international coalition of thinkers, writers, artists, growers, and grassroots policy activists committed to advancing food sovereignty for all people, in all its forms including seed sovereignty, announced the "Seed is Power" fund, which ensures that seeds stay in the hands of the people. It supports seed savers "on their own terms, disrupting the status quo of 'top-down' philanthropy—creating a reciprocal system that redistributes power, building equity, and community among seed savers."

In an act of courageous re-commoning—bringing things of value back into the ancient praxis of communal care and responsibility, with communal and open access—seed keeper Vivien Sansour entrusted Palestinian heirloom Yakteen gourd seeds to the Hudson Valley Seed Company (HVSC), as part of founder K Greene's and HVSC's efforts to support cultural communities restoring and rematriating their heritage seeds. HVSC has provided growing grounds and supportive human community for the seed and other seed people. From 2015 to 2021, Greene, under the auspices of an endeavor known as Seedshed, manifested a midwife role to the seed regeneration and rematriation work of several cultural groups, including Akwesasne and the Saint Regis Mohawk Indian Tribe, working with the Indigenous Seed Keepers Network, whose hunting grounds and trade routes ran from Canada to the Catskill Mountains through where HVSC currently grows; the Lenape Center, representing the Delaware Tribe of Indians in Oklahoma, "enabling leaders in the Lenape

Center to share seeds across the broad diaspora of Lenapehoking so that the seeds can thrive in the hands of their people"; Reclaim Seed NYC, "a women of color led collective working towards community-based seed justice and food sovereignty in New York City, supporting a dynamic community of urban growers growing food on almost 46 acres throughout NYC. The project stewards a free public seed library and ethnobotanical teaching garden hosted by the King Manor Museum in Jamaica, Queens"; and Morton Seed Library, now part of a larger effort called Library of Local, working to share seeds across the Hudson Valley community.

In another act of re-commoning, Fedco Seed has established an alternative to the straight for-profit economic model to incentivize public-access seed breeding and to recognize cultural contributions to the seed and plant breeding commons by paying royalties to Indigenous breeders and keepers of seed. In 2018, Fedco began paying royalties "in recognition of the native breeders and seed keepers of the past and present, whose varieties have endured and continue to sustain us here on Turtle Island [North America]. We are indebted to those keen eyes, practiced hands and seed relationships, so often overlooked. Fedco's catalog is rife with references to probable Native provenances. We will continue to pay royalties for varieties that either hold a Wabanaki [on whose homelands Fedco grows] story or that have a tribal designation in the name. These royalties will go to the Indigenous nonprofit Nibezun ... dedicated to preserving and promoting all aspects of Mi'kmaq, Passamaquoddy, Penobscot, Maliseet, and Abenaki ceremonies, traditions, customs, and language to practice and education."

Further, Fedco has worked to designate and recognize "seeds that were carried with, selected by, and cared for by Black people who were stolen out of Africa and enslaved." To date, Fedco has designated a dozen varieties that originate in Africa, or are part of Black foodways, for Black benefit sharing. Fedco will give 10 percent of the proceeds from sales of those seeds to the Northeast Farmers of Color Land Trust, which assists farmers of color in purchasing their own farms.

And in a meaningful gesture toward incentivizing breeding for the commons, Fedco pays royalties to "backyard breeders" and marks which seeds in the catalog were produced by independent breeders, from whom they purchase seed directly. Fedco notes that independent breeders are "continuing a long tradition of adapting varieties to local tastes and conditions," and as such "are the backbone of culture. For the most part eschewing plant patents, their work is their reward. Fedco is committed to buying seed from small breeders to give economic support to their work. Though we can find cheaper seed elsewhere, we prefer not to compromise on quality or ethics. We hope you agree."

In another striking effort, the US-based Open Source Seed Initiative to date has 415 pledged seed varieties that will remain in the commons in perpetuity for others to grow, save, share, re-grow, and breed with the condition that any offspring are also pledged to the commons. They have 35 plant breeders committed to the OSSI breeding more seed, and 61 seed company partners selling OSSI seed.

Between 2015 and 2018, the Community Seed Network (CSN) was formed by seed savers and seed organizations in the United States and Canada. CSN evolved into a joint initiative of Seed

Savers Exchange and SeedChange, a Canadian seed initiative. CSN's mission is "to support and to connect people to projects, projects to each other, and everyone to seed ... [making] this work visible locally, regionally, and internationally, empowering community seed leaders as trailblazers and movement builders."

In 2020, a coalition of seed-saving activists and national seed-saving groups from 31 European countries, and the European Coordination of Let's Liberate Diversity, came together to form Seeds4All, a website dedicated to seed diversity that aims to "give visibility to all European organizations that collect, enrich, produce, disseminate, and sustainably use traditional and new varieties of seeds belonging to the public domain, freely reproducible and not genetically modified." Twenty-four thousand seed varieties are represented there.

Cultural leadership groups, including the Indigenous Seed Keepers Network and Second Generation Seeds, continue the work of identifying seed of cultural importance in seed-holding groups and institutions such as Seed Savers Exchange and the USDA, and natural history museums and seed banks around the country. Once identified, these cultural seeds are then rematriated back to their people, who re-enliven them through re-growing and sharing them. This whole process ultimately strives to make whole, or as Chris Bolden-Newsome expressed, re-member these seeds with their cultural stories and histories.

In Fort Collins, Drs. Christina Walters and Stephanie Greene with the USDA continue internally to search that collection and its documentation and tag seed that might be of cultural importance, as do staff and volunteers at SSE.

The Germplasm Resources Information Network (GRIN) of the USDA remains an open-source, searchable information site. GRIN "documents animal, microbial, and plant collections through informational pages, searchable databases, and links to USDA-ARS projects that curate the collections."

In 2023, the 11th Annual Seed Library Summit was held online, with no charge for admission as part of their group's belief in the creative commons.

Each act of re-commoning, each act of courage through seed and courage seeded is germinating a different worldview, a different seed narrative. And there is increasing momentum.

OCTOBER 24
After a year of historic drought—one of the driest years on record for more than a century in California, the rains come. Earlier this year than the last three years when we had to wait for real rains deep into November or December even. An epic Category 5 "atmospheric river of moisture" churned itself off the coast and poured six inches of rain into our region in one day.

We are of course worried about flash flooding, mudslides in burn scars, the impact on the still-displaced communities of the Camp Fire let alone those now displaced by the Dixie Fire, which in turn raises questions about and attention to the ongoing battles of identity and restoration for so many ecosystems, economies, cultures and peoples, plants and places the world over.

OCTOBER 31: SAMHAIN—ALL HALLOWS' EVE
Despite recent rains, we are still in a record-breaking drought in a record-breaking epidemic, and everything is stretched. The summer heat has taken its toll on all of us.

Down by the creek, the buckeyes are deep in their normal seasonal summer dormancy, leaves crisp and nutmeg brown. Their seed set is very small—small in number and small in size for this time of year; the plants intuitively know to conserve their resources. Where some years there might be 25 seeds festooning the small trees or large shrubs, this year there are two or three. Which is enough to replace these mother plants.

This creek and riparian corridor—cathedral-like alders and sycamores, willows and cattails, mimulus and watercress, is not just a watershed but a seedshed, a human- and cultureshed as well. It is a conduit for life of all kinds being distributed and redistributed.

In the world beyond the creek, beyond this little canyon, in California's chaparral, October often has a more subtle heat and intense dryness than August and September. This is always an expectant time, waiting for steady winter rains to resume. It might be this month, it might be next month, but as of now the seasonal end to the dry time feels possible with that first drink earlier this month.

The foothills plant community of trees, rugged shrubs, vines, geophytes, herbaceous perennials and annuals, is thick with seed—bright and bold and eye-, wind-, and even water-droplet-catching seed also waiting— hanging in the liminal and beautiful, often messy balance from ripeness to release to start the next round of life.

This whole landscape is vividly and wildly populated: capped acorns fat and thin, dark brown and green; bigleaf maple samaras; glistening silver curlicue wings of feathery clematis; increasingly bright red clusters of toyon; the aging remains of deep purple elderberry clusters; wrinkling orange hips studding the thorny stems of *Rosa californica*; burnished, glossy, fist-sized buckeyes winking from sheaths that dehisce and contract around the large seeds like outgrown winter coats on children irritable at the confinement. Nonnative grass seeds and awns are prickly and brittle in the grasslands. Invasive nonnative blackberries not eaten by us or other mammals and birds are now dried specks on their brown calyces.

On wheat-colored stems, the lilies, fritillarias, and *Calochortus* are almost invisible beneath their sheltering shrub companions. Within their genus-specific seed structures, rows of wizened, dry, black and bronze and chocolate-colored seeds wait in elaborate architectural housings of durable, textural, fibrous vestments—like fine handmade Italian paper—for the time to be right, for an animal or a gust of wind or observant hand to rattle the structure and begin the cycle again.

The seeds are testament to patience, to diversity of ways, means, forms, and methods, to beauty and ingenuity, to adaptation, to resourcefulness, to a dynamic balance of competition and cooperation, to seasonality and cycles, and to generous sharing of all of that—like mothers and daughters, grandparents and grandchildren, gardeners and gardens. Like all family.

Right now, near the deep part of the creek past the old swimming hole, which is currently dense with large woody debris slowing the creek, filtering the creek, cooling the creek, and feeding the riparia, I swim alongside a maturing cattail, beside graceful stems of paper-lantern-like mimulus seed pods. Cottonwood and willow cotton (which wafted downstream like a snowstorm in spring) can still be seen in ragged clumps in little corners of organic litter. The *Darmera*'s large umbrella leaves, looking almost tropical and uncharacteristic for this summer-hot and dry part of the world, are held up downstream from where we swim, like a mother's hands I saw in them earlier, but also alms dishes or crucible staging platforms for the next generation.

Drought, fire, pandemic, environmental and economic disruption—all of these trials are embedded in, softened and supported by the seed-to-seed cycle of the plant world around us, even when we abbreviate this cycle, diminish it. Even when we don't see it. Something about looking at the world from the seed's-eye view, of watching and caring for another, from preparing the first tiny seed to laying down their final form to be upcycled into the lives around them at season's or life's end, makes you see more, diminish less. Invites you and allows you into this longer view, by the year, by the decade, by the millennium—which is slower, but so much bigger.

I wish I could say this was just a tale of California, but it's not.

Perhaps I should rephrase that: I am glad this is not just a tale of California, because it is in fact a tale of life.

It is a tale of what we see and what we don't see, what we seed and what we don't seed. It is a tale of what we nurture and what we don't nurture;

how the world we want and how we want the world is, as always, up to our individual seeds and seedings.

The seeds of change are in all of us if we wish to nurture them, to save them, and grow them out and on. The seeds, even with a small seed set, are still there in the creeks, in the forests, in the meadows, on the mountaintops, in the soil, in the burn scars, in tiny glass jars in people's cupboards, in old tins under beds, in envelopes in drawers, in large seed bank vaults and regional seed banks and public seed libraries, in communal seed swaps, and in sacred buildings of worship. Waiting in the cracks of city sidewalks and on rural roadside edges the world over. We need them all.

A great diversity of seeds and seed people are also miraculously there in academic and traditional ecological science, in spiritual centers, in art studios and craft circles, in agriculture and horticulture of both rural and urban communities. For now.

What exactly are the contours of our humanity? Are they perfectly formed to the texture of a mustard seed? Of an acorn? Of the glossy chestnut handful of a buckeye with its eye-like hilum? Are they the permeating fragrance of basil seed? The elaborate armature of a pipevine? Are they the juicy protein invitation of an elaiosome or sweet flesh of a berry, an apple?

Can the contours of our humanity expand back out to be that infinitely diverse, artful, flavorful, and generative?

The seed and the seed keepers among us believe they can. They see, seed, and re-seed their great expectations and faith that we can meet this moment—these many moments—for and with the seeds in our crops, in our wildlands, in our communal food and festivals, art and ceremonies. For the seeds in our collective hearts, minds, and bodies—our hopes, prayers, and blessings.

ACKNOWLEDGMENTS

First, gratitude to the seeds, their plants, their lands, their animals, and their people.

Second, to the many generous and fierce seed keepers growing and protecting our world—the many who trusted me with their stories, their words, and their intelligence for this book, the many known and unknown, past and present who may not be mentioned here, but who are nonetheless of critical importance—it is your collective work as seed keepers that fed this journey, and feeds our world in ways seen and unseen. Any failures of facts, interpretation, or imagination are mine alone.

I am, as ever, grateful for the seedbed and loving families in which I have been continually nurtured: mother Sheila Balding Jewell, father Samuel Rea Jewell, stepmother Isabel Ewing Jewell, aunt Diana Jewell Bingham; sisters Sabrina Jewell and Flora Jewell-Stern; aunts Bettina, Pammy, Linda, and Sue; uncles Ivor David and Pliny; cousins Lucinda, PJ, Linda, Sheila, and Abigail; and, the entire Simchuk family. Deep gratitude to the incredible, supportive circle of humans who have encouraged me these many seasons: Christl, Amy, Charles, Erik Singer, Gretchen, Sacha, Kim, Jennifer, Mary, Nancy, Lynn, Julie, Lorene, Sunday, Colleen, Adrienne, Mary Rose, Kristen, Keiko, Brandi, Candy, Debra, Mary Ann, Loree, Abra, Wambui, Christin, Pen, Isa. Family and friends alike have each gifted me with love, challenge, creativity, and celebration.

With humble thanks for the hours spent reviewing (and reviewing again) for readability, relevance, and biology, for composition and the complexity of life and punctuation: Sheila Blackford Bloor, Julie Kierstead, and Rob Schlising.

Stacee Gravelle Lawrence, Timber Press editor and friend, and Andrew Beckman, publisher: thank you for believing in this idea and in me as a writer. Laura Whittemore, copyeditor: your bird-sharp eyes and detailed input improved and brought this book to its final maturity. To the rest of the great Timber team—Katlynn, Cobi, and more—your invaluable support is appreciated!

John W. Whittlesey—you have walked beside me and held my hand every step and word of these recent seed-story years, unwavering in your kindness, your patience, and your love. We have and will sow, water, grow, gather, see, and savor many more happy seed days.

SELECTED REFERENCES

PREFACE

Page 10, Since the 1980s, when the first GMO seed patent was issued:

Dharauli, Kyiv, and Rugby Lukashivka. 2022. "The Coming Food Catastrophe."
  The Economist, 19 May 2022. economist.com/leaders/2022/05/19/
  the-coming-food-catastrophe

Page 11, As I write this in mid-2022, I have been struck:

Romero, Simon. 2022. "'Burning Down a Way of Life': Wildfire Rips
  through a Hispanic Bastion," *New York Times*, 5 May 2022.
  nytimes.com/2022/05/05/us/new-mexico-wildfires.html

Page 11, I am struck by the news of Russian forces:

Le Page, Michael. 2022. "Priceless Samples from Ukraine's National Seed Bank
  Destroyed in Bomb Attack." *New Scientist*, 19 May 2022. newscientist.com/
  article/2321008-priceless-samples-from-ukraines-seed-bank-destroyed-
  in-bomb-attack

October: The Energetic Nature of Seed

Page 19, The great oaks of this canyon:

Standiford, Richard B., Douglas McCreary, and Kathryn L Purcell. 2002. "Pro-
  ceedings of the Fifth Symposium on Oak Woodlands: Oaks in California's
  Changing Landscape." 22–25 October 2001, San Diego, CA. USDA, U.S.
  Forest Service, Southern Research Station. srs.fs.usda.gov/pubs/6199

Pavlik, Bruce M., Pamela C. Muick, Sharon G. Johnson, and Marjorie Popper.
  1991. *Oaks of California*. Los Olivos, CA: Cachuma Press, and Oakland, CA:
  California Oak Foundation.

Keator, Glenn, and Susan Bazell. 1998. *The Life of an Oak: An Intimate Portrait*.
  Berkeley, CA: Heyday Books, and Oakland, CA: California Oak Foundation.

Mechoopda Indian Tribe of the Chico Rancheria, Butte County, CA.
  mechoopda-nsn.gov/; mechoopda-nsn.gov/history/euro-american-contact

California Heritage Indigenous Research Project, Nevada City, CA. chirpca.org

Griggs, F. Thomas, and Gregory H. Golet. 2002. "Riparian Valley Oak (*Quercus lobata*) Forest Restoration on the Middle Sacramento River, California." In Standiford, Richard B., et al, tech. editor. "Proceedings of the Fifth Symposium on Oak Woodlands: Oaks in California's Challenging Landscape." USDA, U.S Forest Service, Southern Research Station. srs.fs.usda.gov/pubs/26151

McDonald, Philip M. "Blue Oak." U.S. Forest Service, Southern Research Station publications. srs.fs.usda.gov/pubs/misc/ag_654/volume_2/quercus/douglasii.htm

Page 21, Here in this small canyon:

Speer, Robert. 2008. "Gold Rush on Dry Creek." *Chico News & Review*, 6 March 2008. newsreview.com/chico/content/gold-rush-on-dry-creek/632058

Page 22, The intermingling gray pines:

Lukes, Laura. 2019. "Finding an Ecological Niche: A Three-Part Series on Selected Foothill Woodland and Chaparral Species, Part 2 of 3: The Gray Pine." *The Real Dirt Blog*, 8 March 2019. ucanr.edu/blogs/blogcore/postdetail.cfm?postnum=29577

Brodhead, Laura. 2017. "Native Plant Society: An Appreciation of the Gray Pine." *Record Searchlight*, 4 February 2017. redding.com/story/life/2017/02/04/native-plant-society-appreciation-gray-pine/97436540

Page 23, Plant life grows hand in hand with rock:

Staton, Kelly, and Debbie Spangler. 2014. *Geology of the Northern Sacramento Valley, California*. California Department of Water Resources Northern Region Office Groundwater and Geologic Investigations Section. cawaterlibrary.net/wp-content/uploads/2017/05/Geology-of-the-Northern-Sacramento-Valley.pdf

Bills, Albin, and Samantha Mackey. 2018. *Wildflowers of Table Mountain: A Naturalist's Guide*. Chico: California State University Chico, Studies from the Herbarium.

Page 28, I am very interested in the "moral arc of the universe,":

Worth, Rev. J. Mark. 2016. "The Moral Arc of the Universe." Harvard Unitarian Universalist Church. 13 November 2016. uuharvard.org/services/moral-arc-of-the-universe

Page 29, origins of Halloween:

"Samhain." *Celtic Connection*. wicca.com/pagan-holidays/samhain.html

"The Eight Important and Sacred Celtic Holidays of the Year." *Meanwhile in Ireland*, 18 May 2020. meanwhileinireland.com/eight-important-sacred-celtic-holidays

November: The Circular Setting of Seed

Page 34, According to NASA, Earth:

"How Did Life Begin and Evolve on Earth, and Has it Evolved Elsewhere in the Solar System?" *NASA Science*. science.nasa.gov/solar-system/ big-questions/how-did-life-begin-and-evolve-earth-and-has-it-evolved-elsewhere-solar-system

Pages 35, evidence of vascular plants appeared:

For my discussions on the evolution and biology of the vascular and seed-bearing plants, I have relied on these books:

Hanson, Thor. 2015. *The Triumph of Seeds*. New York: Basic Books.

Thompson, Peter. 2010. *Seeds, Sex and Civilization*. London: Thames & Hudson.

Kessler, Rob, and Wolfgang Stuppy. 2012. *Seeds: Time Capsules of Life.* San Rafael, CA: Earth Aware Editions.

Elpel, Thomas J. 1996. *Botany in a Day: The Patterns Method of Plant Identification*. Pony, MT: HOPS Press.

Page 42, In 2019, the United Nations (U.N.):

United Nations Environmental Programme Annual Report, 2019. unep.org/ annualreport/2019/index.php

Page 43, The iris occurring:

For my detailed discussions of individual California native plant species or genera throughout this book, I have relied on these sources:

The Jepson eFlora, the Jepson Herbarium, University of California, Berkeley. ucjeps.berkeley.edu/eflora

CalScape, the California Native Plant Society's online reference resource. calscape.org

Calflora, a nonprofit database for plants (native and nonnative) growing in California. calflora.org

Flora of North America. flora.huh.harvard.edu/FNA

Page 49, Being competitive in challenging:

Ali Meders-Knight. TEK leader and instructor for the Mechoopda Indian Tribe of the Chico, Rancheria, personal interview and correspondence, 2021.

Page 49, *Pinus longaeva*:

"Bristlecone Pines." National Park Service, Great Basin National Park, NV. nps.gov/grba/planyourvisit/identifying-bristlecone-pines.htm

Page 50, Pine nuts feed a multitude of birds:

Baron, Matthew. 2018. "The History of Pine Nuts." 15 April 2018. Wholesale Nuts and Dried Fruit. wholesalenutsanddriedfruit.com/ history-of-pine-nuts

Darwin, Charles. 1839. *The Voyage of the Beagle*. London: Henry Colburn.

Darwin, Charles. 1859. *On the Origin of Species By Means of Natural Selection*. London: John Howard.

Page 51, Seeds have distinct traits:

Cheryl Birker, personal interview and correspondence, 2021.

Naomi Fraga, personal interview and correspondence, 2021.

Page 52, The sandhill cranes are in.

Cornell Lab of Ornithology. birds.cornell.edu/home

Thompson, Andrea. 2022. "Plants are Stuck as Seed-Eating Animals Decline. *Scientific American*, 14 January 2022. scientificamerican.com/article/ plants-are-stuck-as-seed-eating-animals-decline

Fry, Carolyn. 2016. *Seeds: A Natural History*. Chicago: University of Chicago Press.

Page 54, The roadside toyon:

Rosenthal, Sue. 2018. "Toyon and Cedar Waxwings." *Bay Nature*, 2 January 2018 baynature.org/article/toyon-cedar-waxwings-classic-pairing

Garcia-Rodriguez, Alberto, Jorg Albrecht, Sylwia Szczutkowska, Nina Farwig, and Nuria Selva. 2021. "The Role of the Brown Bear *Ursus arctos* as a Legitimate Megafaunal Seed Disperser." *Nature*, 14 January 2021. nature. com/articles/s41598-020-80440-9

Page 55, Dr. Doug Tallamy:

Tallamy, Douglas W. 2019. *Nature's Best Hope: A New Approach to Conservation That Starts in Your Yard*. Portland, OR: Timber Press.

Douglas W. Tallamy, personal interview and correspondence, 2019–2021.

December: Seedshed

Page 60, Two small packets of Palestinian heritage wheat:

Vivien Sansour, personal interview and correspondence, 2021.

Disarming Design from Palestine: An independent nonprofit platform resisting the dehumanization of Palestinians. Based in Belgium and serves as a design label that "fosters thought-provoking and disarming designs from Palestine." disarmingdesign.com

Page 61, Violence against the seedshed:

United States Environmental Protection Agency, National Priorities List and Superfund Alternative Approach Sites. epa.gov/superfund/ search-superfund-sites-where-you-live

Page 64, Often plants have several methods:

Fry, Carolyn. 2016. *Seeds: A Natural History*. Chicago: University of
Chicago Press.

Kessler, Rob, and Wolfgang Stuppy. 2012. *Seeds: Time Capsules of Life*.
San Rafael, CA: Earth Aware Editions.

Elpel, Thomas J. 1996. *Botany in a Day: The Patterns Method of Plant
Identification*. Pony, MT: HOPS Press.

Page 70, Joe Joe Clark is a native plant enthusiast:

Joe Joe Clark, naturalist, Napa County Open Space District, personal
interview and correspondence, September 2020.

January: Seed Life Linking Us

Page 77, Dormancy, a state of:

Christina T. Walters, supervisory plant physiologist, USDA Agricultural
Research Service, personal interview and correspondence, 2021.

Fry, Carolyn. 2016. *Seeds: A Natural History*. Chicago: University of
Chicago Press.

Page 77, We as humans have throughout time:

Wilson, Diane. 2021. *The Seed Keeper: A Novel*. Minneapolis, MN:
Milkweed Editions.

Christina T. Walters, supervisory plant physiologist, USDA Agricultural
Research Service, personal interview and correspondence, 2021.

Page 78, In wildfire-adapted regions:

Mullen, Luba. 2017. "How Trees Survive and Thrive After a Fire." *Your
National Forest Magazine*, Summer/Fall 2017. National Forest Foundation.
nationalforests.org/our-forests/your-national-forests-magazine/
how-trees-survive-and-thrive-after-a-fire

Page 81, Well-known gardener:

Roach, Margaret. "Estimating Viability: How Long Do Seeds Last?" A Way to
Garden. awaytogarden.com/estimating-viability-how-long-do-seeds-last

Page 82, In February of 2020:

Katz, Brigit. 2020. "Scientists Grew Palm Trees from 2,000-Year-Old
Seeds." *Smithsonian Magazine*, 7 February 2020. smithsonianmag.com/
smart-news/scientists-grew-palm-trees-2000-year-old-seeds-180974164/

Klein, Alice. 2020. "Extinct Date Palms Grown from 2000-Year-Old Seeds
Found Near Jerusalem." *New Scientist*, 5 February 2020. newscientist.com/
article/2232464-extinct-date-palms-grown-from-2000-year-old-seeds-
found-near-jerusalem/

Zang, Sarah. 2020. "After 2,000 Years, These Seeds Have Finally Sprouted."
The Atlantic, 5 February 2020. theatlantic.com/science/archive/2020/02/
how-to-grow-a-date-tree-from-2000-year-old-seeds/606079

Page 84, Friend, fellow gardener, and emeritus:

Robert Schlising, personal interviews and correspondence, 2018–2022.

Schlising, Robert, and Halkard E. Mackey Jr. 2020. "Biology of the Ephemeral
Geophyte, Steer's Head (*Dicentra uniflora*, Papaveraceae) in the Southern-
most Cascade Range, Butte County, California." *Madroño: A West American
Journal of Botany*, Volume 66 (Issue 4), 148–163. 22 January 2020.
bioone.org/journals/madro%C3%B1o/volume-66/issue-4

Page 87, The Bill and Melinda Gates Foundation foment:

Urhahn, Jan. 2020. "Bill Gates's Foundation Is Leading a Green Counter-
revolution in Africa." *Jacobin*, 27 December 2020. jacobin.com/2020/12/
agribusiness-gates-foundation-green-revolution-africa-agra

Page 89, For Dave Smoke-McCluskey:

Dave Smoke McCluskey, personal interviews and correspondence, 2021.
thecornmafia.com/

Patterson, Haddasah. 2020. "Kernels of Truth About Corn." The Bitter
Southerner, 17 November 2020. bittersoutherner.com/feature/2020/
features/2020/kernels-of-truth-about-corn

McCann, James. 2021. "Maize and Grace: History, Corn, and Africa's New
Landscapes, 1500–1999," published online by Cambridge University Press,
6 July 2001. cambridge.org/core/journals/comparative-studies-in-society-
and-history/article/abs/maize-and-grace-history-corn-and-africas-new-
landscapes-15001999/5BA7DF0BFCA80F173E3137A97D530C56

Page 91, Today is National Seed Swap Day:

"History of National Seed Swap Day." National Today. nationaltoday.com/
national-seed-swap-day/#history

Page 92, I attend a virtual lecture:

Ecological Landscape Alliance. ecolandscaping.org/

Heather McCargo, personal interviews and correspondence, 2021.
wildseedproject.net/

Page 92, On Dig Delve:

Dig Delve. digdelve.com/

The Gaia Foundation. gaiafoundation.org/guardian-seed-saving-movement-
calls-for-seeds-to-be-publicly-owned

Genova, Alexandra. 2020. "Seed Saving Movement Calls for Seeds to be Publicly Owned." *The Guardian*, 28 December 2020. theguardian.com/uk-news/2020/dec/28/seed-saving-movement-calls-for-seeds-to-be-publicly-owned

February: Seed Shares and Seed Laws
Page 99, Daniel gave me the perspective:

Daniel Atkinson, personal interviews and correspondence, November 2013–March 2016.

Micaella Colley, Organic Seed Alliance, personal interviews and correspondence, January–March 2016. seedalliance.org

Kimmerer, Robin Wall. 2013. *Braiding Sweetgrass: Indigenous Wisdom, Scientific Knowledge, and the Teachings of Plants*. Minneapolis, MN: Milkweed Editions.

Robin Wall Kimmerer, personal interviews and correspondence, 2018–2021.

Hoover, Elizabeth. *From Garden Warriors to Good Seeds: Indigenizing the Local Food Movement*. gardenwarriorsgoodseeds.com/

Elizabeth Hoover, personal interviews and correspondence, February–April 2016; February–November 2018.

Ira Wallace, Southern Exposure Seed Exchange, personal interviews and correspondence, 2018–2021. southernexposure.com

Penniman, Leah. 2018. *Farming While Black: Soul Fire Farm's Practical Guide to Liberation on the Land*. White River Junction, VT: Chelsea Green Publishing.

Leah Penniman, Soul Fire Farm, personal interviews and correspondence, 2018–2020. soulfirefarm.org

Rowen White, Sierra Seeds, personal interviews and correspondence, 2017; February–November 2018; 2021. sierraseeds.org

Diane Wilson, personal interviews and correspondence, 2021–2022. dianewilsonwords.com

Native American Food Sovereignty Alliance/Indigenous Seed Keepers Network. nativefoodalliance.org/

Kellee Matsushita-Tseng, Second Generation Seeds, personal interviews and correspondence, 2021–2023. secondgenerationseeds.com

LaDuke, Winona. The 32nd Annual Salem Peace Lecture, 21 November 2021, Salem, OR. honorearth.net/. View lecture: youtube.com/watch?v=lvj4w3BgauM&ab_channel=WillametteUniversity

Page 100, The Organic Seed Alliance takes us:

Organic Seed Alliance. seedalliance.org

Dillon, Matthew. "And We Have the Seeds," 22 February 2005. seedalliance.org/
2005/and-we-have-the-seeds

Seminis. vegetables.bayer.com/us/en-us/products/seminis.html

Food and Power. foodandpower.net

Page 103, Beginning in the 1850s:

The American Seed Trade Association. betterseed.org

Louwaars, Niels. 2019. "Open Source Seed, A Revolution in Breeding, or Yet
Another Attack on the Breeder's Exemption?" *Frontiers in Plant Science* 10,
18 September 2019. frontiersin.org/articles/10.3389/fpls.2019.01127/full

Page 105, Subsequently, the USDA still supported:

Seed Savers Exchange. seedsavers.org

Hubbard, Kiki. 2019. "A Short History of Intellectual Property Rights on Seed
and What Farmers Should Know." *Natural Farmer*, Summer 2019.
thenaturalfarmer.org/article/a-short-history-of-intellectual-property-
rights-on-seed-and-what-farmers-should-know

Page 108, In 1999, High Mowing Organic Seeds:

High Mowing Organic Seeds. highmowingseeds.com

Council for Responsible Genetics, Ecology Center, Berkeley, CA. ecologycenter.
org/directory/directory-entries/council-for-responsible-genetics-crg

Wild Garden Seed/Shoulder to Shoulder Farm. wildgardenseed.com

Page 109, While the organic food:

National Organic Program, Agricultural Marketing Service, United States
Department of Agriculture. ams.usda.gov/about-ams/programs-offices/
national-organic-program

Lawn, CR. 2019. "The Fedco Seed Catalog: More than a Marketing Tool."
New Commons Project, University of Maine, Farmington.
newcommonsproject.org/eventvideos

Page 111, In early 2022, I interviewed Dave Melhorn:

Dave Melhorn and Lauren Giroux, Johnny's Selected Seeds, personal
interviews and correspondence, 2021–2022.

Elmore, Bartow, J. 2021. *Seed Money: Monsanto's Past and Our Future.*
New York: Norton Publishing.

W. Atlee Burpee. burpee.com/company-history

NE Seed. neseed.com/commercial-seed-company

DP Seed LLC. dpseeds.com/

Page 114, Melhorn's thinking is largely corroborated:

Sowell, Andrew, and Bryn Swearingen. 2021. "Wheat Outlook 2021." Economic Research Service, United States Department of Agriculture. ers.usda.gov/publications/pub-details/?pubid=102369

Goldman, Suzanne. 2013. "The U.S. Department of Agriculture Probes Oregon Monsanto GM Wheat Mystery." *The Guardian*, 22 June 2013. theguardian.com/environment/2013/jun/22/agriculture-oregon-monsanto-gm-wheat

Global Fortune Insights. Global Seed Market Size, Share, and Industry Analysis 2018–2025. fortunebusinessinsights.com/industry-reports/commercial-seed-market-100078

U.S. Food and Drug Administration. "GMO Crops, Animal Food, and Beyond." fda.gov/food/agricultural-biotechnology/gmo-crops-animal-food-and-beyond

Pitchford, Joey. 2020. "Farmland Under Threat, Part 1." North Carolina Department of Agriculture & Consumer Services, 24 June 2020. blog.ncagr.gov/2020/06/24/farmland-under-threat-part-1-what-is-the-issue/

Agriculture.com staff. 2006. "Monsanto's American Seeds, Inc., Buys Five Seed Companies." Successful Farming, 28 June 2006. agriculture.com/news/business/Monsantos-American-Seeds-Inc-buys-five-seed-companies_5-ar978

Hubbard, Kiki. Summer 2019. "A Short History of Intellectual Property Rights on Seed and What Farmers Should Know." *Natural Farmer*. thenaturalfarmer.org/article/a-short-history-of-intellectual-property-rights-on-seed-and-what-farmers-should-know

Page 117, The seed from these crops and acres:

Knutson, Jonathan. 2018. "31 Million Acres Lost: Development Cuts into U.S. Farmland." *AgWeek,* 9 May 2018. agweek.com/business/31-million-acres-lost-development-cuts-into-u-s-farmland

Page 120, Just 60 years ago:

Carson, Rachel. 1962. *Silent Spring.* New York: Houghton Mifflin.

Page 120, poison oak (*Toxicodendrun diversilobum*):

Dresser, Sierrian. 2012. "Poison Oak Has A Good Side, Too." *Bay Nature,* 12 July 2012. baynature.org/article/poison-oak-has-a-good-side-too

Page 122, The nonnative mustards:

Oregon State University, Extension Service. "Bees in the Vegetable Garden—Mustard." extension.oregonstate.edu/gardening/pollinators/bees-vegetable-garden-mustard

Panzar, Javier. 2019. "This Super Bloom is Pretty Dangerous: Invasive
    Mustard is Fuel for the Next Fire." *Los Angeles Times*, 25 April 2019.
    latimes.com/local/lanow/la-me-ln-mustard-fire-santa-monica-
    mountains-20190425-story.html

California Invasive Plant Council. Brassica Nigra. cal-ipc.org/plants/profile/
    brassica-nigra-profile

Leach, Kristyn. 2020. "Civil Eats TV: Saving Seeds with Kristyn Leach."
    youtube.com/watch?v=jVKtmrrdW3U

Bossard, Carla. "IPCW Plant Report: *Cytisis scoparius*." California Invasive
    Plant Council. cal-ipc.org/resources/library/publications/ipcw/report39

Northwest Treaty Tribes. 2019. "Scotch Broom Beetles Could Help Slow
    Spread of Invasive Plant." *Northwest Treaty Tribes Magazine*,
    22 Jun 2019. nwtreatytribes.org/scotch-broom-beetles-could-
    help-slow-spread-of-invasive-plant

LaBoe, Barbara. 2011. "Beetles Chomp Away at Hardy Scotch Broom."
    Seattle Times, 28 May 2011. seattletimes.com/seattle-news/
    beetles-chomp-away-at-hardy-scotch-broom

March: Seed Commerce

Page 129, By 1849, a year after gold:

Blum, Mrs. Bessie Lyte. 1941. In a written history, in author's personal
    collection.

Page 131, The earliest blooming:

Abrahamson, Ilana. 2014. "Arctostaphylos manzanita." In Fire Effects Informa-
    tion System (online). U.S. Department of Agriculture, Forest Service,
    Rocky Mountain Research Station, Fire Sciences Laboratory (Producer).
    fs.usda.gov/database/feis/plants/shrub/arcman/all.html

Page 136, Oregon State University:

Oregon State University, Corvallis, OR. Special Collections and Archives,
    Research Center

Nursery and Seed Trade Catalogs Collection 1832–1999. scarc.library.
    oregonstate.edu/findingaids/index.php?p=collections/findingaid&id=2552

Smithsonian Institution, Smithsonian Libraries. Seed and Nursery Catalogs.
    library.si.edu/exhibition/seed-and-nursery-catalogs

Atlanta History Center, Cherokee Garden Library. atlantahistorycenter.
    com/exhibitions/cherokee-garden-library-collection-highlights/
    hastings-seed-catalogues/

Page 139, All of this history leads:

Wilde, Matthew. 2012. "Uncertain Future: Lawmakers Try to Find Compromise on Farm Bill Reauthorization." *Waterloo-Cedar Falls Courier*, 20 May 2012. wcfcourier.com/business/local/uncertain-future-lawmakers-try-to-find-compromise-on-farm-bill-reauthorization/article_7885282a-a11c-11e1-bafe-0019bb2963f4.html

Page 139, For example, earlier:

Matthew Martin and Lisa Carle, Pyramid Farms, personal interview and correspondence, January 2021. pyramidfarms.com/

Page 140, In the "independent":

Center for Food Safety. "Food Safety Report for June 2012." cfs.gov.hk/english/programme/programme_fs/files/2012_food_safety_report_06_e.pdf

Rob-See-Co, LLC. Elkhorn, NE. robseeco.com

National Gardening Association. "National Gardening Survey 2022 edition." gardenresearch.com/view/national-gardening-survey-2022-edition

Ferry-Morse Home Gardening. Norton, MA. ferrymorse.com/?msclkid=966a4981e06d1a731b4e2b417e62f27f

Central Garden and Pet. central.com/our-brands

Fedco Seeds. Clinton, ME. fedcoseeds.com/trees/about_fedco.htm

Maine Organic Farmers and Gardeners. Unity, ME. mofga.org

Page 146, Judith Larner Lowry:

Judith Larner Lowry, Larner Seeds, Seeds for California Landscape, personal interviews and correspondence, 2021–2022. larnerseeds.com

California Native Grasslands Association. cnga.org

Page 147, Any power like that:

United States Department of Agriculture. Agricultural Marketing Service, Federal Seed Act. ams.usda.gov/rules-regulations/fsa

California Department of Food and Agriculture. Seed Board and Commissions: ams.usda.gov/rules-regulations/fsa

Page 148, I caught Jillian:

Jillian Hagenston, California Department of Food and Agriculture, Seed Inspection, personal conversation, July 2022. cdfa.ca.gov/plant/pe/nsc/docs/seed/SeedInspRec.pdf

California Department of Food and Agriculture. Regulations and Seed Law. cdfa.ca.gov/plant/regs_seed_law_3899.html

April: Seed's Human Banking History

Page 152, John and I join Elena Gregg:

Elena Gregg, personal conversation, July 2021.

"Butte County Meadowfoam (*Limnanthes floccosa* ssp. *californica*."
California Department of Fish and Wildlife. wildlife.ca.gov/Conservation/
Plants/Endangered/Limnanthes-floccosa-ssp-californica

Page 156, Human seed banks:

John B. Dickie, senior research leader, Royal Botanic Gardens, Kew, personal
interviews and correspondence, 2020–2021. kew.org/science/our-science/
people/john-b-dickie

Page 157, The oldest such agricultural:

Loskutov, Igor; "Vavilov and His Institute a History of the World Collection of
Plant Genetic Resources in Russia." International Plant Genetic Resources
Institute, 1999.

Nabhan, Gary Paul. 2011. *Where Our Food Comes From: Retracing Nikolay
Vavilov's Quest to End Famine*. Washington, D.C.: Island Press.

Stout, Arlow Burdette. 1913. "The Imperial Botanic Garden of Peter the Great
at St. Petersburg," *Journal of the New York Botanical Garden* 14: 195.

Page 158, The institute is famous:

Gary Paul Nabhan, personal interviews and correspondence, 2021.

Stephanie Greene, supervisory plant physiologist, USDA Agricultural Research
Service, personal interviews and correspondence, 2021.

Page 159, It's essentially the backup reserves:

Christina T. Walters, supervisory plant physiologist, USDA Agricultural
Research Service, personal interviews and correspondence, 2021.

Page 161, Dickie points out:

Parson, Edward A., Peter M. Haas, and Marc A. Levy. 1992. "A Summary of the
Major Documents Signed at the Earth Summit and the Global Forum."
Environment Science and Policy for Sustainable Development, October 1922,
34(8):12–36 researchgate.net/publication/233115003_A_Summary_of_the_
Major_Documents_Signed_at_the_Earth_Summit_and_the_Global_Forum

Page 162, This was not a huge surprise:

The Consultative Group on International Agricultural Research (CGIAR).
cgiar.org

Svalbard Global Seed Vault. seedvault.no

International Center for Agricultural Research in the Dry Areas (ICARDA).
icarda.org

Page 163, In 1996, following:
The Crop Trust. croptrust.org

Page 164, Although the unpredicted:
Wendle, John. 2018. "'Doomsday Vault' Protects Earth's Food Supply—Here's How." *National Geographic*, 20 March 2018. nationalgeographic.com/environment/article/norway-svalbard-global-seed-vault

Page 166, As of early 2022:
Sengupta, Somini. 2017. "How a Seed Bank, Almost Lost in Syria's War, Could Help Feed a Warming Planet." *New York Times*, 13 October 2017. nytimes.com/2017/10/13/climate/syria-seed-bank.html

Sullivan, Helen, 2021. "A Syrian Seed Bank's Fight to Survive. *New Yorker*, 19 October 2021. newyorker.com/news/annals-of-a-warming-planet/a-syrian-seed-banks-fight-to-survive

Page 166, In another interplay:
Christina T. Walters, supervisory plant physiologist, USDA Agricultural Research Service, personal interview and correspondence, 2021.

National Laboratory of Germplasm Research & Preservation and California Botanic Garden. "A Study for the Ages." Center for Plant Conservation. saveplants.org/a-study-for-the-ages

Page 174, Seed Savers Exchange's mission:
Interview with Diane Ott Whealy, *Seed Phytonutrients*, 14 June 2019. seedphytonutrients.com/seed-diversity-cultural-diversity-diane-ott-whealy-of-seed-savers-exchange

Fowler, Cary, and Pat Mooney. 1990. *Shattering: Food, Politics, the Loss of Genetic Diversity*. Tucson: University of Arizona Press.

Page 175, When I speak with Tim:
Tim Johnson, personal interview and correspondence, 2020–2021.

Page 178, Thinking again:
Seed Savers Exchange. seedsavers.org

Nabhan, Gary Paul. 1989. *Enduring Seeds: Native American Agriculture and Wild Plant Conservation*. New York: North Point Press.

Gary Paul Nabhan, cofounder of Native Seed/SEARCH, personal interview and correspondence, 2021–2022.

Alexandra Zamecnik, executive director, Native Seed/SEARCH, personal interview and tour of Native Seed/SEARCH, 2021.

May: The Wild Side of Seed Banks

Page 185, Since 1886, May Day has:

CNN 2020 Haymarket affair; history.com/topics/19th-century/haymarket-riot

Page 187, The Kew seed bank:

Millennium Seed Bank, Royal Botanic Gardens, Kew. kew.org/science/
collections-and-resources/research-facilities/millennium-seed-bank

John B. Dickie, senior research leader, Royal Botanic Gardens, Kew, personal
interviews and correspondence, 2020–2021. kew.org/science/our-science/
people/john-b-dickie

Page 190, The first known formalized US native seed bank:

Portland State University, Rae Selling Berry Seed Bank & Plant Conservation
Program. pdx.edu/seed-bank/history-0

Julie Kierstead, personal interviews and correspondence, 2018–2022.

Page 190, every effort helps:

Other wild biodiversity seed bank models can be found around the country,
often associated with regional botanic gardens, such as the Ladybird
Johnson Wildflower Center in Austin, Texas; the Native Plant Trust in
Massachusetts; and the Atlanta Botanic Garden in Atlanta, Georgia.

Page 193, While seed saving:

Naomi Fraga, director of conservation, California Botanic Garden, personal
interview and correspondence, 2021.

Cheryl Birker, seed conservation program manager, California Botanic Garden,
personal interview and correspondence, 2021.

California Botanic Garden. Seed Conservation, Seed Storage and Curation:
calbg.org/conservation/seed-conservation

Page 195, Evolving parallel to seed banking:

Lowry, Judith Larner. 1999. *Gardening with a Wild Heart: Restoring California's
Native Landscapes at Home.* Berkeley: University of California Press;
and Lowry, Judith Larner. 2007. *The Landscaping Ideas of Jays: A Natural
History of the Backyard Restoration Garden.* Berkeley: University of
California Press.

Judith Larner Lowry, personal interview and correspondence, 2021–2022.

Gail Haggard, Plants of the Southwest. plantsofthesouthwest.com

Alan Wade, Prairie Moon Nursery. prairiemoon.com/

Page 197, At the highest global-network levels:

Convention on Biological Diversity: About the Nagoya Protocol. cbd.int/
abs/about/

Page 198, As reported by the Agrarian Trust:
Feldman, Ari Ephraim. 2021. "City Council Bans Use of Chemicals in
    Public Areas," *Spectrum News, NY1*, 23 April 2021. ny1.com/nyc/
    all-boroughs/news/2021/04/22/city-council-bans-use-of-chemical-
    pesticides-in-public-areas

Page 198, The Center for Biological Diversity:
For the most up-to-date statistics as of printing on the data around the impacts
    of pesticides, insecticides, and coated seeds, I relied on these sources:
Center for Biological Diversity press release, 16 June 2022. biologicaldiversity.
    org/w/news/press-releases/epa-confirms-three-widely-used-
    neonicotinoid-pesticides-likely-harm-vast-majority-of-endangered-
    plants-animals-2022-06-16
Mineau, Pierre. 2020. "Neonicotinoids in California, Their Use and Threats
    to the State's Aquatic Ecosystems and Pollinators, with a Focus on Neonic
    Treated Seeds," 22 September 2020. biologicaldiversity.org/campaigns/
    pesticides_reduction/pdfs/Report-Neonicotinoids-in-California.pdf
Nunez, Damien, and Madeline Potter. 2020. "Neonicotinoids: The Good,
    the Bad, and the Ugly." University of Maryland, Department of
    Entomology, 21 December 2020. entomology.umd.edu/news/
    neonicotinoids-the-good-the-bad-and-the-ugly
National Pesticide Information Center: Treated Seeds. npic.orst.edu/ingred/
    ptype/treated-seed.html
California Department of Food and Agriculture: California Agricultural
    Production Statistics. cdfa.ca.gov/statistics/
Ungelsbee, Emily. 2021. "Treated Seed Troubles, Seed Treatment Overload:
    The Unintended Consequences of a Popular Treatment," *Progressive
    Farmer*, 14 July 2021. dtnpf.com/agriculture/web/ag/crops/article/
    2021/07/13/seed-treatment-overload-unintended

Page 199, As of 2004, more than 18,000 pesticides:
Pesticide Action Network of Europe. pan-international.org/europe/
Donley, N. 2019. "The USA lags behind other agricultural nations in
    banning harmful pesticides." *Environmental Health* 18, 44.
    ehjournal.biomedcentral.com/articles/10.1186/s12940-019-0488-0#citeas
European Parliament. Fact Sheets on Chemicals and Pesticides
    europarl.europa.eu/doceo/document/E-9-2020-000845_EN.html
European Commission Farm to Fork Strategy. food.ec.europa.eu/horizontal-
    topics/farm-fork-strategy_en

June: Seed Libraries and Literacy

Page 204, An article in *Modern Farmer*:

Helmer, Jodi. 2021. "This Teenager Helped Launch Seed Libraries in Every
State." *Modern Farmer*, 8 February 2021. modernfarmer.com/2021/02/
this-teenager-helped-launch-seed-libraries-in-every-state

Page 204, These so-called seed libraries:

Roach, Margaret. "Seed Libraries in the Headlines: Some Grounding
Perspective from Ken Greene." A Way To Garden. awaytogarden.com/
seed-libraries-headlines-perspective-ken-greene/

Page 207, people are receptive to learning about seed:

Community Seed Network. communityseednetwork.org/

SeedChange, Canada. weseedchange.org/

Page 208, By mid-2014, a coalition mobilized:

Richmond Grows Seed Lending Library. richmondgrowsseeds.org/

Sustainable Economies Law Center. "Online Seed Law Tool Shed." theselc.org/
seed_law_resources; github.com/neilthapar/Seed-Law-Tool-Shed

Sustainable Economies Law Center. "Save Seed Sharing! Campaign."
theselc.org/save_seed_sharing

Page 209, Unanimously, the group passed:

"Seed Libraries in Pa. Now Exempt from Costly Law," *Allied News*. alliednews.
com/news/lifestyles/seed-libraries-in-pa-now-exempt-from-costly-law/
article_4e769364-e86d-5964-9ebb-f18deacca83d.html

Page 211, Reading Gary Nabhan and Stephen Buchmann's:

Buchmann, Steve, and Gary Paul Nabhan. 1996. *The Forgotten Pollinators*.
Washington, D.C.: Island Press.

Page 212, Nabhan's interest in seed:

Carson, Rachel. 1962. *Silent Spring*. New York: Houghton Mifflin.

Page 213, The unique natural history of this area:

Vale, Thomas R. 1977. "Forest Changes in the Warner Mountains, California."
Annals of the Association of American Geographers. onlinelibrary.wiley.com/
doi/abs/10.1111/j.1467-8306.1977.tb01118

USDA, Forest Service, Warner Mountain Ranger District. fs.usda.gov/recarea/
modoc/recarea/?recid=71242

USDA, Forest Service, Wilderness Act of 1964. fs.usda.gov/Internet/
FSE_DOCUMENTS/fseprd645666.pdf

Page 220, February 2021 saw the first Slow Seed Summit:

Slow Food USA, Slow Seed Summit 2021. slowfoodusa.org/gatherings/
seed-summit-2021/

Jeff Quattrone, personal interview and correspondence, 2021–2022.
    Library Seed Bank. libraryseedbank.info/
Slow Food USA, Ark of Taste. slowfoodusa.org/ark-of-taste
Page 222, Quattrone's community garden:
Quattrone, Jeff. 2022. "How Campbell Soup Turned New Jersey into
    a Tomato-Growing State," *Smithsonian Magazine*, 14 January 2022.
    smithsonianmag.com/innovation/how-campbell-soup-turned-new-
    jersey-into-tomato-growing-state-180979397/
Weaver, William Woys. "Heirloom Tomato Varieties," *Mother Earth News*.
    motherearthnews.com/organic-gardening/heirloom-tomato-
    varieties-zewz1310zpit
Page 225:
Ken Greene, cofounder Hudson Valley Seed, personal interview and
    correspondence, 2021–2022
Hudson Valley Seed. hudsonvalleyseed.com/
Friedlander, Blaine. 2001. "Cornell delicata squash, disease-resistant ver-
    sion of heirloom winter variety, named 2002 All-America Selection,"
    Cornell Chronicle, 22 October 2001. news.cornell.edu/stories/2001/10/
    cornell-delicata-squash-named-2002-all-america-selection

July: Seed Conservation

Page 231, Many botanic and public gardens:
Atlanta Botanical Garden, Conservation Seed Bank, Atlanta, GA. atlantabg.
    org/conservation-research/science-and-research/biodiversityresearch/
    conservation-seed-bank-and-cryobank/
Desert Botanical Garden, Ahearn Desert Conservation Laboratory, Phoenix,
    AZ. dbg.org/
Page 232, Take *Pediocactus knowltonii*:
Hahne, Claire. 2019. "A Backstop to Extinction," *Sonoran Quarterly*, Winter
    2019. dbg.org/a-backstop-to-extinction
Page 233, The USDA maintains an active:
USDA, Agricultural Research Service, Plant Genetic Resources Unit
    (PGRU), Geneva, NY. ars.usda.gov/northeast-area/geneva-ny/
    plant-genetic-resources-unit-pgru/apple-collection/apple-collection/
Page 234, Seedswoman and gardener Shanyn Siegel:
Shanyn Siegel, personal interview and correspondence, 2021–2022.
Page 235, preserving the wild species of cranberry:
Canaday, Autumn. 2021. "USDA Research Seeks to Strengthen Resiliency
    as Climate Change Affects Production," *ARS News*, 14 December 2021.

ars.usda.gov/news-events/news/research-news/2021/usda-research-
seeks-to-strengthen-cranberry-resiliency-as-climate-change-affects-
production/

USDA, Forest Service, and ARS. 2014. "USDA Forest Service and
Agricultural Research Service Strategy for the Complementary
Conservation of Wild Cranberry (*Vaccinium macrocarpon* Ait.
and *V. oxycoccos*) Genetic Resources and Protocols for Collecting
Genetic Material, Germplasm, and Herbarium Vouchers."
fs.usda.gov/wildflowers/ethnobotany/documents/cwr/
StrategyProtocolsComplementaryConservationWildCranberry08192014.pdf

Page 237, Today, eerily close to the point:

CalFire. fire.ca.gov/incidents/2021/7/13/dixie-fire

Page 237, A report published recently:

Anderson, Mark, Michael Piantedosi, and William Brumback. 2021.
"Conserving Plant Diversity in New England," a joint project of
The Nature Conservancy and The Native Plant Trust.
nativeplanttrust.org/plant-diversity-report; nativeplanttrust.org/
documents/827/ConservingPlantDiversity_FullReport_Final_6.19.21.pdf

Mark Anderson and Michael Piantedosi, personal interview and correspondence, 2021.

Page 239, This is clear in Gary Nabhan's work:

Nabhan, Gary Paul, 1989. *Enduring Seeds: Native American Agriculture and
Wild Plant Conservation*. New York: North Point Press.

Colin Khoury, personal interview and correspondence, 2021.

Page 244, According to Forest Service tables:

USDA, Forest Service, Fire Regime Tables. fs.usda.gov/database/feis/fire_
regime_table/fire_regime_table.html#California

Shrogren, Elizabeth. 2017. "A Century of Fire Suppression in Why California
Is in Flames." *Mother Jones*, 12 December 2017. motherjones.com/
environment/2017/12/a-century-of-fire-suppression-is-why-california-
is-in-flames

Page 245, Yampah is a magnet:

William Whitson, seed breeder at cultivariable.com/about-us/; osseeds.
org/ossi-breeders/william-whitson/; cultivariable.com/instructions/
root-crops/how-to-grow-yampah/

Page 245, Wild crop relatives:

Colin Khoury, personal interview and correspondence, 2021.

Page 251, Plants- and seedswoman Heather McCargo:

Heather McCargo, founder of Wild Seed Project, personal interview and correspondence, 2021. wildseedproject.net/

Xerces Society, Portland, OR. xerces.org

Doug Tallamy, cofounder of Homegrown National Park. homegrownnationalpark.org

Edwina Von Gal, founder of Perfect Earth Project and Two Thirds for the Birds. perfectearthproject.org/; 234birds.org/about-us/

Page 257, Seedswoman Shanyn Siegel:

Shanyn Siegel, personal interview and correspondence, 2021–2022.

August: Seed Memory

Page 264, Many cultures still honor:

Chris Bolden-Newsome, personal interview and correspondence, 2021–2022.

Rowen White, Sierra Seeds. sierraseeds.org/blog/

Prechtel, Martin. 2012. *The Unlikely Peace at Cuchumaquic: The Parallel Lives of People as Plants: Keeping the Seeds Alive.* New York: Penguin Random House.

Vivien Sansour, founder of Palestine Heirloom Seed Library, personal interview and correspondence, 2020–2022. viviensansour.com/ Palestine-Heirloom

Page 265, Rowen White, to my mind:

Rowen White, personal interview and correspondence, 2018–2022.

Sierra Seeds, Seed Seva. sierraseeds.org/seed-seva

Page 270, Elizabeth Hoover is another:

Hoover, Elizabeth. *From Garden Warriors to Good Seeds: Indigenizing the Local Food Movement.* gardenwarriorsgoodseeds.com/

Elizabeth Hoover, personal interview and correspondence, 2018–2022.

Page 272, Another active contributor:

Gwin, Pat. 2019. "What If the Seeds Do Not Sprout? The Cherokee Nation SeedBank & Native Plant Site." In *Indigenous Food Sovereignty in the United States: Restoring Cultural Knowledge, Protecting Environments, and Regaining Health,* edited by Devon Mihesuah and Elizabeth Hoover. Norman: University of Oklahoma Press.

Cherokee Nation SeedBank. secure.cherokee.org/seedbank

Page 273, I have a slurry of black cherry:

Mam, Kalyanee, Lisa Lee Herrick, and Rowen White. 2021. "The Cultural Healing Power of Food." *Emergence Magazine*, 21 April 2021. emergencemagazine.org/event/the-cultural-healing-power-of-food

Page 278:

Owen Smith Taylor, cofounder of True Love Seeds, personal interviews and correspondence, 2021–2022. trueloveseeds.com/

Page 279, Prior to cofounding Truelove:

William Woys Weaver, Roughwood Seed Collection. williamwoysweaverepicurewithhoe.com/roughwood-seeds

Page 280, Simultaneous to Taylor's:

White Earth Land Recovery Project, Great Lakes Indigenous Farming Conference. welrp. org/2023-20th-annual-great-lakes-indigenous-farming-conference/

Page 281, He is also cofounder and codirector:

Chris Bolden-Newsome, personal interview and correspondence, 2021–2022. trueloveseeds.com/

Bartram's Garden, Sankofa Community Farm, Philadelphia, PA. bartramsgarden.org/farm/

September: Seeds of Culture

Page 289, Seed Program Manager Genevieve:

Genevieve Arnold, seed program manager, Theodore Payne Foundation, personal interviews and correspondence, 2017–2023. theodorepayne.org/seed-program

Page 290, TPF's Seed and Bulb:

Seed LA. seedla.org/

Page 290, In 2020, the nearly:

Evan Meyer, executive director, Theodore Payne Foundation, personal interviews and correspondence, 2021–2023. theodorepayne.org

Page 291, Kitazawa Seed was founded:

"Kitazawa Seeds: Maya Shiroyama and Jim Ryugo on 100 Years of Selling Asian Vegetable Seeds." Episode 46 of *Delicious Revolution* podcast, 11 September 2017. iheart.com/podcast/256-delicious-revolution-31080042/episode/46-kitazawa-seeds-maya-shiroyama-38938392

Kitazawa Seed. kitazawaseed.com/

Page 292, A next-generation person:

Kellee Matsushita-Tseng, Second Generation Seeds, personal interviews and correspondence, 2021–2023. secondgenerationseeds.com

Page 295, Today is Rosh Hashanah:
Rabbi Arthur O. Waskow, personal interview and correspondence, 2021.
Waskow, Rabbi Arthur O. 2012. *Seasons of Our Joy: A Modern Guide to the Jewish Holidays*. Lincoln: University of Nebraska Press.
My Jewish Learning. myjewishlearning.com/
Page 296, I'm reading a recent analysis:
"Ownership & Control, Mergers & Acquisitions." Food & Power.net. foodandpower.net/ownership-control
Page 298, Questioning the global agricultural:
Vandana Shiva, personal interviews and correspondence, 2018–2022.
Shiva, Vandana. 2014. *The Vandana Shiva Reader*. Lexington: University Press of Kentucky.
Shiva, Vandana. 2016. *The Violence of the Green Revolution*. Lexington: University Press of Kentucky.
Shiva, Vandana. 1993. *Monocultures of the Mind*. New Delhi, India: Natraj Publishers.
Vandana Shiva, recorded talks 2020, 2021. navdanya.org
The Neem Foundation. neemfoundation.org/about-neem/history-of-usage
Neemworld.com
U.S. Department of Health and Human Services, National Center for Complementary and Integrative Health, "Ayurvedic Medicine: In Depth." nccih. nih.gov/health/ayurvedic-medicine-in-depth
National Crime Records Bureau: Crime In India. Annual Reports 1994–2021. ncrb.gov.in/en/crime-india
The Seeds of Vandana Shiva. 2021. Becket Films. vandanashivamovie.com/
Page 301, The Coachella Valley:
Coachella Valley Water District. cvwd.org
The Cahuilla Band of Indians. cahuilla.net/
"The Salton Sea: An Ecological Disaster." 2011. University of California Berkeley, Department of Environmental Science, Policy, and Management: "Salton Sea is a shallow hypersaline lake . . . because of its location in an area of high evaporation [i.e., the desert], it has been accumulating soluble salts and insoluble constituents in its bottom sediment for more than 100 years . . . The Salton Sea is now impaired, and selenium is one of many constituents threatening its health."
Coachella Valley Agriculture. coachellafarms.com/coachella-valley-agriculture
Colorado River Basin Water Quality Control Board. waterboards.ca.gov/coloradoriver/

U.S. Department of the Interior, Bureau of Land Management. Imperial Sand
   Dunes. blm.gov/visit/imperial-sand-dunes

NASA Earth Observatory. The Algodones Dunes. earthobservatory.nasa.gov/
   images/49896/the-algodones-dunes

Page 307, The Tohono O'odham culture:

National Park Service, Tucson Mountain District. "Saguaro Fruit: A Traditional
   Harvest." nps.gov/sagu/learn/historyculture/upload/Saguaro-Fruit-A-
   Traditional-Harvest-Brief.pdf

Page 308, We arrive in Tucson in the midst:

"Tohono O'Odham and Basket Claw Cultivation." Native Seeds/SEARCH.
   nativeseeds.org/pages/tohono-oodham-domesticated-devils-claw

DesertUSA, Devil's Claw. desertusa.com/flowers/devil-claw.html

Page 310, The walls of the NS/S offices:

University of Arizona, Tucson, Tumamoc Hill Desert Laboratory. tumamoc.
   arizona.edu/tumamoc-hill/overview; americansouthwest.net/utah/
   capitol_reef/wildflowers.shtml

Vivien Sansour, founder of Palestine Heirloom Seed Library, personal
   interview and correspondence, 2020–2022. viviensansour.com/
   Palestine-Heirloom

Page 316, We, along with a multitude of birds:

"Western bumble bee, *Bombus occidentalis*." Xerces Society. *iucnredlist.org/
   species/44937582/46440211*; xerces.org/endangered-species/
   species-profiles/at-risk-bumble-bees/western-bumble-bee

October: Going to Seed

Page 322, In California, the so-called water year ends:

California Department of Water Resources, California Data Exchange Center.
   drought.ca.gov/media/2021/10/CA-Drought-Update-10-4-21.pdf

Page 323, Some days the world seems viewable:

Diane Wilson, personal interview and correspondence, 2021.
   dianewilsonwords.com

Wilson, Diane. 2021. *The Seed Keeper*. 2021. Minneapolis, MN:
   Milkweed Editions.

Page 323, Plants- and seedsman:

Jeff Quattrone, personal interview and correspondence, 2021.
   libraryseedbank.info

Tim Johnson, personal interview and correspondence, 2021–2023.

Page 331, Recently, A Growing Culture:

"Seed is Power" fund. A Growing Culture. agrowingculture.org/seed-is-power/;
    agrowingculture.org/vision/

Page 331, In an act of courageous re-commoning:

Ken Greene, cofounder of Hudson Valley Seeds, personal interviews and
    correspondence, 2021–2023.

Page 331, In another act of re-commoning:

Fedco Seeds, benefit sharing royalty payments. fedcoseeds.com/trees/
    indigenous-royalties.htm; fedcoseeds.com/black-history-month.htm;
    fedcoseeds.com/seeds/catalog_codes.htm

Page 333, In another striking effort:

Open Source Seed Initiative. osseeds.org/

Page 333, Between 2015 and 2018:

Community Seed Network. communityseednetwork.org/

SeedChange. weseedchange.org/

Page 334, In 2020, a coalition:

Agricultural and Rural Convention. Seeds4All. arc2020.eu/
    new-seed-platform-seeds4all-launches/

Let's Liberate Diversity. liberatediversity.org/

Page 335, The Germplasm Resources Information:

USDA, ARS, Germplasm Resources Information Network (GRIN). ars-grin.gov/

Page 335, In 2023, the:

11th Annual Seed Library Summit. seedlibraries.weebly.com/

ADDITIONAL READING
AND RESOURCES

BOOKS

Baskin, Carol, and Jerry M. Baskin. 2014. *Seeds: Ecology, Biogeography, and Evolution of Dormancy and Germination* (2nd ed.). San Diego, CA: Academic Press.

Bewley, J. Derek and Michael Black. 1985. *Seeds: Physiology of Development and Germination* (2nd ed). New York: Plenum Press.

Black, Michael, J. Derek Bewley, and Peter Halmer, eds. 2006. *The Encyclopedia of Seeds: Science, Technology and Uses*. Wallingford, UK: CABI.

Buchmann, Steve, and Gary Paul Nabhan. 1996. *The Forgotten Pollinators*. Washington, D.C.: Island Press.

Buttala, Lee, and Shanyn Siegel, eds. 2015. *The Seed Garden: The Art and Practice of Seed Saving*. Decorah, IA: Seed Savers Exchange, Inc.

Chace, Teri Dunn. 2015. *Seeing Seeds: A Journey into the World of Seedheads, Pods, and Fruit*. Portland, OR: Timber Press.

Darwin, Charles. 1839. *The Voyage of the Beagle*. London: Henry Colburn.

Darwin, Charles. 1859. *On the Origin of Species By Means of Natural Selection*. London: John Howard.

Elmore, Bartow J. 2021. *Seed Money: Monsanto's Past and Our Food Future*. New York: W. W. Norton.

Elpel, Thomas J. 1996. *Botany in a Day: The Patterns Method of Plant Identification*. Pony, MT: HOPS Press.

Emery, Dara E. 1988. *Seed Propagation of Native California Plants*. Santa Barbara, CA: Santa Barbara Botanic Garden.

Fenner, Michael, and Ken Thompson. 2005. *The Ecology of Seeds*. Cambridge, UK: Cambridge University Press.

Fowler, Cary, and Pat Mooney. 1990. *Shattering: Food, Politics, and the Loss of Genetic Diversity*. Tucson: University of Arizona Press.

Fry, Carolyn. 2016. *Seeds: A Natural History*. Chicago: University of Chicago Press.

Hanson, Thor. 2015. *The Triumph of Seeds*. New York: Basic Books.

Hoover, Elizabeth. 2017. *The River Is in Us: Fighting Toxics in a Mohawk Community*. Minneapolis: University of Minnesota Press.

Kessler, Rob, and Wolfgang Stuppy. 2012. *Seeds: Time Capsules of Life*. San Rafael, CA: Earth Aware Editions.

Kloppenburg, Jack Ralph Jr. 2004. *First the Seed: The Political Economy of Plant Biotechnology* (2nd ed.). Madison: University of Wisconsin Press.

Loewer, Peter. 1995. *Seeds: The Definitive Guide to Growing, History and Lore*. Portland, OR: Timber Press.

Lowry, Judith Larner. 1999. *Gardening With a Wild Heart: Restoring California's Native Landscapes at Home*. Berkeley: University of California Press.

Lowry, Judith Larner. 2007. *The Landscaping Ideas of Jays: A Natural History of the Backyard Restoration Garden*. Berkeley: University of California Press.

Martin, Alexander C., and William D. Barkley. 1961. *Seed Identification Manual*. Berkeley: University of California Press.

McDorman, Bill. 1994. *Basic Seed Saving*. Cornville, AZ: Seeds Trust.

Mihesuah, Devon. A, and Elizabeth Hoover, eds. 2019. *Indigenous Food Sovereignty in the United States: Restoring Cultural Knowledge, Protecting Environments, and Regaining Health*. Norman: University of Oklahoma Press.

Nabhan, Gary Paul. 1989. *Enduring Seeds: Native American Agriculture and Wild Plant Conservation*. New York: North Point Press.

Nazarea, Virginia D., Robert E. Rhoades, and Jenna E. Andrews-Swann, eds. 2013. *Seeds of Resistance, Seeds of Hope: Place and Agency in the Conservation of Biodiversity*. Tucson: University of Arizona Press.

Prechtel, Martin. 2012. *The Unlikely Peace at Cuchumaquic: The Parallel Lives of People as Plants: Keeping the Seeds Alive*. Berkeley: North Atlantic Books.

Ray, Janisse. 2012. *The Seed Underground: A Growing Revolution to Save Food*. White River Junction, VT: Chelsea Green Publishing.

Shiva, Vandana. 2014. *The Vandana Shiva Reader*. Lexington: University of Kentucky Press.

Silvertown, Jonathan. 2009. *An Orchard Invisible: A Natural History of Seeds*. Chicago: University of Chicago Press.

Thompson, Peter. 2010. *Seeds, Sex, and Civilization: How the Hidden Life of Plants Has Shaped Our World*. London: Thames & Hudson.

Thoreau, Henry D. 1993. *Faith in a Seed: The Dispersion of Seeds and Other Late Natural History Writings*. Edited by Bradley P. Dean. Washington, D.C.: Island Press.

Wilson, Diane. 2021. *The Seed Keeper: A Novel*. Minneapolis, MN: Milkweed Editions.

ORGANIZATIONS AND WEBSITES

California Botanic Garden

Seed Conservation Program, calbg.org/

California Native Seed Supply Collaborative,
canativeseedcollaborative.wordpress.com/

Cherokee Nation Heirloom Seed Bank, secure.cherokee.org/SeedBank

Community Seed Network, communityseednetwork.org/

Crop Trust, croptrust.org/

Dream of Wild Health, dreamofwildhealth.org/

Experimental Farm Network, experimentalfarmnetwork.org/

Gaia Foundation, gaiafoundation.org/

Institute for Applied Ecology, appliedeco.org/

and their Native Seed Network, appliedeco.org/nativeseednetwork

Library Seed Bank, Jeff Quattrone, libraryseedbank.info/

Millennium Seed Bank, Kew, kew.org/wakehurst/whats-at-wakehurst/
millennium-seed-bank

Native American Food Sovereignty Alliance/Indigenous Seed Keepers Network,
nativefoodalliance.org/

and their Seed Hub Grants in Partnership with the USDA's Indigenous Food
Sovereignty Initiative, usda.gov/tribalrelations/usda-programs-and-
services/usda-indigenous-food-sovereignty-initiative

National Seed Strategy Report 2015–2020, blm.gov/sites/default/files/
docs/2021-08/Progress%20Report%2026Jul21.pdf

Nevada Seed Strategy, partnersinthesage.com/nevada-seed-strategy

Olericulture and Seeds, Shanyn Siegel, shanynsiegel.com/

Open Source Seed Initiative, osseeds.org/

Organic Seed Alliance, seedalliance.org/

Plant Conservation Alliance, blm.gov/programs/natural-resources/
native-plant-communities/national-seed-strategy/pca

Richmond Grows Seed Lending Library, richmondgrowsseeds.org/

Rocky Mountain Seed Alliance, rockymountainseeds.org/

SeedChange, weseedchange.org/

Seeds of Success, blm.gov/programs/natural-resources/native-plant-communities/native-plant-and-seed-material-development/collection

Seed Savers Exchange, seedsavers.org/

Seeds, Soil & Culture, seedssoilculture.org/

Sierra Seed, Rowen White, sierraseeds.org/

Slow Food USA, slowfoodusa.org/

The Southwest Seed Partnership, southwestseedpartnership.org/

Thomas Jefferson Center for Historic Plants, monticello.org/house-gardens/center-for-historic-plants/

Ujamaa Cooperative Farming Alliance, ujamaafarms.com/

U.S. Department of Agriculture-Agricultural Research Service, National Laboratory for Genetic Resources Preservation, ars.usda.gov/plains-area/fort-collins-co/center-for-agricultural-resources-research/paagrpru/

SEED COMPANIES

Arizona
DP Seeds LLC, dpseeds.com/
Native Seeds, nativeseeds.org/
Terroir Seeds, underwoodgardens.com/

California
Everwilde Farms, Inc., everwilde.com/
Heritage Growers Native Seed and Plant Supply, heritagegrowers.com/
J. L. Hudson, Seedsman, jlhudsonseeds.net/
Larner Seeds, larnerseeds.com/
Peaceful Valley Farm & Garden, groworganic.com/
Redwood City Seed Company, ecoseeds.com/
Redwood Seeds, redwoodseeds.net/
Renee's Garden , reneesgarden.com/
Seedhunt, seedhunt.com/
Swallowtail Garden Seeds, swallowtailgardenseeds.com/
The Living Seed Company, livingseedcompany.com/
Theodore Payne Foundation Store, store.theodorepayne.org/
Thrive Heirloom Seed, thriveheirloomseed.com/

Colorado
Botanical Interests, Inc., botanicalinterests.com/
Burrell Seed Growers LLC, burrellseeds.us/
High Desert Seed and Gardens, highdesertseed.com/
Seeds Trust, seedstrust.com/

Connecticut
John Scheepers Kitchen Garden Seeds, kitchengardenseeds.com
New England Seed Company, neseed.com/

Iowa
Sand Hill Preservation Center, sandhillpreservation.com/
Second Generation Seeds, secondgenerationseeds.com/
Seed Savers Exchange, seedsavers.org/

Kansas
Heritage Heirloom Seed Company, heritageheirloomseedcompany.com/

Maine
Fedco Seeds, fedcoseeds.com/
Johnny's Selected Seeds, johnnyseeds.com/
Pinetree Garden Seeds, superseeds.com/
Wild Seed Project, wildseedproject.net/

Maryland
Reimer Seeds, reimerseeds.com/

Massachusetts
Ferry-Morse Home Gardening, ferrymorse.com/

Michigan
Nature & Nurture Seeds, natureandnurtureseeds.com/

Minnesota
Prairie Moon Nursery, prairiemoon.com/seeds/
Jordan Seeds, jordanseeds.com/

Missouri
Baker Creek Heirloom Seeds, rareseeds.com/
Morgan County Seeds, morgancountyseeds.com/
White Harvest Seed Company, whiteharvestseed.com/

Montana
The Good Seed Company, goodseedco.net/

New Mexico
Plants of the Southwest, plantsofthesouthwest.com/

New York
Fruition Seeds, fruitionseeds.com/
Harris Seeds, harrisseeds.com/
Hudson Valley Seed Company, hudsonvalleyseed.com/
Salt of the Earth Seed Company, saltoftheearthseeds.com/
Turtle Tree Seed, turtletreeseed.org/
Ujamaa Seeds, ujamaaseeds.com/

North Carolina
Eden Brothers, edenbrothers.com/
Sow True Seed, sowtrueseed.com/

Oregon
Adaptive Seeds, adaptiveseeds.com/
Nichols Garden Nursery, nicholsgardennursery.com/
Peace Seeds and Peace Seedlings, peaceseedslive.com/ and
    peaceseedlingsseeds.blogspot.com/
Restoration Seeds, restorationseeds.com/
Siskiyou Seeds, siskiyouseeds.com/
Strictly Medicinal Seeds, strictlymedicinalseeds.com/
Territorial Seed Company, territorialseed.com/
Victory Seed Company, victoryseeds.com/
Wild Garden Seed, wildgardenseed.com/

Pennsylvania
Experimental Farm Network Seeds, experimentalfarmnetwork.org/
Rohrer Seeds, rohrerseeds.com/
Truelove Seeds, trueloveseeds.com/
W. Atlee Burpee & Company, burpee.com/

South Carolina
Park Seed, parkseed.com/

Texas
Mary's Heirloom Seeds, marysheirloomseeds.com/
Wildseed Farms, wildseedfarms.com/
Willhite Seed, willhiteseed.com/

Utah
Kitazawa Seed Company, kitazawaseed.com/
True Leaf Market , trueleafmarket.com/

Vermont
Earthbeat Seeds, earthbeatseeds.com/
High Mowing Organic Seeds, highmowingseeds.com/
Vermont Bean Seed Company, vermontbean.com/

Virginia
Monticello and Thomas Jefferson's Center for Historic Plants,
    monticelloshop.org/garden/heirloom-seeds/
Southern Exposure Seed Exchange, southernexposure.com/

Washington
Ed Hume Seeds, humeseeds.com/
Floret , shop.floretflowers.com/
Irish Eyes Garden Seeds, irisheyesgardenseeds.com/
Uprising Seeds, uprisingorganics.com/

West Virginia
Two Seeds in a Pod, twoseedsinapod.com/

Wisconsin
A. P. Whaley Seed Company, LLC, awhaley.com/
Annie's Heirloom Seeds, anniesheirloomseeds.com/
Jung Seed Company, jungseed.com/
St. Clare Heirloom Seeds, stclareseeds.com/

INDEX

1941 Garden Guide, 135

ABG (Atlanta Botanical Garden),
    231–232
abscission (dispersal method), 68
Abundant Life Seed Foundation, 110
accessory fruit, 58
Acer macrophyllum, 47
achene, defined, 58
acorns, 26–28
    defined, 58
    growth of, 18–19, 75, 80, 81, 277, 285
    in mast years, 21–22, 25
    as part of forest, 51
    production, 20
    size of, 23
acorn woodpeckers, 53, 277
Adinkera, King, 282
Aesculus californica, 122
Africa, 87–88, 98, 99, 123, 170, 224,
    281–283, 333
Agastache, 91
agave species, 232, 306
Agavoideae, 133
Age of Loneliness, 56
AGRA (Alliance for a Green Revolution
    in Africa), 88
Agrarian Trust, 198
agribusiness, 87–89, 209, 249, 296–298
Agricultural Extension office (Oregon
    State University), 122
Agricultural Marketing Service, USDA
    (AMS), 106, 148
agriculture. *See* agribusiness; farmers
    and farming; organic farmers and
    farming

Ahearn Desert Conservation Laboratory
    (DBG), 232
Akan people and language, 282
Akwesasne Task Force on the Environ-
    ment (ATFE), 270
alder trees, 47–48, 76, 200, 252
Aleppo, Syria, 162, 166
algal blooms, 303
Algodones Dunes, 305
'Ali Baba' watermelon, 191
Alliance for a Green Revolution in
    Africa (AGRA), 88
allium / *Allium* spp., 153, 219, 220
Alnus rhombifolia, 48
American Association of Seed Control
    Officials, 209
American Farmland Trust, 117
American Indians, 77, 130, 179–180, 182,
    207, 245, 272, 305. *See also* Indige-
    nous peoples
American Seeds, Inc. (ASI), 112
American Seed Trade Association
    (ASTA), 103, 104, 115
AMS, USDA (Agricultural Marketing
    Service, USDA), 106, 148
Anderson, Eugene, 241
Anderson, Mark, 238, 239, 241
anemochory (dispersal method), 64–65
angiosperms, 36, 37, 38–40, 48
annual plants and seeds, 18, 310–311
Annual Seed Library Summit (2023),
    335
ant dispersal, 68, 85
Anthropocene, 29, 55
Apiaceae, 177
Apocynaceae, 58

apple trees, 233–234

Arctostaphylos manzanita, 131

Arctostaphylos viscida, 131

arid landscapes, 126, 180–181, 188, 301

Aristolochia californica, 94

Arizona (state), 309

Ark of Taste, 91, 221

Arnold, Genevieve, 289–290

Arquette, Dave, 270

Arquette, Mary, 267, 270

ARS, 236, 335

art and artists, 221–222, 224–227

Artemisia spp., 306

Artemisia cana, 214

Artemisia tridentatae, 214

artpacks (HVSC), 227

arugula, 191, 192

Asclepias spp., 219

Asclepias fascicularis, 45

Ashland, Mount, 91

ASI (American Seeds, Inc.), 112

Asian diaspora, 100, 123, 135, 224, 291

ASTA (American Seed Trade Association), 103, 104, 115

Asteraceae, 58, 65, 126

astragalus, 219

ATFE (Akwesasne Task Force on the Environment), 270

athletics, seeding in, 13

Atkinson, Daniel, 98–99

Atlanta Botanical Garden (ABG), 231–232

Atlanta History Center's Cherokee Garden Library, 136

Atlantic (magazine), 82

author

  ancestors of, 274–275

  as garderner, 13, 45

  as mother, 45

  and seed, 12–16

author's father, 32

author's grandfather, 185, 274

author's mother, 31–32, 145–146, 147, 173, 184

autumnal equinox, 144, 314

awns, 58, 69

Ayurvedic medicine, 299

Azadirachta indica, 298

Baccharis pilularis, 56, 62

'*baladi*' tomato, 313

ballistic dispersal, 69, 155, 275

ballochory (dispersal method), 69, 155, 275

Barnes, Carl Leon "White Eagle," 273

barn owls, 277

Bartram, John and William, 282

BASF (multinational company), 297

basket claw, 308–309

basket designs, 309

Batalin, A. F., 157

'*Battir*' eggplant, 313

Battus philenor, 95

Bay Area Seed Interchange Library (BASIL), 206

Bayer (pharmaceutical company), 101, 102, 110, 118

Bayer-Monsanto (corporation), 114, 115, 296–297

bay trees, 79, 200

beans, 98, 207, 247

bees, 84, 86, 121, 154

Beltane (Celtic festival), 185

berry, defined, 59

Berry Botanic Garden (Portland, Oregon), 190

Bhopal, India, 297

Bidwell, John, 129

bigleaf maple, 47

Bill and Melinda Gates Foundation, 87–88, 249

biodiversity

  and CBD treaty, 161–162

  climate and, 237–240

  cloning and, 254

  depicted at Native Seeds/SEARCH headquarters, 308

  fire and, 243

in mountain areas, 216
promotion of, 334
seeds and, 39–42, 334
wild crops and, 245–246
biodiversity hotspots, 24
biodiversity loss, 25, 53–56, 164, 187, 251
biotechnology industry, 161–162
birds, 23, 50, 66–67, 194–195, 200, 302, 318
Birker, Cheryl, 51–52, 193
bitterroots, 218
blackberries, 291
'Black Chestnut' soybeans, 294
black crowders, 98
black-eyed peas, 283
black mustard, 122–123
black oaks, 21
Blennosperma nanum var. *nanum*, 152
blue oaks, 21, 22, 23, 33, 48–51
"boarding school era," 179
Bolden-Newsome, Chris, 265, 278, 279, 280, 281–283, 334
Bombus spp., 317
Bombus occidentalis, 316, 317
botanical Latin, 37–38
Braiding Sweetgrass (Kimmerer), 99
Brassicaceae, 177
Brassica family, 60, 143
Brassica nigra, 123
bravery, 314
breast cancer, 145
broadcast sowing, 143–144
brodiaea, 79
broom, 124, 231. *See also* Scotch broom
brown bears, 55
Brown Envelope Seed, 93
Buchmann, Stephen, 211–212
buckeyes
dispersal of, 46
dormancy of, 76, 335
flowers of, 186
growth of, 45, 75, 80, 81, 122, 285
presence of, 25
sound of, 27

buff-tailed bumble bee, 317
bulbs, 79–80
bumble bees, 126, 131, 155, 202, 210, 316–317
bunchgrass ecosystems, 146
Burpee, W. Atlee, 222–223. *See also* W. Atlee Burpee (seed company)
burr, defined, 59
Bush, George H. W., 162
bush poppy, 64, 78
Butte County meadowfoam, 152
butter beans, 98
butterflies, 200–201, 210. *See also specific butterfly species*
buzz pollination, 126, 131

cabbage seed, 104
Cahuilla peoples, 300, 301
calamintha, 170
California
agriculture in, 199–200, 287
conservation in, 259–260
and COVID-19, 8
droughts in, 15, 19, 86, 335–336
fire in, 15. *See also specific named fires*
Seed Advisory Board, 148
wheat in, 60
California bee plant, 121
California Botanic Garden (CalBG), 52, 167, 193, 194, 291
California Department of Food and Agriculture (CDFA), 148, 287
California dove, 53
California Drought Report, 322
California Floristic Province, 20, 24, 218, 259
California fuchsia, 170
California Gold Rush (ca, 1849), 129, 130
California Invasive Plant Council, 123
California native pipevine, 94–95
California Plant Rescue, 259–260
California poppies, 203
California quail, 53
California Seed Law, 148

California towhee, 121
California Water Board, 303
Calochortus, 43–44, 56, 63
Calochortus albus, 43
calyx (plant part), 65, 287
Camp Fire (2018), 15, 27, 79, 202, 237, 284, 285, 335
campsites and camping, 314
canyon live oak, 33
capsules (fruits), 59, 69, 76, 309
Cardamine californica, 80
cardinal/scarlet monkeyflower, 51, 52
Carle, Lisa, 140
Carlock, Danielle, 208
Carnegiea gigantea, 306
carpels (plant parts), 40, 58, 59
carpenter bees, 170–171, 287, 306
carpology (seed ecology), 41
carrots, 140, 263–264
Carson, Rachel, 120, 213
Carter, Majora, 186
caryopsis, defined, 59
Catawba Nation, 91
catkins, 48, 76, 155
cattails, 230, 276
caves, 129
CBD (1992 Rio Earth Summit; Convention on Biodiversity), 161, 163, 188–189
CDFA (California Department of Food and Agriculture), 148
ceanothus / *Ceanothus* spp., 79
Ceanothus cuneatus, 121
cedar waxwings, 53, 54–55, 67
Celtic cultures, 29, 72, 96, 150, 185, 261
Center for Biological Diversity, 198
Center for Plant Conservation, 167, 232, 259
Central Garden & Pet, 141
Central Valley (California), 287
Centro Internacional de Mejoramiento de Maíz y Trigo (International Maize and Wheat Improvement Center, CIMMYT), 162, 165

century plants, 306
Cercis occidentalis, 46, 202
Cercocarpus ledifolius, 216
CGIAR (Consultative Group on International Agricultural Research), 162–163
'Cha Jogi' red perilla, 294
Chakrabarty, Diamond v., 107
chaparral wild buckwheat, 86
chefs, 89–91
Chemamagi Du'ag (Horned Lizard Mountain), 310
Cherokee Nation Seed Bank (CNSB), 272–273
cherry tomatoes, 273, 317
Chevron Conservation Award, 190
Chico, California, 129
China, 140
Chiricahua Desert Museum, 233
Chlorogalum pomeridianum, 79, 202
Christmas trees, 57
Chuseok (Korean harvest festival), 311
CIMMYT (Centro Internacional de Mejoramiento de Maíz y Trigo (International Maize and Wheat Improvement Center)), 162, 165
circumscissile, defined, 125–126
citrus industry, 130
Civil Eats website, 123
Clark, Joe Joe, 70
Clarkia elegans, 135
Clark's nutcracker, 67
Claytonia perfoliata, 75–76
Clematis lasiantha, 121
Clif Bar Family Foundation, 208
climate and climate change, 250
  biodiversity loss and habitat loss and, 9–10, 53, 237
  challenges of, 183
  and cranberries, 236–237
  evolution and, 35
  impact of, 89, 161, 164, 242, 322
cloning (propagation method), 170, 253, 254, 255, 307

clovers, 143, 153
CNSB (Cherokee Nation Seed Bank), 272–273
Coachella Valley (California), 300–301
Coachella Valley Water District (CVWD), 302–303
coconuts, 65
coevolutionary partnerships, and angiosperms, 38
coffeeberry, 79
Cold War (1942–1989), 175
colonialism / colonization, 242, 269, 304
Colorado River Basin Water Quality Control Board, 303
coma (plant part), 220
common manzanita, 131
Community Seed Network (CSN), 207, 333–334
Condea emoryi, 64
cone-bearing plant species, 36–37
Conservation Seed Bank (Atlanta, Georgia), 231–232
Conserving Plant Diversity in New England (report), 237, 242
consolidation of seeds, 177
Consultative Group on International Agricultural Research (CGIAR), 162–163
contamination of crops, 328–329
contracting dispersal, 69–70
Convention on Biodiversity (CBD, 1992 Rio Earth Summit), 161, 163, 188–189, 197
Convention on Biological Diversity. *See* Convention on Biodiversity (CBD, 1992 Rio Earth Summit)
corn, 88, 112–113, 182, 198–199, 207, 240, 327, 328
'Cornell Bush Delicata Squash', 225–226
Cornell Lab of Ornithology, 53
Corn Mafia, 90
Corteva (corporation), 101–102
corymbs (plant parts), 172
cotton, 199

cottonwood trees, 155
cotyledons (plant parts), 37, 41
Council for Responsible Genetics, 108
COVID-19 pandemic, 8–10, 15, 97, 99, 144, 207, 305, 335
coyote brush/bush, 56, 62–63
cranberries, wild, 235
creek and riparian corridor, 276, 336, 337
creosote bush, 306, 307
crop gene banks. *See* seed banks
Crop Trust (Global Crop Diversity Trust), 164, 165, 247–248
CSN (Community Seed Network), 207, 333–334
Cultivating Place (public radio program and podcast), 15, 16, 97, 98, 118–119
cultural connections, 222, 297
cupule (acorn part), 26, 27
Curcubitaceae, 191
curl-leaf mountain mahogany, 216
CVWD (Coachella Valley Water District), 302–303
cyanogenic glucosides, 54
Cylindropuntia bigelovii, 306
Cytisus scoparius, 79, 124

daggerpod, 219, 220
Dakhóta peoples, 169
Darmera, 172, 231
Darmera peltata, 172
Darwin, Charles, 44, 50, 102
date palms, 82–84
datura species, 286–287, 288
Datura stramonium, 287
Datura wrightii, 286, 289
Daucus carota, 264
Daucus carota var. *sativus*, 263
Davidson College, 91
Day of the Dead (Dia de los Muertos), 29
DBG (Desert Botanical Garden), 232–233
DDT (pesticide), 120
deer, 192
deergrass, 133

dehisced fruits, 44, 58, 59, 60, 69, 71, 307, 336
Delphinium variegatum, 203
Dempsey, Wes, 33, 97
Dendromecon, 78
Dendromecon rigida, 64
De Ruiter (seed supplier), 110, 114
Desert Botanical Garden (DBG), 232–233
desert lavender, 64
desert scrub landscapes, 306
devil's claw, 308
Diacon (pesticide and fungicide producer), 141
Dia de los Muertos (Day of the Dead), 29
Diamond v. Chakrabarty, 107
diaspora, defined, 99
diaspores, 41, 58, 70, 99, 218–220
Dicamba (herbicide), 118
Dicentra uniflora, 85
Dichelostemma volubile, 186
Dickie, John, 156
  on the CBD treaty, 161
  on plant breeding, 159
  on rhe Russian empire, 157
  on seed banks, 187, 188–189, 197–198, 255
  on seed saving, 193–194
Dig Delve (online magazine), 92
Dillard, Annie, 210
Dillon, Matthew, 100, 102–103, 107
dioecious, defined, 83
Disarming Design, 61
distress signal, 185–186
diversity. *See* biodiversity
diversity loss. *See* biodiversity loss
Dixie Fire, 237, 239, 243, 244, 261, 284, 315, 318, 335
Doomsday Vault. *See* Svalbard Global Seed Vault (SGSV)
dormancy, 76–81, 84, 85
doves, 67
DowDuPont (corporation), 297

D. Palmer Seed, 113
DP Seeds LLC, 113
dragonflies, 201, 211
Dream of Wild Health, 169, 271
droughts, 15, 19, 21, 86, 277, 284, 285, 304, 322, 335
drupe (fruit type), 59, 65, 121
dryland milkweed, 219
Dungy, Camille, 250

Eastern Deciduous Forest, 251
Ecological Landscape Alliance, 92
ecosystems, 24, 211–212, 215
ecotones, 23
elaisomes, 64, 68
Emergence Magazine, 274
empty-nester syndrome, 283
endangered species, 212
endosperm, 37, 41
endozoochory (dispersal method), 67
Enduring Seeds (Nabhan), 247
'Enorma' runner bean, 94
environmental cues, germination and, 77, 78
Environmental Health (journal), 199
EPA Superfund sites, 62
epicotyl (plant part), 41
Epilobium canum, 170
Epipactis gigantea, 64
Eriogonum dasyanthemum, 86
Eruca vesicaria, 191
Erythranthe, 52
Erythranthe cardinalis, 51
Erythranthe glaucescens, 52
Erythranthe guttata, 52, 230
Eschschlozia californica, 203
Eschscholzia lobbii, 153
eukaryotes, 35
European Coordination of Let's Liberate Diversity, 334
European honeybees, 122
European settlers, 129–130, 179, 234
evolution, 41–42

ex situ conservation practices, 156, 187, 235–236, 258
extinction, 42, 53, 86, 165, 298

F, 170
fairy lantern, 44
Farm Act (1996), 114
Farm Action, 102
farmers and farming, 87–89, 249–250, 333
Farm to Fork Strategy (European Commission), 199
fava beans, 283
FDA (Food and Drug Administration), 112, 115
feather grass, 147
Feather River Canyon, 237, 243, 316
Fedco Seed, 141–142, 332–333
Federal Seed Act (1939), 106, 147–148
Ferry-Morse (seed company), 141
fertility signs, 128
field peas, 98
finches, 50
fire, 11, 21, 25–26, 27, 50, 78–80. *See also* named fires
fire, prescribed, 243–244
fire followers, 78
fire regimes, 20
fire season, 28
fire suppression, 79, 214, 244
fish, drought impacts on, 322–323
F. Lagomarsino & Sons (seed company), 135
flash flooding, worries about, 335
"float test" (viability test), 81
Florilegia, 136
flowers. *See* wildflowers
follicle, defined, 59
Food & Power (website), 101–102, 296
Food and Drug Administration (FDA), 112, 115
food security, 161, 168, 197, 242
foothill clematis, 121
Forest Service (USDA), 57, 214, 235, 236, 244

The Forgotten Pollinators (Nabhan and Buchmann), 211
Fork Fire (2020), 215
Fort Collins, Colorado, 159–160, 233, 234
Fouquieria splendens, 306
Fowler, Cary, 178, 247
Fraga, Naomi, 52, 193
Frangula californica, 79
Fraser Valley (Colorado), 126
Fred Meyer Foundation, 190
Friends of the Ahart Herbarium, 152
fringepod, 143
From "Garden Warriors" to "Good Seeds" (Hoover), 271
fruit (plant part), 40, 59
Fry, Carolyn, 54
frying pans, 153
fungus gnats, 95

The Gaia Foundation, 92
Gal, Edwina von, 253
gametophyte phase, 36–37
Gandhi, Mahatma, 299
Garcia, Paula, 11
Garden Guide (1941), 135
gardening and gardeners
    author's mother as, 31–32, 145, 147
    author's role as, 14–15, 16, 45, 60–61
    during Depression era, 138
    Hoover's mother as, 270
    Johnson on, 260–261, 324–325
    and native plants, 254
    and "participatory conservation," 173
garden journals, 31–32
Gardiner Public Library, 204, 206
Gates Foundation, 87–88, 249
Gateway Science Museum (Chico, California), 15
gene banks. *See* seed banks
General Foods (corporation), 112
genetically engineered (GE) seeds and/or plants, 101, 108–109, 111–112, 113, 114, 159, 165, 325

genetically modified organisms (GMOs), 10, 101, 111–112, 115–118, 165, 325, 327

genetic diversity. *See* biodiversity

Geneva, New York, 233–234

genocide and attempted genocide, of land-based peoples, 28, 180, 224, 304, 329

Gentiana, 66

geologic age, shown by landscape, 315

geophytes, 44, 85, 128

George Ball, Inc. (horticultural business), 112

geranium species, 69

germination-stimulating enzymes, 78

germplasm, 160

Germplasm Resources Information Network (GRIN), 334, 335

Gettle, Jere and family, 46

Gibbons, Euell, 251

Giroux, Lauren, 111, 112, 118–119

Global Crop Diversity Trust (Crop Trust), 164, 165, 247–248

Global Plan of Action (1996), 163

GMOs (genetically modified organisms), 10, 101, 111–112, 115–118, 165, 325, 327

GNPC (Greenbelt Native Plant Center), 258–259

God, nature of, 144

goldfields, 152

Goldman, Amy, 178, 191

Gold Rush (ca. 1849), 129, 130

gooseberries, 220

grasses, 306, 315, 318

gravity dispersal, 68

gray pine cones, 25

gray pines, 22–23, 33, 48–51, 130

grazing, in Warner Mountains, 214–215

Great Basin, 218

Great Basin bristlecone pines, 49

Great Eastern Hardwood Forest, 251

Greenbelt Native Plant Center (GNPC), 258–259

Greene, Ken "K," 204–207, 222–225, 331–332

Greene, Stephanie, 158, 160, 233, 234, 334

Green Garden Products, 141

Green Gulch Farm, 191

Green Revolution, 87–89, 163, 298

greens, winter, 18

Gregg, Elena, 152–153, 154

GRIN (Germplasm Resources Information Network), 334, 335

Grothaus, Molly, 190

A Growing Culture (international coalition), 331

G. Thorburn & Sons (seed seller), 136–137

Gwin, Pat, 272–273

gymnosperms, 36–37, 39

habitat loss, 53

Hagenston, Jillian, 148–149

Haggard, Gail, 195

'Handsome Dark One' wheat, 313

Hanson, Thor, 41

haploid cells, 40

Harrington's rule, 194

Harvard Arboretum, 252

harvest moon, 311

Hashañi Mashad (saguaro harvest month), 307

hawk moths, 287

Hazon (environmental organization), 295–296

heirloom seeds, 114

hellstrip planting, 86, 133

herbals (books), 136

herbicides, 102, 113, 118, 119, 198, 211

Heritage Seeds, 113

heritage seeds and plants, 179, 271, 331

herpochory (dispersal method), 69–70

Herrick, Lisa Lee, 274, 275–276

Hesperaloe parviflora, 133

hesperidium, defined, 59

Heteromeles arbutifolia, 54
Heuchera sanguinea, 135
H. G. Hastings seed and garden company, 136
High, Kat, 287
high fire season, 21
High Mowing Organic Seeds, 108
high seed season, 21
hiking, 120–121, 215–216
hilum (seed part), 40
Himalayan blackberry, 79, 231
'Hime Kansen' watermelon, 192
Holmberg, Tyler, 281
"home" concept, 279
Homestead Act (1869), 129
honeybees, 211, 287
Hoover, Elizabeth, 99, 270–272
Horned Lizard Mountain (Chemamagi Du'ag), 310
horsemint, 91
hot weather, 276
Hubbard, Kiki, 105, 107, 112, 118
Hudson Valley Seed Company (HVSC), 205, 223–227, 331
human impact, on seeds and plants, 128–129, 147, 156, 196, 213, 214–215
hummingbirds, 131, 306
'Hungarian Blue' breadseed poppy, 86
hunger problem, 87–88, 116, 163, 178, 247, 274
Hunt, Ginny, 86
hybrids, 104–105, 257
hydrochory (dispersal method), 65–66
hypocotyl (plant part), 41

ICARDA (International Center for Agricultural Research in the Dry Areas), 162, 165, 166
Iceberg roses, 95
ides of March, 134
'ihuk (devil's claw), 309
I'itoi (Great Spirit), 309
Imbolc (Celtic festival), 96, 120

Imperial Botanical Gardens of Saint Petersburg, 157
In a North State Garden (public radio program and podcast), 97
inbreeding depression, 153, 255, 256–257
Indigenous Farming Conference, 280, 282
Indigenous peoples. *See also* American Indians; Native Americans; *and specific group names*
ancestral seeds of, 224
and cranberries, 235
and Fedco Seed, 332
foodways of, 89–91, 99–100, 103–104, 178–183, 186, 278
landscape management by, 20, 215
as seed teachers, 266
sunflower image and, 222
Indigenous Seed Keepers Network (ISKN), 169, 268, 269, 331, 334
insect pollinators, 126, 131, 153, 155, 211
insects, 56, 131–132, 153–154, 154–155, 191, 198
in situ conservation practices, 231–232, 233, 235–236, 237
interior live oak, 21, 33
International Center for Agricultural Research in the Dry Areas (ICARDA), 162, 165, 166
International Maize and Wheat Improvement Center, 240
International Rice Research Institute (IRRI), 162, 165
International Seed Library Forum (2015), 209
International Treaty on Plant Genetic Resources for Food and Agriculture (2004), 164
invasive plants, 122–124, 146–147, 215, 231, 264
Ipomea alba, 32
Iris douglasiana, 43
irises, 43–44, 56, 63

IRRI (International Rice Research Institute), 162, 165

ISKN (Indigenous Seed Keepers Network), 169, 268, 269, 331, 334

Ithuriel's spear, 186

Jacobin magazine, 87

'Jadu'I' watermelon, 313

Jahn, Molly, 225

Japanese flag, 135

Jefferson, Thomas, 102

Jentz, Kathy, 91, 94

Jepson eFlora database, 125

Jersey tomato, 223

"Johnny Appleseed gene pool," 234

Johnny's Selected Seeds, 111, 113–114

johnny-tuck, 152

Johnson, Joel, 181

Johnson, Tim, 175, 176–178, 260, 323–325, 326–330

Johnston, Rob, Jr., 113

Joint Resolution in Support of Seed Libraries, 209

'Joseon Shorty' Korean cucumber, 294

Joy, Sheryl, 181

juniper, 214

Kanien'kéha peoples, 89–91

Kapuler, Alan and Linda, 267

Kenya, AGRA projects in, 88

Kew Gardens (Royal Botanic Gardens, Kew), 187–190

Kharkiv, Ukraine, 11

Khoury, Colin, 245–250, 326, 327

'khyar abyad' cucumber, 313

Kierstead, Julie, 91, 190

Kimmerer, Robin Wall, 99

King, Martin Luther, Jr., 28

King Manor Museum, 332

Kitazawa, Gijiu, 291–292

Kitazawa Seed, 100, 191, 291–292

"Klondike University Strain" watermelon, 135

Koppenjan, Gary, 100

Kumin, Maxine, 283

labor movement, 185

lacepod, 143, 149

LaDuke, Winona, 99, 267

'Lady Choi' peppers, 294

Lamb Nursery (Spokane, Washington), 97

land-based cultures, 115, 179, 243, 278

Land Girls, 94

land-grant universities (LGUs), 105

land plants, 35–36

landscape managers, 290

larkspur, 203

Larner Lowry, Judith. *See* Lowry, Judith Larner

Larner Seeds, 146, 196

Larrea tridentata, 306

Lasthenia californica, 152–153

LA Times, 122

Latin botanical names, 37–38

Lawn, C. R., 110, 111, 141

Leach, Kristyn, 100, 123

legumes, 59

Lenape Center, 331–332

Leopold, Aldo, 196, 277

Let's Liberate Diversity, 334

lettuce seedlings, 170

Lewis and Clark expedition, 102

Lewis Hybrids, 113

Lewisia rediviva, 218

LGUs (land-grant universities), 105

Library of Local, 332

Library Seed Bank project and research, 223

lilies, 70–71

lilies of the valley, 173

Lilium spp., 70

Limnanthes floccosa subsp. *californica*, 152

Linnaeus, Carolus, 38, 44

livestock, in Warner Mountains, 214–215

local food, 204

loculicidal follicle, 58
lodgepole pine trees, 214
Long Live LA Conservation Seed Bank, 290
Louis L. Borick Natural Medicine Research Center, 82
Louwaars, Niels, 104
love-in-a-mist, 84, 86
"Lovejoy Formation" basalt, 23–24
Lowry, Judith Larner, 146, 195
lumber industry, 129–130
Lunar New Year, 123

Mackey, Halkard, 85
Maiduan peoples, 27, 50. *See also* Mechoopda Maidu people
Maidu grinding stones, 128
mail order sales of seeds and plant material, 137
Maine (state), 251, 253
Maine Organic Farmers and Gardeners, 141–142
malaria outbreak, 130
Malus spp., 233
Malus ×*domestica*, 234
Malus sieversii, 233
Mam, Kalyanee, 274, 275–276
mammals, 251
manzanitas, 55, 131–132, 142
maple samaras, 60, 65
Maricopa County (Arizona), 208
Marie (fictional character), 169
Martin, Matthew, 140
Martin, Sandi, 86
mass seed production, 262
Masters Choice (seed grower), 140
mast years and masting, 21, 28
Matsushita-Tseng, Kellee, 100, 292–293, 294, 295
May Day, 185
McCargo, Heather
    on broadcast sowing, 143–144
    on gardening with seed, 260, 290
    on genetic diversity, 254–255
    on native seeds and plants, 92, 251–253
    on seed collection, 255
    sharing and, 94
McClellan-Welch, Sarah, 273
meadowfoam, 153
Meals for Millions project, 178
Mechanicsburg, Pennsylvania, seed library, 208
Mechoopda Maidu people, 19, 20, 129
Meders-Knight, Ali, 50
medicinal plants, 137, 298–299
Mediterranean climate, 75, 85
Mediterranean sweet orange, 130
Melhorn, Dave, 111, 112, 114, 119
The Melon (Goldman), 191
melons, 191–192
Mendel, Gregor, 44, 104
Messervy, Julie Moir, 173
Methuselah (date palm), 83
Mexican cultures, 29
Mexico, corn in, 327
Mexico–United States border, 305
Meyer, Evan, 290
microclimates, 24, 238, 242
Mid-Atlantic Regional Seed Bank, 258
milkmaids, 126
milkweed family, 58
Millennium Commission grants, 188
Millennium Seed Bank Project (MSBP), 188
Milton, John, 186
miner's lettuce, 75–76
mitigation protocols, 154
Modern Farmer, 204
Modoc Plateau, 213
monkeyflowers, 51–52, 218, 230
mono-crop agriculture, 303
Monocultures of the Mind (Shiva), 298
Monsanto Corporation
    and American Seed Trade Association, 103
    and De Ruiter, 110
    and Heritage Seeds, 113

Monsanto Corporation (cont'd)
  patents, 248, 296–297
  and Seminis, 100–101, 109, 111–112, 142
moon cycles, 18, 89, 96, 122, 264. *See also*
  journal sections
moonflowers, 46
moral arc of universe, Parker on, 28
Morgan, Huw, 92–94, 99
Moriarty, George, 225
Morton, Frank, 109, 267
Morton, Karen, 267
mother, author's role as, 45
"mothering" concept, 277–278
moths, 210
mountain mahogany seed, 220
Mount Ashland. *See* Ashland, Mount
MSBP (Millennium Seed Bank Project),
  188
Muhlenbergia rigens, 133
Muller, Doug, 223
Munz, Philip, 167
mustards, 122
'Mutsu' apple tree, 318
myrmecochory (dispersal method), 68

Nabhan, Gary, 158, 181–182, 211–213,
  239–242, 246, 247, 319
Nagoya Protocol, 197
narrowleaf milkweed, 45, 46, 285
NASA, and evolution of plant life, 34–35
Nassella tenuissima, 147
nasturtiums, 97
National Bioengineered Food Disclo-
  sure Standard (NBFDS), 116
National Genetics Resource Advisory
  Committee, 327
National Laboratory for Genetic
  Resources Preservation (NLGRP),
  159–160. *See also* U.S. Seed Bank
  (NLGRP)
National Organic Program, 109, 113
National Seed Swap Day, 91
National Wilderness System (United
  States), 214

Native American Food Sovereignty
  Alliance, 169, 268
Native Americans, 207. *See also* Indigenous peoples
native bees, 84, 86, 154, 210
Native Plant Landscaper Certificate
  Program (TPF), 290
native plants
  with American Indian culinary
    history, 245
  Clark and, 70
  garden design for, 194–195
  for home landscapes, 254, 289–290
  McCargo and, 251–253
  in New York City, 258–259
  seed libraries for, 208
Native Seeds/Southwestern Endan-
    gered Aridland Resource Clearing
    House (Native Seeds/SEARCH or
    NS/S)
  about, 180–183
  beans at, 247
  building resiliency, 239–240
  founding of, 178, 212–213
  Three Sisters garden concept, 207
  visit to, 291, 308–310
navarretia / *Navarretia* spp., 218
Navdanya, 298, 299–300
Navy officers, 104
NBFDS (National Bioengineered Food
  Disclosure Standard), 116
nectarines, 291
neem tree, 298–299
NE Seed (seed company), 113
neurological diseases and development
  disorders, 198
Nevada (state), 216
Newburn, Rebecca, 208
Newcomb's Wildflower Guide, 255
New England, 237–238, 240
New Jersey (state), 221, 323
New Mexico Acequia Association, 11
New Scientist (magazine), 82
Newsom, Gavin, 261

New York City, 198, 258–259

New York Times, 11, 82

Nibezun (Indigenous nonprofit), 332

Nicotiana rustica, 308

Nigella damascena, 84

night-blooming moonflower, 32

nightshade family, 126

N. I. Vavilov All-Russian Institute of Plant Genetic Resources (VIR), 157, 158, 161

NLGRP (National Laboratory for Genetic Resources Preservation), 159–160. *See also* U.S. Seed Bank (NLGRP)

North American Orchid Conservation Center, 233

Northeast Farmers of Color Land Trust, 333

Northern California (United States)
  author in, 15, 32, 171
  citrus industry in, 130
  heat in, 19, 76
  names for basket claw in, 308
  trees in, 49
  view of, 216
  western bumble bee in, 316
  wheat in, 61
  White in, 267

Nosema bombi, 317

NSPR (public radio station), 98

NS/S (Native Seeds/Southwestern Endangered Aridland Resource Clearing House (Native Seeds/SEARCH or NS/S)). *See* Native Seeds/Southwestern Endangered Aridland Resource Clearing House (Native Seeds/SEARCH or NS/S)

nut, defined, 59

oak trees, 18–23
  acorns on, 277
  and moonlight, 150
  poor health of, 285
  shade from, 276

in spring season, 200
  varieties of, 33, 47

ocotillo cactus, 306, 307

Office of Special Studies, 162

O'Keeffe, Georgia, 286

olive trees, 128

Open Source Seed Initiative (OSSI), 111, 141, 333

oracle oak, 21

orchards, 287

Orchidaceae, 37

orchids, 65, 81, 233

Oregon State University (Corvallis, Oregon), 122, 136–138

organic farmers and farming, 109–110, 327–328

Organic Grower Supply (Maine Organic Farmers and Gardeners), 141–142

Organic Seed Alliance, 99, 100, 110

Oroville, California, 130

Oroville dam, 284–285

OSSI (Open Source Seed Initiative), 111, 141, 333

Ott Whealy, Diane, 106–107, 174, 179

outbreeding depression risk, 259

ovaries, 59, 71, 172

ovules, 34, 40, 71

Pacific Flyway, 53, 302

Pacific Gas and Electric Co., 237

Palestine, 60–61, 91, 312–314

Palestine Heirloom Seed Library (PHSL), 60

pandemics. *See* COVID-19 pandemic

PAN Europe (Pesticide Action Network of Europe), 199

pansies, 173

papante tobacco, 308

Papaver somniferum, 86

pappus (seed part), 56, 58, 65

Paradise, California, 27

Paradise Lost (Milton), 186

Parker, Theodore, 28

Parnassian butterfly, 85

Parnassius clodius, 85
parsley, 191
"participatory conservation," 173
Passover (Pesach), 295
Patagonia, Arizona, 181–182
patents and seed patenting. *See also*
    Plant Patent Act (1930); U.S. Patent
    and Trade Office (PTO)
    GMOs and, 10, 117
    large corporations and, 248, 296–297
    for neem tree, 298–299
    Quattrone and Johnson on, 325–327
    SSE and, 205
    Supreme Court ruling on, 107
pathology, study of, 257
Payne, Theodore, 289
pea family, 124
Pearson, Dan, 92, 93
pea seeds, 134
Pediocactus knowltonii, 232–233
Penniman, Leah, 99, 281
Pennsylvania Department of Agricul-
    ture, 208
penstemon seed, 220
pepo, defined, 59
perennial plant mail-order businesses,
    131
Perers, Kristin, 144
Pérez-Escobar, Oscar Alejandro, 83–84
pericarps (fruit parts), 26, 27, 40
Perideridia spp., 245
Pesach (Passover), 295
Pesticide Action Network of Europe
    (PAN Europe), 199
pesticides, 198–199
Petroselinum crispum, 191
Phoenicaulis cheiranthoides, 219
Phoenix Zoo (Arizona), 233
PHSL (Palestine Heirloom Seed
    Library), 60
pine nuts, 50–51, 97
pine trees, 79, 150
pink checkerbloom, 153
Pinus, 33

Pinus albicaulis, 214
Pinus contorta, 79, 214
Pinus jeffreyi, 214
Pinus longaeva, 49
Pinus ponderosa, 214
Pinus sabiniana, 22–23
pipevine seed pods, 204
pipevine swallowtail butterfly, 94–95
plant and/or seed catalogs, 46, 89, 96,
    134–139
Plantation Products, 141
"plant blindness," 29–30
plant communities, 24
plant families, 38, 39
plant genera, 38
plant genetics, 256–257
Plant Patent Act (1930), 105. *See also*
    patents and seed patenting
plants
    evolution of, 34–36, 134
    in Feather River Canyon, 316
    in foothills, 336
    propagating, 134, 145, 193, 233, 252,
        255, 273, 330. *See also* cloning
        (propagation method)
    rare plants, 255, 259
    species of, 38, 310–311
    in Warner Mountains, 214, 216
Plants of the Southwest (seed/plant
    source), 196
Plant Variety Protection Act (1970), 106
Platanus racemose, 47
Pleiades/Seven Sisters constellation, 89
plug trays, 170
Plumas National Forest (United States),
    57, 315
plumule, 41
poison oak, 120–121, 171
pollen and pollen tubes, 40, 71, 76, 155
pollination contamination, 117, 118
pollinators, 195, 198, 210–211, 311. *See
    also* insect pollinators
pomes, 54, 58, 59
Populus fremontii, 155

Prairie Moon Nursery, 196
Prechtel, Martin, 265, 319
precipitation averages, 304
prescribed fires, 243–244
"preserve" land, 152–153
Primula clevelandii, 125
Proboscidea parviflora, 309
propagules, 67, 80, 233
PTO (U.S. Patent and Trade Office), 103, 107. *See also* patents and seed patenting
pumpkins, 191
Pyramid Farms, 139–140

quail, 67
Quattrone, Jeff, 220–222, 227, 323, 325–326, 330
Queen Anne's lace, 264
Quercus douglasii, 22
Quercus lobata, 21
Quincy, California, 316
quinolizidine alkaloids, 124

radicles, 41, 80
Rae Selling Berry Seed Bank and Plant Conservation Program, 190
rainfall, 86, 335–336
rain lily bulbs, 32
Rancho Arroyo Chico, 129, 130
Rancho Santa Ana Botanic Garden (RSABG), 167
rare plants, 255, 259
The Real Seed Company, 93
Reclaim Seed NYC, 332
Recommended Universal State Seed Law, 209
recordkeeping, 192
redbud trees, 46, 202
red oak group, 47
red perilla, 294
redundancy, 160, 161, 242
Redwood Seeds, 86
red zippers, 98
rematriation of seeds, 224, 269, 270, 334

resilient landscapes, 238–239, 241–242
rice, 130
Richmond Grows Seed Lending Library, 208
Rio Summit (1992), 161, 163, 188–189
riparian communities, 48
Roach, Margaret, 81–82
Robert, Tom, 141
Roberts, Glenn, 90
robins, 53, 54, 121
Rob-See-Co (seed grower), 140
Rockefeller Foundation, 88
Rosa 'April Love', 203
Rosa californica, 203
Rosa 'Gertrude Jekyll', 203
Rosa 'Lady Emma Hamilton', 203
Rosalie Iron Wing (fictional character), 169
rose family, 58
rose hips, 59, 95, 203, 336
Rosenthal, Sue, 54–55
roses, 173
Rosh Hashanah, 295
Roughwood Center for Heritage Seed-ways, 280
Roundup (herbicide), 119, 198
Royal Botanic Garden of Madrid, 187
Royal Botanic Gardens, Kew (Kew Gardens), 187–190
RSABG (Rancho Santa Ana Botanic Garden), 167
Rubus armeniacus, 79
Russia, seeds and plants in, 157
Russian Bureau of Applied Botany, 157
Ryugo, Jim, 292

Sackler family, 140
sacred thornapple, 287
Safe Seed Pledge, 108–109, 141
Sagan, Carl, 33
sagebrush, 214, 216, 306
saguaro cactus, 306–307
Sallon, Sarah, 82–83
Salton Sea, 300, 301, 302–303

salvias, 91, 170

samaras, 60, 65

Samhain (Celtic festival), 29, 335

A Sand County Almanac (Leopold), 196

sandhill cranes, 52–53

sandstone, 24

Sankofa Community Farm, 281–282

Sansour, Vivien, 60, 173, 265, 312–314, 331

Santa Rosa Village, 309

Save Seed Sharing Campaign, 208

scarification, 67, 78, 132

scarlet/cardinal monkeyflower, 51, 52

schizocarp, defined, 60

Schlising, Robert, 84–85

Schutz, Kenneth, 232

Science Museum of Minnesota Native American exhibition, 273

Scotch broom, 79, 124–125. *See also* broom

Scotch broom seed beetle, 125

screech-owls, 277

Scrophularia californica, 121

Second Generation Seeds, 293–294, 334

Sedum, 66

Seed Act (1939). *See* Federal Seed Act (1939)

Seed Advisory Board (California), 148

Seed and Bulb Program (TPF), 289, 290

seed and/or plant catalogs, 46, 89, 96, 134–139

Seed Bank for Rare and Endangered Species of the Pacific Northwest, 190

seed banks, 187–190, 192–194, 197, 232–233

ex situ conservation, 156

international, 162–168, 248, 300

at NS/S, 178, 180, 181–182

origin dates of, 324

and "participatory conservation," 173

at SSE, 258

standards for genetic diversity, 255

seed banks, natural, 170, 231

seed capsules, 71, 84, 95, 121, 133

SeedChange (Canadian seed initiative), 207, 334

seed coats, 40–41, 66, 77, 78, 81

seed companies, 142, 324, 329–330

seed diversity, 39, 158, 182, 334

seed ecology (*carpology*), 41, 51

The Seed Garden (book), 258

seed genetics, Wilson on, 325

seed growers, origin dates of, 324

seed heads, 121–122

seed historians and history, 176, 312, 313

Seed Hunt, 86

seed industry, 148, 149

"Seed is Power" fund, 331

The Seed Keeper (Wilson), 77, 169, 323, 325

seed keepers, 338

Seed LA (Los Angeles Regional Native Seed Network), 290, 291

Seed Law Tool Shed, 208–209

seed libraries, 204–209, 220–222, 223, 227, 313, 332

seedlibraries.net, 208

Seed Library Summit (2021), 220

seedlings, potting on of, 171

seed pods, 69, 143, 155, 219–220, 230–231, 287

seed propaganda images, 221–222

seeds, 33–34, 319

Seeds4All (website), 334

Seed Savers Exchange (SSE), 174–178

Asian varieties at, 294

crop contamination at, 328

and CSN, 333–334

and cultural connections, 222, 334

founding of, 106–107

and seed libraries, 205, 207

Siegel at, 258

seed saving and seed savers, 103, 227

and Cold War, 175

and CSN, 207

importance of, 93, 205–206, 331

methods, 191

scarlet monkeyflower, 51
and *The Seed Garden*, 258
and seed storage, 192
seed seasons, 21, 51
"seed security," 156
Seed Seva, 267–268
seed sharing, 312, 313, 325, 332
Seedshed (project), 331
seedsheds, 61–62, 329, 336
The Seeds of Vandana Shiva (documentary film), 300
SeedSongs (White blog), 264
seed songs and prayers, 264–265
Seed Stewards (online network), 294–295
seed stories, 276, 280–281, 332
seed swaps and swapping, 91, 174, 206
Seed Week (U.K.), 92
SELC (Sustainable Economies Law Center), 208–210
self and place, understanding of, 184
self-pollination, 117, 153, 155
Seminis (seed supplier), 100–101, 109, 111, 114, 142
serotinous cones, 79
serpentine soils, 49
Serratos, Alicia, 204, 207
settlers, European, 129–130, 179, 234
Seven Sisters/Pleiades constellation, 89
Sevin (pesticide and fungicide producer), 141
SGSV (Svalbard Global Seed Vault), 164–166, 178, 248, 272
Shattering (Fowler), 247
Shehadeh, Ali, 166
shield-bracted monkeyflower, 52
'Shirogoma' white sesame seeds, 291
Shiroyama, Maya, 292
Shiva, Vandana, 297–300
Shmita (2021), 295–296
shooting star, 155
shrubs, 33, 318
Sidalcea calycosa ssp. *calycosa*, 153
Siegel, Shanyn, 175, 234, 257–260
Siege of Leningrad (1941 to 1944), 158

Sierra Seeds, 267
Silent Spring (Carson), 213
silicle/silique, 60, 64, 69
Sixth Extinction, 55
Slow Food's Ark of Taste, 91, 221
Slow Food USA, 220, 221
Slow Seed Summit (2021), 220, 222
Smithsonian (magazine), 82
Smithsonian Institution Libraries Trade Literature Collection,, 136
Smoke-McCluskey, Dave, 89–91, 94
snakes, 233
soaproot, 79, 202–203
soil fertility, 138–139
solanums, 126
sonication, defined, 126
Sonoran Desert, 232, 300, 301, 308, 311
Southwest United States, crops and seeds in, 180, 188
Soviet-bloc regions, 175
soybeans, 113, 118, 198–199
'Sparks Earliana' tomato, 222
sparrows, 67
spermatophytes, defined, 36
Spicer, Edward, 241, 330
spices, 295
spinach, 170, 263, 291
spore-bearing plants, 35, 36–37
spring ephemerals, 153
springs (water sources), 43, 285
squashes, 176, 191–192, 207
SSE (Seed Savers Exchange). *See* Seed Savers Exchange (SSE)
Stalking the Wild Asparagus (Gibbons), 251
steer's head, 85–86
storage of saved seeds, 192
stream orchid, 64
styles (plant parts), 65, 84, 122
sugar beets, 327
suicide rates, among farmers, 299
Sukkot (Jewish harvest festival), 311
Summit for Seeds and Breeds for the 21st Century, 110

sun cycles, 18
sunflowers, 221–222
'Sunnybrook Earliana' tomato, 222, 223
Sunnybrook Farm (Burpee experimental station), 222
Superfund sites, 62
Sustainable Economies Law Center (SELC), 208–210
Sutter, John, 129
Svalbard Global Seed Vault (SGSV), 164–166, 178, 248, 272
sweet peas, 77, 97, 134
Syngenta (corporation), 140, 248, 249, 297
synzoochory (dispersal method), 67
syrphid flies, 86
Systema Naturae (Linnaeus), 38

Tallamy, Doug, 55–56, 253
Tamar Organics, 93
tassel, 155
taxonomy, 37–38
Taylor, Owen Smith, 278–283
teddy-bear cholla cactus, 306
teosinte corn, 327
tepals, 202
Terremoto (design firm), 290, 291
tetrazolium salt compounds (for viability testing), 81
"The Envelope" (Kumin), 283
Theodore Payne Foundation for Wild Flowers and Native Plants (TPF), 287, 289–291
Thorburn, G., 136–137
Thorp, Robbin, 317
Three Sisters planting method (corn, beans, and squash), 90
"Three Sisters Seed Boxes," 207
Thysanocarpus curvipes, 143
Tippett, Krista, 28
Tohono O'odham Nation, 178, 179, 307, 309
tomatoes, 221, 222–223, 266, 317, 323
Torrey, John, 252

Toxicodendrun diversilobum, 120
toyons, 54–55, 121, 285
TPF (Theodore Payne Foundation for Wild Flowers and Native Plants), 287, 289–291
trees, 57–58, 251, 315, 316, 318
Trifolium spp., 153
Triphysaria eriantha, 152
Trisler Seeds, Inc., 112–113
triteleia, 79
Triteleia laxa, 186
True Leaf Market Seed Company, 292
true lilies, 70–71
Truelove Seeds, 278, 279, 280
Tucson, Arizona, 181, 182, 308
tule fog, 76
Tumamoc Desert Lab, 311
Tumamoc Hill (near Tuscon, Arizona), 310–311
tumbleweeds, 65
turf grass, 42, 87, 119, 135, 194–195, 211, 287
turkeys, 128
Tuscan Formation lava cap, defined, 23
twining brodiaea, 186
Typha spp., 276
Typha latifolia, 230

Ujamaa Cooperative Farming Alliance, 329
Ukraine, Russian invasion of, seed impact, 10, 11
Umbellularia californica, 79
umbrella plant, 172–173
unicorn plant, 308
United Nations (U.N.), 42
United States, 30, 161–162, 199–200
urbanization, 25, 117
Urhahn, Jan, 87–88
U.S. Customs, 61
USDA (Agricultural Marketing Service), 106, 148
USDA (US Dept. of Agriculture), 114, 116, 161, 190, 233, 327–328

USDA, and seed distribution, 103, 104, 105, 106

USDA-ARS, 236, 335

USDA Forest Service (USDA-FS), 57, 214, 235, 236, 244

USDA plant hardiness zones, 75, 96, 147

U.S. Patent and Trade Office (PTO), 103, 107. *See also* patents and seed patenting

U.S. Seed Bank (NLGRP), 159–160, 167, 334

U.S Southwest, crops and seeds in, 180, 188

U.S. Treasury Department, 104

Vaccinium macrocarpon 'Aiton', 235

Vaccinium oxycoccos, 235

Vale, Thomas R., 213–215

valley oak, 21, 22, 23, 25, 33

vascular plants, 35–36

Vavilov, N. I., 158

Vavilov Institute (seed bank), 157, 158, 161

Venable, Larry, 311

vernal equinox, 144

viability, 80–81, 84

The Violence of the Green Revolution (Shiva), 298

VIR (N. I. Vavilov All-Russian Institute of Plant Genetic Resources), 157, 158, 161

Vitis californica, 200

von Gal, Edwina, 253

The Voyage of the Beagle (Darwin), 50

Wade, Alan, 196

Wallace, Ira, 99, 191, 281

walnut trees, 195

Walters, Christina, 159, 160, 166–168, 192–193, 194, 234–235, 334

Warner Mountains (California), 213–220

watercress, 231

water dispersal of seeds, 65–66

Waterloo-Cedar Falls Courier (newspaper), 139

watermelons, 191–192

water year, 322

W. Atlee Burpee (seed company), 112, 136, 141. *See also* Burpee, W. Atlee

A Way to Garden (public radio program and podcast), 82

Weaver, H. Ralph, 280

Weaver, William Woys, 280

weedy cress, 155

Welch, Kevin, 273

Went, Frits Warmolt, 166–167

western bumble bee, 316, 317, 318

western lodgepole pine, 79

western sycamore, 47

Whealy, Diane Ott. *See* Ott Whealy, Diane

Whealy, Kent, 106–107, 174

wheat, 60–61, 81, 91, 112, 114, 130, 199, 313

White, Rowen, 100, 264, 265–270, 274, 275–276, 278, 281

white alder, 48

white bark pine trees, 67, 214

white fir trees, 214

whiteleaf manzanita, 131, 132

white milkmaids, 80

white oak group, 47

white shooting stars, 125

Whitson, William, 245

Whole Seed Catalog (2021), 46

wild crop relatives, 245–246

Wilde, Matthew, 139

wilderness areas, 214–215

wildfires, 11, 21, 25–26, 27, 50, 78–80. *See also named fires*

wildflowers, 128, 152–153, 200, 217–218, 311, 315, 316

wild grape vines, 200

wildland restoration, 80

wildlife, 22, 24, 55, 253, 254, 322–323

wildlife dispersal (seed dispersal method), 66–67

Wild Seed Project, 92, 251, 253
wild turkeys, 53
William Malcolm and Company, London, 137
willow trees, 79, 200
Wilson, Diane, 77, 99, 169–170, 271, 323, 325
Wilson, E. O., 55–56
'Wilson Sweet' watermelon, 192
wind dispersal, 64–65, 219
wind pollination, 117, 155
winter greens, 18
'Winter Luxury' pumpkin, 191
wisteria, 275
woody buckbrush shrub, 121

Xerces Society, 253, 316

Yakteen gourd seeds, 331
yampah, 245
yellow carpet, 152
yellow pine trees, 214
yoga, 144
yucca, 306
Yuma Indian Nation, 305

Zamecnik, Alexandra, 181, 183
Zephranthes spp., 32
zoochory (dispersal method), 66–67